Rx:
PEACE

The Promise and The Future

Rx:
PEACE
The Promise and The Future

Sylvia Hornstein

NuAge Books
Van Nuys, California

Published in the United States of America
by NuAge Books
    P.O. Box 7535
    Van Nuys, CA 91409

Library of Congress Catalog Card Number: 87-91233

ISBN 0-9619265-0-3

To my children,
Don, Jim and Debbie,
their children,
their children's children...

CONTENTS

PREFACE

Peace can be a startlingly hostile subject. Although images of peace are entirely different from images of war, they are linked finely together. Regular linkage places peace and war back to back—on opposite sides of the same coin, so to speak. This perspective appears to indicate that the space between peace and war is narrow, that alternatives are shallow, and that at any given moment there is danger of falling into the dreaded state of war.

Peace is precarious in this fragile view, and only the firmest safeguards, the utmost vigilance, and the strictest posture can maintain the peaceful condition. Constant readiness for war is an absolute requirement, for it is ever imminent. Peace, in this understanding, can scarcely be contemplated without invoking the terrible propensity for war.

Peace can be an uncomfortable subject. Discussing peace brings into question an entire array of matters—matters fundamental to our social order and to our collective well-being; matters that many feel have already been delegated to the correct authorities, that are out of the ordinary domain and with which they need not bother—indeed, should not have to concern themselves. That is the proper business of the politicians, defense people, and the clergy. That's what they are there for. Continued discussion causes a certain sense of indignation and irritation. The instigator is disdainfully categorized as "unrealistic", "idealistic", "utopian", or worse, and summarily dismissed from consideration, if not from presence.

Lingering doubts may remain, however. The discussions have not been entirely fruitless, since, almost without exception, peace is the desired state. Yet peace remains elusive. An interesting phenomenon suggests itself in this regard. Scarcely anyone is against peace, in principle. All want it. There is implicit social agreement, and the political endeavor ostensibly supports it. Nevertheless, in spite of its widespread desirability and noteworthy purpose, peace remains a volatile subject.

Buried deeply in hearts and psyches, it seems, peace has been privately nurtured but carefully screened from view. It has not been subjected to intense scrutiny nor, for some, brought to conscious awareness. Discussions of peace may disturb the equanimity of the individual. Still, of late, doubts have been raised in the mind. The senses are alerted. Conflicting messages are impinging and colliding that raise questions about the basic world order, its system of maintenance, and the ability to sustain or reach desired goals that are fundamental to the heart and essence of human and environmental life and survival. The subject cannot, will not, go away.

Suddenly, peace in the world has shifted from a private dream or vision and from an academic, religious, or political question to a matter of critical and collective urgency. All other matters are relegated to secondary standing. The issue of survival has become primary.

Awarenesses have been sharply awakening these past few decades—particularly these years, the space years—that indicate the common tenancy of earth, the finiteness of its borders, limited resources, and fragile environment. Developments have been acutely experienced worldwide, and the impact and importance of global interactions have been daily brought home. Interdependence is a word with increasingly new examples and meanings. The question of needs and goals is no longer an academic subject relegated to philosophical discourse, nor is the bedrock certainty of survival absolutely taken for granted any longer. The resulting effect is a deepening disquietude and heightened unease.

For all that there is agreement on the desirability of peace, notes of dissension and fear can soon be detected. It is observed that there is agreement on one fundamental level, that of survival. If war is the cause of annihilation and if peace is needed to ensure survival, then peace must be instituted. But—and it is a "but" of monumental proportions—what is peace? Has peace ever been known? And one must ask the ultimate question: Why are we collectively pursuing a course of militaristic action that is perceived to be fraught with the greatest peril for all of life on earth, whose tragic consequences can be foreseen and foretold by the common man and woman on the street, whose continued path flies in the face of sanity, rational argument, and morality, as well as knowledge of economics, technology, and history? The answer, of course, is that we have not yet substituted another system for the war system for the collective preservation of life.

The war system was devised and refined over millennia for protection of a people, for resisting aggression, for expansion of goods and territory on an infinite globe. But what appeared to be a natural extension of the authority of kings, barons, and states has, upon current knowledge and perception, become a possible deathtrap for the world populace. Priorities and conditions mitigate now for fundamental change and adaptation. But is there a substitute for the war system? Peace is desired, but is it possible?

In categorically stating that warfare is an invention that can be replaced by another preferred social invention, Margaret Mead, anthropologist, stipulated that the defects of the old system must first become apparent and acknowledged. A new social system is entirely possible that would make warfare as obsolete as the passenger car has made the horse and carriage.[1]

This new system, however, must fit the questing mind, no matter how urgent the need. It must be a path that flows with history—with evolution, change, and growth. It must transcend time—that is, be part of the past, the present, and the future. It must fulfill the requirements of the space age, unifying humanity and insuring respect and responsibility for earth. In short, it must hold the promise of life and evolution—that is, of survival. What could possibly fulfill this exacting criteria? Something incredibly complex, or something simple, already familiar, experienced? The latter, of course, is the case. The answer lies in the extension of peace, substituting a system of peace for the war system.

(Peace? What do you mean, peace? How is peace known, familiar, experienced? Isn't human nature hostile, aggressive, warlike? Haven't there always been wars and always will be wars?)

The premise is stated forthwith: *There has always been peace.* Peace is part of our heritage, our practice, and our projection. It has come from the depths of our origins, has been nurtured and sustained over millennia, and is now sufficiently developed to be formally acknowledged, embraced, and extended. The pages that follow bear out this theme, and admit the notion of peace from the confines of the unconscious to enlightened cognitive awareness.

There is no disclaimer of the fact that war has been an age-old system of conduct between disputants. That is a fact. But it must no longer be permitted to obscure the peace initiatives and practices that have been upheld and maintained, and that have flourished over time, resulting in dispersed peace networks now awaiting sturdy connections. It is maintained that the concept of peace has been seeded and practiced through the ages, and it is submitted that this practice has sufficiently germinated for propagation and active cultivation, if not harvesting.

The desire for peace has been variously fired and motivated; ideas and experiences, as well as ideals, hopes, and prayers, have contributed to the concept. An understanding of attitudes, habit, and change is necessary. And, while one can apply common sense and logic to the subject of peace and war, there are some matters fundamental to it that are not necessarily logical. Nor are they insignificant to our topic, many seemingly unrelated fields lying immediately adjacent, if not intertwined, in the whole peace—war syndrome.

In perceiving the subject matter over time, one notes that peace has been a part of human consideration and behavior for centuries on end. This seems to have been lost sight of, or perhaps it has been obscured by weighted war information. Humankind has been interacting peacefully for ages of time, even as warfare has become the specifically sharpened threat it is. The effort herein attempts to balance the matter and to project peace as a viable system for serious consideration.

The time has come when the possibility of peace must be considered as a living reality *in our lifetime*. Reasoning that there must be a "new manner of thinking" to guarantee human life and survival, Albert Einstein foresaw that it was necessary for human beings to reach the level of belief and confidence in the possibility of peaceful solutions.[2] It is submitted that now is that time.

Should peace actively be waged and become increasingly accepted in human negotiations—and I believe we can make it happen, humankind being ingenious as it is—it is entirely possible that we will overcome the pressing predicament that threatens all of us. Together, we may yet safely pass this dark night. We must, of course.

Sylvia Hornstein

Where there is no vision
the people perish

Book of Proverbs, 29:18

THE SCENARIO

$\mathcal{T}$he situation must be perceived in utmost clarity. This moment upon which our future hinges is one of infinite hope and utter despair. In stark relief, the scenario presents itself: life or death, survival or extinction, evolution or entropy. The decision is absolute.

A

The world is poised at the edge of a huge abyss. Wars and hostile encounters between nations have placed all of humankind in jeopardy. There is threat to survival. No longer confined to military targets and military personnel, sophisticated nuclear weapons and armaments threaten existence of all life, human and environmental. Since the terrible destruction of Hiroshima and Nagasaki over forty years ago, the power to wreak havoc has increased many times. One speaks in terms of mega-destruction or macro-destructiveness. World warfare would now encompass the extinction of millions of lives. Genocide is the possibility—the mass murder of countless people—as is the resultant devastation of vast areas of land. Radiation would contaminate the environs and, by wind, rain, animal or insect life, as well as by food, drink, and human contact, spread unpredictably and uncontrollably.

The Mutual Assured Destruction (MAD) pact, now sanctioned by the major powers (United States of America, Union of Soviet Socialist Republics), would guarantee retaliation in kind, thereby insuring both genocide and suicide to an initiator of nuclear warfare. The possibility of a first-strike attack is nervously in the wings, the fearful action of a maddened people threatened beyond endurance.

The situation grows ever more tense. In 1969, U Thant, then-Secretary General of the United Nations, warned that the world had critically few years in which to resolve its terrible problems.[3] None has repudiated the statement. Valuable time has passed. Unbelievably, since then, there have been greatly increased budgets for military expenditures, greater sums for more and bigger weapons, continued marshaling of economics, intelligence, and resources for defense and "security"; in short, more of the same. But there is no security. Indeed, there is less security than ever.

The threat to life, to human survival, and, possibly, to earth itself is from nuclear war, no matter who instigates it. And the threat is multiplying as other nations rush to emulate the "powers", role models—to purchase the same destructive armaments, to secure their own "defense". The more weapons that are available, it has been stated, the more likely is their use. The greater the proliferation of warmaking powers, the greater are the possibilities of blackmail, terrorism, guerrilla tactics, suicide missions, human error, preemptive attack, madness, etc. The evil is spreading and infecting the world.

Inexplicably, the populace of nations is strangely silent, unwilling, if not unable, to admit that the basic system of warmaking is inexorably grinding toward disaster. Sensing, rousing, feebly becoming aware of impending doom, an impotent people is frighteningly observing the oncoming obliteration. Incredibly, talk continues of "man's hostile nature", "limited warfare", bigger bombs, or, perhaps, laser beams, MX missiles, neutron bombs, and other exotic armaments. So-called defense experts continue to discuss ever more inhuman means for better "security".

Blind allegiance to an obsolete system has rendered us defenseless in the real sense. The hierarchy of our political system has given the power over our collective lives to a few men, and we are dependent on them for existence in the ultimate sense. Our lives hang by a thread and the sword of Damocles is suspended over it. Any gusty wind in the form of any of the above and/or unknown perils could sever that thread and plunge humankind into hell.

B

The profound departure from all that has been previously known, the change that eclipses every former experience, the pivot on which time springs from the past into the future, is the birth and emergence of the space age. With this advent, the windows of the world have been opened to the panorama of the universe. For the first time in all of time, it is possible to go out of this world, to leave earth at will. It is possible to penetrate beyond earth's confines, to travel into and through the void of space, to connect with other islands of matter in the universe. The earth is no longer the totality of existence for humankind; its boundaries are no longer rigidly defined. The future has been extended indefinitely.

The changes that have been engendered since the onset of the space age have caused, and are continuing to cause, paroxysms of preparation within the human species in acknowledgment of this startling event. It is a profound and fundamental change, encompassing the most basic reorganization of perception, adaptation, and direction of the organism. Analogous to other known fundamental shifts in human perception and human organization, such as the change engendered from food hunting and food gathering to food-producing; perceiving the shape of the earth to be round rather than flat; awareness that the earth revolves around the sun rather than vice versa, etc., the shift in human accommodation to the space phenomenon is of tremendous significance.

Earth-shattering conceptions and dilemmas are presenting themselves within the mind for future resolution. Questions leap to mind: Are there other beings in space, and are they peaceful or hostile? What do they look like? Will humans travel routinely in space in the future? How long can an earthling leave earth's atmosphere and remain in space before physical or psychological changes occur? Can human life be extended? These and myriad other questions abound in creative profusion and press enthusiastically for more information and experiences.

Spatial perception has afforded the exquisite view of earth as the beautiful globe it is, suspended in the rarefied biosphere—fragile, vulnerable, resourceful, teeming. The human family is seen as one unit on one earth. Time and space are sensed in universal proportions, and all things are writ large in the greater arc of timelessness. It is a moment of awe, a moment of grace, the lifting of the veil, and before the awesome splendor, an ennobled human species needs rise to true humanhood. The wonder and excitement generated beyond former perceptions is without compare, warranting excesses of self-praise.

The human mind that conceived and made this infinite mystery possible to experience is surely a marvel. Congratulations are in order, but they pale before the accomplishment. How marvelous is humankind to have made the future accessible, to have spread wide the magnificent vista before one and all. What was formerly fantasy is proven reality. Spurred by whatever divine inspiration, intrepid imagination, and indomitable will, the skill, technique, and loving cooperation required for realizing the space achievement has succeeded in piercing the bounds of earth, yielding infinity. We are indeed a magnificent species, earth's finest specimen, worthy of the future. The spectrum of hope, strength, purpose, mystery, and adventure is vividly ahead. The universe, no less, is humanity's playground.

PART I

PEACE:

TRANSCENDING

TIME

CHAPTER ONE

PEACE ACTIVITIES IN THE RELATIVE PRESENT

$\mathcal{T}$he effects over time on behalf of peace are cumulative. Like individual flakes of snow that mound in collective profusion, the efforts and experiences of cooperative and peaceful events have settled on earth and begun to leave their imprint in a thickening mantle of depth and broadening impact. It is not possible to consider the subject of peace from the point of view of this moment only, as though nothing has led to it and more will not follow. It is necessary to widen the array and effect of peace efforts, and to note some of the innumerable actions and events that have led, and are leading, to the establishment of peaceful interaction as a normative pattern of behavior between the peoples of earth.

Incorporated in our perspective is the sweeping notion of time itself. This moment is center stage in our lives, the spotlight of Now shining brightly; all else is darkened, swathed, or closed from view. One is immersed in this moment, caught up in it, and the play looms large. But of course there is implicit the drama of earlier events and the excitement of coming situations. Past and future are molded on that stage, their presence felt even as the present is illuminated. So, too, with the searchlight on peace. Was the Vietnam War the only expression against war? Was the explosive sentiment for peace at that time the only voice that ever erupted for peace? Were the peace enthusiasts alone in their shout, railing against the establishment, against their elders, against the rigid senselessness and brutality of an inhuman war? In a sense, and for a moment, it seemed they were. Cutting themselves adrift from established pattern, the peace advocates clung together and, mercury-like, formed their own body and fused their voices into one long shout for peace. Theirs was a great communal victory.

We owe this great firebrand generation a tremendous debt, and our gratitude and appreciation is hereby acknowledged, late as it may be. They had the heart and stamina and courage to stand up against the machine of war, against inhumanity, and to utter a great guttural shout. Unbidden, spontaneous, it arose from the depths and erupted. They were our voice, although it took a while to realize it. They shouted what was in our hearts, submerged and mute as it was. They were the voluble catalysts, the spur that caused an end to a war in which five American presidents had been involved.[4]

They were magnificent. But they were not alone in their desire for peace. Without diminishing or detracting from their achievements and their catalytic effect, it is necessary to realize that there have been, and presently are, a great host of individuals, groups and organizations active on behalf of peace. Located all over this country, and in countries throughout the world, multitudes of private, nongovernmental (and governmental) people have been and are actively working to promote peace and to end or diminish wars. Simultaneously, they are earnestly and dedicatedly engaged in the rational and civilized effort of promoting peaceful cooperation as the standard for human behavior in the world. Worldwide, there are hundreds upon hundreds of peace and disarmament groups, their numbers growing continually, and their message appealing to ever-growing segments of the population.[5] And they, in turn, rest on a great backlog of human efforts for peace that recedes ever more distantly in time. The phenomenon of peace activists and group activities in and on behalf of peace suggests that there is extant a great equalization of people's efforts for peace.[6] Bubbling just under the surface, a widespread roil is beginning to pick up momentum as passions and actions are being energized in this direction. Appendix A, at the back of this book, includes some listings of groups, organizations, and institutes active in this area.

For proper perspective and clarity of understanding, it is necessary to acknowledge the varied events and efforts that have been instrumental in turning the human race to peace, however slowly it may seem. However, at this point, a note of caution is inserted: The word "peace" is replete with semantic confusion. It has been bandied, romanticized, parodied, prophecized, slandered, and demeaned. Popular language usage has placed peace in multiple conjunctions of meanings with, for example, quiet, rest, mental repose, passivity, love, greetings, prayers, etc., as well as with treaties, war, police, presidents, councils, conferences, prizes, and so on, not to mention in association with dreamers, visionaries, and religionists. Some commonly known words and phrases in daily use are listed in Appendix B.

The varied usage in our language is indicative of, and has contributed to, vague and amorphous ideas about peace. But the widespread multiplicity of meanings attached to it indicates the pervasiveness and internalization of ideas and values connected with the peace concept, ranging from religious, philosophical, and psychological associations to educational and political meanings. Actually, far from being unknown, peace has a place in our minds, our conversations, habits, and plans—a place that is widely diversified, frequently unconsciously so, sifting through actions and thoughts, coloring the spectrum of human interactions.

The rash of daily negative news would seem cause for near-despair of peace, however. Battle lines are being drawn, positions are hardening, and prospects for peace seem to be rapidly diminishing. Military budgets are the highest they have ever been in peacetime, sophisticated weapons are openly discussed and stocked, and terrorism and nuclear proliferation are worrisome news items. Yet, despite all this, despite a militaristic milieu (or perhaps because of it), much has been quietly happening in the field of peace. Largely hidden from public view, a field of peace and peace-related matters has been developing.

A persistent searcher finds a comparatively large array of material within the peace field. This may be rather shocking. From the generally negative societal view of peace as a legitimate subject for rational consideration or serious study, and from the narrowing focus of the subject matter itself (as with all specific research, but certainly as much or more so with peace, since it isolates the researcher from prevailing thought), the discovery of the far-reaching scope of the peace field is almost overwhelming.

But, it has been asked, what is the peace field? Of whom and what does it consist? Where is it taking place? Some background material is necessary in order to recall the roots of the now-established peace research and peace studies movements, and the field of which it is a growing part.

PEACE RESEARCH AND PEACE STUDIES

Peace research is the name that was applied to the focus of a small band of scientists and researchers who decided that the subject of peace and war was not exempted from serious examination. Collective human behavior could be subjected to critical review no less than individual behavior. It is the scientific and academic forerunner of current peace and world order studies whose appearance on American campuses, and elsewhere in the world, has generally followed the growth of the movement.

The peace research movement preceded the advent of current peace studies by some thirty years, dating back to the early 1950s. Although young in years, it has been fruitful, engaging researchers worldwide in scholarly debate and scientific investigation on the vitally important and provocative subject of peace, a matter to be researched in similar manner to war and other phenomena involving human beings. However, because there was little or no educational outlet at the time for peace education in universities or teaching institutions, its strength grew in research and scientific format in scholarly journals. It had to be factual, empirical, and analytical in order to find a receptive market. (And, because journals are not general reading material, the work is unknown to the public at large.)

Academic interest along these lines was furthered in no small measure by some pioneering work done by Theodore Lentz, often cited as the father of the peace research movement, with publication of his book, *Towards a Science of Peace* (1955).[7] Two other noted authors are also mentioned in this context: Quincy Wright for his prodigious work entitled, *A Study of War* (1942),[8] and Lewis F. Richardson for his two works, *Arms and Insecurity: A Mathematical Study of the Causes and Origins of War* (1960)[9] and *Statistics of Deadly Quarrels* (1960).[10] Their works added sustenance and motivation to the movement and to the academic search that has consciously laid open the follies of war and aspirations of peace by scientifically focusing on the ever-widening field of human relations that have periodically erupted into "deadly quarrels."

In 1952 a group of psychologists formed in Washington, D.C., for the study and prevention of war.[11] Their publication, *Bulletin*, attracted important intellectual participation, and further research was promoted. (Interestingly, in 1980, another group of doctors, Physicians for Social Responsibility—now international, and the recipient of the 1985 Nobel Peace Prize—was formed in the United States to warn the world's inhabitants of the consummate danger from nuclear war.)[12]

The *Journal of Conflict Resolution* was published in 1957 at the University of Michigan, Ann Arbor, Michigan, and two years later The Center for Research on Conflict Resolution was opened at this same university, remaining actively engaged for twenty-two years. In Norway, the Peace Research Institute at Oslo was established in the late 1950s, is still active today, and publishes the noted *Journal of Peace Research*. Also the University of Pennsylvania, Philadelphia, Pennsylvania, instituted the Department of Peace Science, and findings are published in its *Journal of Peace Science* (an institute, by the way, where one can earn a Ph.D. in Peace Science).

The 1960s saw international consolidation between fledgling peace organizations through meetings and conferences that provided opportunities for viewpoints and printed materials to be exchanged. Historians met in Philadelphia, Pennsylvania, in 1963 to encourage research on war, peace, and conflict for a better understanding of peace, and the Conference on Peace Research in History (CPRH) was born.[13] Its official publication is *Peace and Change*, a quarterly issue formerly published at Sonoma State University, Rohnert Park, California, but now published at Kent State University, Kent, Ohio, under the aegis of the Consortium for Peace, Research and Education (COPRED), an umbrella organization founded a few years later in 1970, headquartered at George Mason University, Fairfax, Virginia.

The subject of peace was the topic of a conference in Switzerland in 1963, and, one year later, in London, England, at which the International Peace Research Association was established.[14] Its official publication, the *International Peace Research Newsletter*, is issued four times a year. The Canadian Peace Institute, in Dundas, Ontario, has been variously associated with several universities and has successfully held many summer institutes. It publishes the *Peace Research Abstracts Journal* and *Peace Research Reviews*.

The Stockholm International Peace Research Institute in Sweden has been active in this area of interest, operating with the help of government funding—a situation that most other peace institutes and organizations do not share, since the majority are privately funded, leading, at times, to periods of insufficient funds and personnel.

There are many other peace education and research institutes outside of the United States, ranging from Finland to Latin America and from Japan to Canada. Approximately one-third of all such institutions are in North America, one-third in western Europe, and the balance in India,

Israel, Japan, etc.[15] Appendix C identifies some centers outside of the United States that are united in their concern for world peace.

Overall, although generally starved for earned acknowledgment from academia and the community and frustrated by inaction on revealed data and research, yet persisting in analyses of human conflicts and interactions, these intrepid researchers have continued to scrutinize the problems and potentials of clashing humanity. Whereas, ideally, educated insights should be reaching the public at large and their designated policymakers—at the least, being openly debated—peace research findings continue to be confined largely within the movement. Dogmatically persisting and quietly growing, however, dedicated scholars have been unveiling the behavior of societies, domestically and internationally, in order to give intellectual credence to an old idea: peace on earth as a normal basis for human interaction.

The emergence and advent of current peace studies and peace research classes on college campuses has been a growing phenomenon in the present time. (The term "peace studies" is differentiated from the peace research movement, although there are overlappings, insofar as it is no longer confined to scientific journals.) Credit must be given to the peace research movement, of course, which has been filtering down to the undergraduate level. It has become a small but quietly active part of the academic scene (still largely unpublicized). The previous and ongoing work and journals of the scholarly and scientific researchers are being tightly scrutinized by many students of today and being added to. Credit must go, too, to the students who have sought such classes for their innate sense of relevant and futuristic study matter.

No longer found only in departments of religion or political science, although these traditional areas continue to have important roles in the overall picture, persistent students have been seeking or self-directing studies on peace in a truly grass-roots approach. The insistent demand for peace studies has opened up a variety of programs in this area, and today many colleges and institutions of higher learning in the United States, as well as elsewhere in the world, are offering interrelated studies on peace, problem solving and conflict resolution, world order, interdependence, global perspectives, etc.

College programs are attempting to meet the need in an unfolding manner. As interest has grown and as facts have begun to collide or merge with one another, not only students are being educated. Instructors, too, are finding themselves faced with facts and viewpoints that differ from previously held notions and, in a great surge of fresh thinking, old and outworn theories are being firmly laid to rest as the new perspectives sweep in. In the wash of change, the rein of education has been loosened to permit the free association of facts and ideas to intermingle. In its wake, instructors must act as facilitators of learning even as they themselves learn in an exchange with their students.

As for the pupils themselves, their freedom to both learn and synthesize was perhaps never greater. At this moment of open question and search in the field of peace studies, the purpose and meaning of education may never have been more *égalitarian* than is the mutual learning process that is occurring in those classrooms where honesty demands acknowledgment of the new ground that is being trod alike by those who restlessly enter the classroom and those who command it.

Facts and information are spilling over and overlapping from the various disciplines. Greater diversity and understanding is offered and permitted as knowledge accrues. Crossing disciplines, it is apparent that the subject of peace is as important to studies in sociology, economics, and law as to history, psychology, foreign languages, and foreign affairs. Although political science and religion remain pivotal areas of study and reference, they are no longer the exclusive departments for studying peace.

A burgeoning bibliography has been developing from individuals, educational sources, and organizations. Noteworthy lists of reading material have been compiled, and where there was formerly a dearth of peace-related material, there are growing numbers of reference and bibliographical literature and visual materials on peace.[16] These, in turn, are sparking additional research and books.

There is work in this field at the Institute of Behavorial Science, University of Colorado at Boulder (source of an extensive bibliography covering the field of peace and conflict), at the University of Hawaii in Honolulu, at Kent State University in Ohio, and at other important centers both in and out of the United States. Appendix D lists many educational institutions in this country where peace studies may be pursued, in most cases for academic credit.

The field has been widening perceptibly these past few years, and the relative abundance of material is encouraging and enlightening. It does not compare to the amount of material on war, having a long way to go to equal it, but there is already enough material to suggest several directions within the field. It is more than adequate to inform and stimulate the interested searcher. The appetite whetted, it is soon realized that the "new" direction has solid foundation. In addition, almost as a bonus, each student brings to bear his or her own interest and enthusiasm, if not self-concern (all are interested in survival), and creative response infuses the effort.

But valid employment opportunities have yet to keep pace. And diminished or canceled funding for innovative studies has serious negative effects on this neophyte academic breakthrough. However, the die has been cast, and the prognosis is positive and hopeful. In a world beset by conflict and militarism and sorely in need of meaningful change, valid and studious interest in peace comes none too soon.

PEACE DEFINITIONS

Peace means many things to different people, researchers and students included. Whereas meanings classically stretch dichotomously from association with war to complete rejection of all conflict and violence everywhere, an informed consensus on the meaning of peace is being arrived at from the various descriptions and definitions that have been advanced.

Bypassing popular slogans and notions of peace, and removing the layers of emotion and myth generally surrounding the subject, clarifications on peace and conflict are emerging and being refined. It is edifying to note that such a broad (and emotionally laden) subject is lending itself to analysis and rational description, while still leaving room for creative interpretation. The need is to include all that peace stands for—that which is felt "in the bones"—and that which is becoming relatively obvious from observation and awareness of interdependent relationships.

Although peace has more frequently been described negatively as non-war (which, at the least, it is), broadened emphasis has widened understanding of the concept and admitted less limited viewpoints. It is becoming clearer that peace is a condition in and of itself, with its own retinue of needs and supports. Various degrees of peace have been categorized and described, from *negative peace*, the absence of organized violence of one group against another, to *positive peace*, the achievement of cooperation and conflict resolution, renouncing war between groups.[17] Peace has been described as a balance between multiple forces,[18] and as that condition when order and justice are both internalized within a group and externalized in its relationships with others.[19]

The concept of peace is broad, stretching to accommodate many variations. A continuum with flexible bounds, it may be seen that *peace is an overall active state of nonviolent behavior and interaction between human beings, and between humans and the environment, with attendant needs, actions, and consequences.*[20] It has its own requirements and is its own condition. One perceives, albeit imperfectly, that the peace concept or continuum is a fundamental condition and system with all the inherent complexities attached thereto. No one act, deed, or treaty, peace is a process upheld by common agreement and bolstered by societal support.

Like any relationship, an agreement for sustained peace is conditional on the partners to the agreement, their motivation, good will or intent, and commitment to the process. Naturally, common interests must be served all around and ground rules established. What are the basic needs? What support systems are needed? What will sustain the condition? And so on. An understanding of one's own humanity and of the general human condition is presupposed. For example, survival of the group is a given need, as is the value of individual life. If survival, community, and individual life are seen as fundamental requirements for all states and peoples, an agreement for peace may be enlisted. A living pact, subject to stresses and strains no less than to good intentions, it requires the dedicated care, support, and maintenance of the total community.

Justice, order, and positive meanings are embodied in descriptions of peace and are considered necessary if the concept is to have general public acceptance and support. The peace concept conveys a sense of well-being and equitable living. Religious principles of kindness and mercy are not far from these meanings, being encompassed, perhaps, in the term "justice". Within the broad range of peace is enveloped the full gamut of human relations. The group's behavior is an extension of individual need: to be free of the scourge of war, to bring improved living conditions to the world's inhabitants, and to implement conditions for optimal development. Hegemony over others is no more acceptable than loss of one's own freedom.

In this context, admitting the common need, it is logical (and imperative) to advocate the spreading of peace networks as bridges between the peoples of the world. The establishment of "peace for all mankind" is no longer seen as merely a messianic ideal—although the combined weight of our ideals has sustained the dream—but as a viable condition and system for human interaction on a finite globe. As such, it is clear that a greater degree of maturity and sophistication is needed in instituting required reforms for enlarging and maintaining peace as a bona fide foundation between the peoples of the world.

These definitions and concepts do not obscure the fact, however, that peace has been a difficult concept for many to envision. "Peacelessness" has been cited as the ongoing condition or continued crisis of war-prone societies. The "absence of peace" has been decried as the condition that exists as long as atomic warfare is considered and condoned.[21] Complete breakdown of peace culminating in outright war is "organized group violence" enacted against another group.

The subject of violence is no stranger to contemporary times and has been researched in depth, generating considerable analyses. Degrees of violence have been cited, from "direct violence" (gunshot, bomb, physical harm by intent, etc.) to "structural and/or system-caused violence" (inequality, unemployment, discrimination, etc.). There is also "incidental" violence that is struck against unrealized potential, the potential for individual and group growth in attaining humanhood and striving for the universal ideals of love, truth, goodness, and peace.

The absence of overt violence in the form of declared militarized and organized warfare does not mean the absence of all conflict, since conflict may be an expected condition between different (and differing) human beings and groups. Resolution of conflict cannot remain dependent on direct violence and war, which eliminate rather than solve the problem. Since conflict is an expected condition requiring consideration and qualification, averting and defusing stressful situations would be preliminary and not unexpected tactics. Recognition of the escalation of tensions is necessarily important, and turning to nonviolent courses of action for resolution is actively seeking an end to the problem. Only the method is modified or changed.

The urgency of correcting social injustices and achieving equitable solutions is an essential step in human affairs. Many nonviolent means are available and effective in resolving human problems—means involving mediations, sanctions, rewards, and punishments. Widespread recognition of such means and greater international use of them would enhance their global effectiveness. Of course, such usage presupposes a commitment to finding resolutions to disputes and conflicts without resort to armed conflict and war. Since the result of organized warfare in the present age is clearly recognized as nihilating—of creating havoc and destruction greater than the problem ("the cure is worse than the disease")—it is obviously an incorrect solution and nonviable option.

The nations of the world are plainly at a crossroads. A past method of settling disputes by force of arms has become untenable. A new pathway is needed. But confusion is resulting from refusal to recognize or admit the scale of the impasse and the need for radical change. War can no longer "solve" national problems. Since war is unacceptable, the difficulties must be settled peacefully and nonviolent methods of conflict resolution raised to a higher degree of refinement and usage. Certainly, creative use of such ways and means is not beyond the capability of a people who has survived countless ordeals throughout time.

It must be expected that humankind will rise to the challenge of facing itself, of finding acceptable means for resolving its problems, and of instituting measures for anticipating and deflecting crises and violence (whether direct, structural, or incidental). Avoiding war and "keeping the peace" is an expression of civilized behavior between peoples. And a concerted effort to unify individuals and groups under the banner of peace would galvanize the entire movement, if not the world at large.

It is readily observed that, overall, peace studies on campuses have opened the field of peace and war to a greater degree of contemplation and discussion than heretofore, broadening viewpoints considerably. Nevertheless, optimistic and futuristic as it is, the entire matter of peace studies and creative futures seems to be a closely guarded secret that is relegated to some area of secondary, tertiary, or lesser emphasis insofar as publicity and general awareness are concerned. It hasn't become fashionable to forthrightly broadcast peace studies programs; incredibly, even at many participating institutions, comparatively few people (students and educators alike) are aware of the program's availability. Some myopic tendency seems to be holding sway, and there is a strange reluctance to publicize these studies. It is shyness misspent. There is every reason for pride and approval in making the public aware of studies concerned with world peace.

The subject of wars and their history, causes, and involvements has long been researched in depth and taught diligently in classrooms—and has too long held a monopoly of perspective. Whereas the need is for more cooperation, resolution of conflicts, and judicious understanding of the multiplicity of world needs, an untoward amount of war information still seems to be disseminated to students. But unless a military career is intended, of what use is such specialized knowledge? Is it not the reverse education that is actually needed? Should not minds be concentrating on peace, on maintaining cordial or, at the least, civil relations, and on instituting support for the continuation of the needed condition? Certainly, greater understanding of people—their histories, cultures, languages, and perspectives—is needed in today's and tomorrow's world.

On a globe of finite borders and increasingly close contact, the need for peaceful solutions to human problems is becoming more obvious with each passing day—not just as a wish, dream, or token condition, but as an actual basis for human interchange. And it is apparent that developing, instituting, and maintaining peace between peoples is not necessarily a given, but is an ongoing and continuous human effort requiring intensive education and support from the community, which is, after all, the prime object and beneficiary of the entire endeavor.

(Educators, students, and community members: It is suggested that you familiarize yourself with the area of peace studies, global research, world order analyses, etc. taught at your local institutions. Ask for it. Publicize it. It is not a matter for reticence or privacy; quite the contrary. Nothing could be more vital to students, colleges, and society than relevant education and enervating public involvement in pursuit of peace, life, and survival. The future depends on it. Literally.)

WORLD PERSPECTIVES

Internationalism, international relations, interdependence, global perspectives, world order, etc. are all expressions devoted to identifying the fact that there are interrelated aspects and problems of inter- and supranational dimensions that require global considerations. Various suggestions have been put forth for some form of world organization. Whereas this notion may formerly have had connotations of loss of national identity or sovereignty, there clearly are certain commonalities between peoples and nations that need responsible investigation. Matters of worldwide import abound and are overlapping, causing growing concern and deepening dissension. Problems of population, food, and economics cross borderlines, as do pollution, fouled seas, or insect proliferation. Impacts are felt globally, and negative effects may be borne unfairly.

As inhabitants of earth, all people share the common habitat. There are common needs and conditions requiring enlightened education, if not some common rules of governance. There are areas that supersede national and international boundaries, such as forests, seas, deserts, atmospheric conditions, natural resources, etc. This naturally uneven distribution of resources frequently results in global "feast or famine" conditions and, possibly, in international irresponsibility. Perhaps the consequences of use and behavior in these areas should be considered from a comprehensive perspective. Unlimited use or abuse of finite resources, for instance, would be ultimately disabling for all. But is there responsibility to member states in the world? If so, what is it? Are tenancy and possession "nine-tenths of the law", and stewardship the rest? Or is it the reverse? There are important questions to be considered.

The lack of global restraint on the military might of individual nations is yet another problem of international concern, and closely linked to the subject of this book. A world people is held captive with bated breath, dependent on the whims and passions of ambitious or desperate leaders. Can this condition (be permitted to) continue?

There are many facets to the concept of international peace, and cooperation is implicit. It is not a simple notion. To become an established pattern of internationally accepted behavior, peace must be broadly considered and systems of maintenance widely institutionalized. The idea of extended organizations for handling global concerns and comprehensive world affairs has been advanced by prominent persons and organizations. An attempt to consider the matter from a worldwide perspective was made.

The World Order Models Project (WOMP) was an assignment directed by the then-Institute for World Order (now World Policy Institute) involving researchers worldwide. It was felt that there was not so much a question of world government by the beginning of the twentieth century as its manner of coming—that is, by force, drift, or design—and its type of instigation and support membership.[22] A suggested timetable considered consciousness-raising in the 1970s, mobilization in the 1980s, and implementation and system transformation in the 1990s.[23] Design and analysis for alternative or preferred world systems was requested, with strategies for their achievement. After several years of regional meetings and planning from 1968 to 1973, various plans were submitted, and many future systems were projected.[24] Differences in cultural perspectives and global locations accounted for varying suggestions as researchers pointed out that certain systems were desired by some cultures but not necessarily by others. Commonalities would have to be found.

Generally, the many proposals were and are grandly concerned with global policies and global systems in an understanding that the world is one unit whose citizens are reaching for peaceful linkages. Yet these same citizens must awaken to the opportunities, hazards, and decisions that lie before them.

The idea of a centralized world government has been proposed—not a new notion, but startling nonetheless. It seems too huge to consider. The world, no less! Preposterous! However, upon reflection, awareness creeps in of the multiplicity of global relationships, of the interdependence of economics and energy, environment and resources, technology and science, etc., and, of course, of all the human factors, such as population, food, living standards, health, and so on. One is enlightened (and relieved) that there is some precedent for the whole idea—some *de facto* world arrangements already exist.

There is the United Nations, of course, and the International Court of Justice, which has permanent status and is "the principal judicial organ" of that body. Although rarely publicized, the World Court has jurisdiction for dealing with treaties, international law, breaches thereof, and reparations thereto. There are also worldwide economic, religious, and scientific bodies. Daily interactions bring international repercussions continually before the public mind, and awareness is advancing of the global consequences of many local and regional acts. There is not, however, an enforcing agency of international status and consequence.

INTERNATIONAL LAW

The field of law is established the world over, albeit practiced differently in various parts of the world according to custom and culture. It is relied upon to settle areas of disputes, grievances, and crimes and has been proposed as an aid in furthering world peace.

Since powers of destruction have become so vast, making war intolerable, the principle of law was suggested as the only alternative to mass ruin.[25] Justice William O. Douglas of the United States was convinced that the role of law in international affairs required strengthening and broadening, and, if brought to bear on a world scale, legal international justice could act to supplant warfare and lawlessness and reduce this deadly habit and option of nations. He pointed out that much law is already international. The more global the activities of a country, the more likely are established international patterns of law.[26]

As noted, there is some precedence and procedure already established in courts of law for handling international disputes, and, indeed, they are doing so at this time. Take, for example, the relatively recent case of American hostage-taking by militant Iranians in violation of international norms. The matter was presented by the United States before the World Court in The Hague, Netherlands, in winter, 1979. At the same time, sanctions against the offending country were requested by America of world member states. World opinion and action was mobilized in a nonviolent manner in order to find resolution and an end to the provocative act. This country attempted a reasoned approach to an overtly hostile act.

The frustration may still be too active for objective analysis; however, some points are clear. A large country, a world power, the United States of America, was willing to show physical restraint against an offending smaller nation. The civilized nonviolent method of bringing the case before the judge and jury of the world was deemed a mode worthy of this country's moral mandate and purpose.

That there *is* a World Court was sharply brought before public awareness. The fact that an international legal system exists may have been a surprising revelation to many. And, whereas this incident would have been a proper time and opportunity for the United Nations to indicate its *raison d'être*, the inaction of this world body and its lack of adherence to its own purposes was also revealed.

A properly functioning world forum seems to be a reasonable place for international grievance charges. Should not such an option be widely available and upheld as the legitimate right of nations to make charges and press for justice? That there should be international integrity and responsibility seems as logical to expect from global member-states as it is from local citizens. Thomas Jefferson foresaw the need for the nation, but it applies equally to the international arena:

> "...laws and institutions must go hand in hand with the progress of the human mind. As that becomes more developed, more enlightened, as new discoveries are made, new truths disclosed, and manners and opinions change with the change of circumstances, institutions must advance also, and keep pace with the times."[27]

The contemporary suggestion for the greater use of law between nations by Justice Douglas and so many others—notably Grenville Clark and Louis B. Sohn, with their suggestion for achieving *World Peace Through World Law*,[28] and Benjamin B. Ferencz in *A Common Sense Guide To World Peace*,[29]—has broadened another avenue for peaceful negotiation. It opens up an entire range of world behavior, from accountability and responsibility to sanctions and reparations. World opinion is a powerful voice, and the weight of the international body in bringing its collective "eye" and scales of justice to bear on national and between-nation disputes, as well as on multinational problems, could be a forceful deterrent to violating the peace and rights of others.

The precarious condition of the world, its lack of sufficient concern for human life, its preponderance of military force and lack of faith and understanding in reaching binding agreements without it, mitigate for critical concern and change in creating a stable world milieu. The need is rife for greater use and reliance on reasoned international settlements and resolutions of disputes, guarding of human rights, life, properties, etc., and for the acceptance of the rule of law in general matters of boundaries, air, maritime controversies, etc., as well as for the myriad problems of interacting peoples. It is an acceptable and timely suggestion for consideration. It must, however, admit to a widening of perspective concerning global citizenry.

WOMEN'S ROLE

In considering global conditions, one is fully aware that the world's population consists only and wholly of two genders, male and female. Two. It is clearly evident that the female is not adequately represented anywhere in proportion to her equal numbers. She is half of all humanity and brings to the world a distinctly oriented perception of it. Her approach is urgently required for a balanced perspective in living naturally and symbiotically on earth. Attempts are being made to redress this imbalance in some places, but the lack of true feminine representation in matters concerning the state of the world is evident in its deficiency.

The role and participation of women in world affairs must be anticipated and planned by women, as well as by men. No longer can woman's vital world outlook be stifled or vicariously represented. Humankind must not be robbed of fifty percent of its perception and experience; *nor may half of humanity have hegemony over the other half.* Sole responsibility for the world must not sit heavily on men's shoulders, as if they alone existed—nor may it be usurped by them. Women must be *expected* to participate fully in all matters and must receive the education and opportunity to become experienced in role fulfillment.

Change in the years ahead, in the coming twenty-first century, is clearly going to be a viable part of existence. Rigidity in outlook and static and patriarchal bureaucracy must not be permitted to web the globe in moribund restriction. There must be room for individual human expansion and free expression of the spirit. The need for balanced perception, for imaginative foresight, and for creative planning will be more necessary than ever before for survival and adaptation in the space age. "What should be" in human relations has every right to be explored and strived for, even as "what is".

There will be greater need for development of all aspects of ourselves, both men and women, than is now the case. Every opportunity for unhampered development of the potential human being must not only be permitted, but must be actively expected, promoted, and nurtured. An era of greatness in human history has every reason to be anticipated and expected with the full and active participation of all members of human society. Whereas war has predominated for centuries upon end, peace must be welcomed for all that it implies and entails.

In this, our age, the relative present, innumerable attempts at peace-making and peace promoting are taking place. Great clusters of people and actions, seemingly unrelated, *are* related in common endeavor in pursuit of peace. What some perceive as wishful thinking, naive rhetoric, and fruitless striving in the face of harsh militaristic patterns are far more than coincidental events. What is occurring is a great upwelling of definitive actions on behalf of peace. What is being heard and witnessed is truly "the voice of the people".

To a jaded, fearful, power-mad and disjointed world, such ideas and behavior may seem simplistic and difficult to accept. Because these events are related to the so-called softer senses, hard-liners are having difficulty in relating to these efforts-in-common. But relate they must, living in the same world, or they will be swept away into the mists of time as anachronisms unfit for survival. A new set of values is being forged and upheld—values to which some have given lesser service in the past, perhaps, but which are essential now and in the times ahead for the survival and advancement of our species.

CHAPTER TWO

PEACE EFFORTS IN THE RECENT PAST

One might say that current efforts for peace are mere reactions to an unstable world situation. Fear is a powerful motivator, and often reactions to perceived danger are emotional, impulsive, and irrational. Certainly, the desire for peace has some roots in our emotions; however, this in itself is scarcely to be condemned, since emotions are valid human characteristics and serve a useful purpose. As for being impulsive, a desire that is as age-old as the wish for peace can never claim that action in its behalf is "impulsive". And as for irrational behavior, the world citizenry is anything *but* irrational in the face of a real possible cataclysm. The fact that the perceived danger of nuclear holocaust is absolutely real and under the control of a few fallible humans is reason enough for all manner of demonstrable behavior. That the people of the world are *not* acting in terrorized fashion is cause for deeper probing.

That many people of the world are acting in concert, yet discretely, in behalf of peaceful resolution of human conflicts gives rise to thoughtful consideration, if not applause. That many are furthering the cause of peace in simultaneous yet differing exercise is evidence of an outpouring of hope and love, and gives pause and respectful interest to the whole endeavor. Surely they are acting out of some inner directive. Surely they are measuring their actions against experience. Surely the certainty of peace-directed behavior is built on a solid foundation reaching back further than "the relative present" of this particular time. Immersion in the present moment—our time, that of immediate experience and memory—must not obscure earlier events that transpired and that have added solid substance and foundation to the structure of peace. The search and work for peace does indeed recede in time. It is necessary to peer more deeply into the recent past.

Great individuals have stirred minds and events on behalf of peace. The effect of one as prominent as Albert Einstein cannot be measured or denied. Imbued with universal insight, Albert Einstein declared his belief in the need for peaceful resolution of human conflicts for half a century. He early understood that noble attitudes are not confined to universities but flourish equally among the general population.[30] A humanist and pacifist in addition to being a famous scientist, Einstein foresaw the importance of world peace, even world government. He was convinced that wars are not less likely to happen because war rules are drawn up. First it must be determined to settle international strife by arbitration.[31] And he was certain that, on the whole, solutions must not be left to governments. Independent people must join together to fight militarism.[32]

Emphatically opposed to warfare (socially condoned mass murder), Einstein nevertheless temporarily set aside his pacifistic beliefs to counter the evil of Hitler and nazism. The time for building peace was clearly during peacetime, before the madness of dehumanizing organized aggression swept through a people, holding it hostage and laying waste a multitude.

Mahatma Gandhi, another world-renowned personage, typified the spirit of nonviolence in private and public life, practicing it in the social and political sphere of his native India. Extending the search and maintenance of truth and nonviolence into worldly affairs, Gandhi understood that humanism and patriotism were consistent with internationalism, since it was important to consider the global human population as one and to be friendly to all.[33] He felt that nonviolence was the greatest force at humankind's disposal, and that human beings were continually progressing towards the search for justice, harmony and friendship, components of *ahimsa* (no harm to living beings in mind, speech, or action).[34] Mahatma Ghandi observed that in the world at large there was not general acceptance of nonviolence, although, he noted, social structures were bound together by bonds of love and applied cooperation.[35]

Gandhi was devoted to the cause of peace and, in 1936, stated that if world leaders who control the destructive weapons were to completely reject their use, world peace could be achieved.[36] Gandhi's influence has been felt far and wide. Many students and adherents are poring over his works and studying the methods of *ahimsa,* nonviolence, and *satyagraha,* reliance on truth as a matter of principle, in order to establish social and political methods for effective accomplishment of international control without resort to violence.[37]

Perceiving nonviolence as an active force in social affairs, a proponent for peace existed in the form of Martin Luther King, Jr. In attempting to right the wrongs done to black America, King focused attention on their plight by holding shameful behavior and discrimination before the eyes of the world, taking the cause to the United Nations. Verbalizing eloquently, and with printed exhortations, King led followers in nonviolent action through organizational and legal maneuvers, marches, sit-ins, boycotts, prayer meetings, freedom rides, etc., unifying and shaping potentially volatile behavior in reasoned and creative directions.

Alternately raising white consciousness and black pride, Martin Luther King, Jr., also came to understand the need for international methods of nonviolence.[38] Achieving world outlook, he believed that the potential for destruction ruled out warfare as a means of obtaining "a negative good".[39] He felt that alternatives to war and destruction must be found.

The role of President Woodrow Wilson was instrumental in establishing peace as a world possibility. Upon conclusion of World War I, which America had entered on the side of the Allies in 1917, President Wilson envisioned a peace that would be permanent, that would restore dignity to the losers as well as to the victors, that would ensure future peaceful interaction. This idealistic spirit was contained in the "Covenant", as it was privately called,[40] a proposal for a federation of nations—a proposal that was a call for a united world.

On January 18, 1918, Woodrow Wilson delivered his famous Fourteen Points address before Congress. The peace he was advocating would put an end to secret diplomacy, uphold national self-determination, eliminate economic obstacles between nations, ensure freedom of the high seas, diminish armaments, etc. The Fourteenth Point, the "heart" of the program, called for an organization of nations with guaranteed political independence and national boundaries for large and small countries equally.[41]

The idea of a world confederation to end the threat of future wars fanned the imagination of many and was initially received with enthusiasm. In attempting to implement this plan for a League of Nations, however, Wilson suffered many political setbacks. In the end, although the

United States did not ratify it, the League of Nations was organized. This, in turn, established the mood and form for the later founding, in 1945, of the present United Nations, whose charter expressly states the determination "to save succeeding generations from the scourge of war,"[42] and whose purpose and principles are:

> 1) "To maintain international peace and security, and to that end: to take effective collective measures for the prevention and removal of threats to the peace, and for the suppression of acts of aggression or other breaches of the peace, and to bring about by peaceful means, and in conformity with the principles of justice and international law, adjustment or settlement of international disputes or situations which might lead to a breach of the peace...."[43]

The United Nations is a collective body of 159 nations, large and small. Although imperfectly attuned and in need of reform, it is nevertheless a struggling sanctuary imbued with a sense of mission and acceptance by the world body politic. Within its framework, many agencies have specialized roles in promoting peaceful international cooperation. For example, there is the World Health Organization (WHO), in Geneva, Switzerland, which desires the best health level for all people; the International Civil (Aviation) Organization (ICAO), Montreal, Canada, whose concern is for international air travel and transport; the Universal Postal Union (UPO), Berne, Switzerland, established in 1874, which greatly increased communication between all peoples.

International relationships can be cited, from exchange of students to international sports competition, from world fairs to global weather and space cooperation, from international art, music, and fashion exchanges to worldwide communications. These and more are all witness to, and experience of, ongoing peaceful interchanges and relationships. The world of business cuts across all lines in daily international transactions as trade plies the four corners of the earth. And, not to be discounted, travelers and local townspeople have met in face-to-face encounters, gaining an immediate experience and understanding of cultural and global differences (and similarities).

The reiteration of these facts of public knowledge is to pinpoint the fact that peaceful relations in the world are not a sudden action, simply a matter of reaction to the perceived threat of war, no matter how urgent that may be. Peace has been established and is being practiced in many forms other than via formal diplomatic niceties of international politics. Abundant contact has been established, and ample precedence set, for peaceful interactions to be formalized between the peoples and nations of the world.

As the idea for sustained peace gains wider public acknowledgment and acceptance, and as its supporters become more sophisticated and experienced in understanding methods for promoting and maintaining the valued condition, there will be citizens of the world, undoubtedly, who will choose to become involved in the United Nations (and like bodies that may arise). They will strive to strengthen, improve, and uphold the ideals and purposes of that potentially august institution, to imbue it with a sense of commitment to its own charter and purposes, and to create of it a proud model and forum for the nations of the world to emulate and in which to gather together in honored company.

The individuals mentioned above have been actively outspoken on behalf of peace. Ideals and efforts have been boldly stated and acted upon. Peace has been the unifying theme, openly and unequivocally declared, without pretense and, certainly, without shame or embarrassment—in contrast to popular cynicism that disdainfully implies that feelings and beliefs in a peacefully operating world are unrealistic, impossible, and "contrary to human nature". The time for individuals to be isolated within themselves, privately nourishing their dreams and beliefs about peace, but feeling helpless before the weight of closed thought and inhibiting mentalities, is as outdated as the time before unions helped to weld and unify separate individuals into a united powerhouse to be reckoned with.

PIONEER EFFORTS FOR PEACE

A prodigious amount of work for peace has been performed by pioneering and courageous people in earlier times, when it was undoubtedly more isolated and less apparent that results would bear fruit. Their efforts cannot be denied, however; in taking note, realization accrues that sturdy peace activities have been building steadily, affording us strong stepping stones upon which to stand and continue.

The cause of peace was strengthened by the Briand-Kellogg Pact (Paris Pact) between the United States and France when it was signed in August, 1928, and ratified by this country in January, 1929. This historic agreement was eventually signed by sixty-three nations.[44] It declares in

Article 1 that

> "...they condemn recourse to war for the solution of
> international controversies, and renounce it as an instrument
> of national policy in their relations with one another...Article
> II...that the settlement or solution of all disputes or conflicts
> of whatever nature or of whatever origin they may be, which
> may arise among them, shall never be sought except by
> pacific means..."[45]

An effective grass-roots campaign for peace was stimulated in the
United States by the founding of an organization in 1921, the National
Council for Prevention of War. Active for twenty-five years, the organization claimed credit for assisting in averting hostilities with Mexico in
1927.[46]

The Women's International League for Peace and Freedom, founded
in 1915, has stated its purpose as the peaceful attainment of world
conditions to guarantee "peace, freedom and justice for all."[47] Lauded by
Albert Einstein, this national and international organization is still highly
active.

The Carnegie Endowment for International Peace was established by
the Carnegie Foundation in 1910 to hold various research and communications programs on war and peace-related matters.[48] And the famed Nobel
Peace Prize was offered by Alfred Nobel, Nobel Foundation, Stockholm,
Sweden, before the turn of the century, to the individual who, in part,
most furthered friendship between nations and most promoted peace
meetings.[49]

The first Nobel Peace Prize was actually granted in 1901 and, of
course, the prize is still being awarded. (It will be recalled that the 1978
Peace Prize was awarded jointly to Prime Minister Menachem Begin of
Israel and President Anwar Sadat of Egypt for their mutual peace agreement.) Other national and international grants, awards, and honors have
been and are still being offered to individuals and organizations in behalf
of peace.

But it must be acknowledged that there were peace activities and
movements before 1900. The first International Peace Congress was held
in London, England, in 1843.[50] The American Peace Society was formed
in 1828; earlier, in 1815, peace societies had formed in New York and
Massachusetts. The British Society for the Promotion of Permanent and
Universal Peace followed shortly thereafter.

This is not an in-depth account of each and every peace movement or organization that existed, for there were, and are, many others that are not here accounted for. Rather, the intent is to focus awareness on peace efforts that have been building over time. It cannot be, of course, that the intrepid pioneers mentioned here created the idea of peace any more than did the Vietnam protesters of our "relative present" day.

In contemplating the earliest date mentioned above, 1815, and the formation of peace groups in New York and Massachusetts, this date is but thirty-nine years from the founding of this country in 1776. Assuredly, many of the settlers of those early days came to this land with the notion of peace deeply imbedded in their hearts. Surely the dreams of those who came and settled and founded this nation manifested themselves in the document called the American Declaration of Independence, which proclaimed

> "That all men are created equal; that they are endowed by their Creator with certain unalienable rights; that among these are life, liberty, and the pursuit of happiness. That, to secure these rights, governments are instituted among men, deriving their just powers from the consent of the governed..."[51]

What, after all, is this document if not a declaration of peaceful intent for men and women to live together in common pursuit of those goals and values deemed most dear to life? Was the experiment successful? We know it was—the thirteen original states growing to the present fifty, and the entire nation living in peaceful nexus with its neighbors to the north and to the south. Is it an isolated miracle? Is the United States of America the only country where citizens live in common agreement, pooling their labor and resources for peaceful self-government? Of course not. But obviously, not all nations enjoy the same internal and external peaceful connections. Because peace norms are not yet a universally accepted standard between nations, however, does not mean that peace does not exist.

There is ample evidence of the binding phenomenon and networking by human beings into socially organized entities to indicate successful peaceful patterns for living cooperatively and communally. Multiple peace exists, of course, in discrete clumps and patches all over the world. And almost everywhere there are feelers, branches, and antennae all exposed and waiting for connections to bridge the gap. Continued successful reaching out, fence-mending, and bridge-building between the nations and peoples of the world are vital components of peace building reaching solidly back into time.

CHAPTER THREE

THE MATTER OF TIME AND THE RECEDING PAST

*T*he matter of time is central to peace and to this thesis. The emphasis on the present is so profound, experiencing it acutely as one does, that the further past fades from memory. Yet it must not be lost completely to mind, especially in our quest for human connections and peace. Mentioning time and its relevance to peace is inadequate by itself, however, without spending some time on it. Accordingly, we shall seemingly digress in order to more nearly grasp time's essence and significance in this account. It is hoped that the short diversion will enhance the matter and place peace and time in greater perspective.

The western concept of time has made its adherents near-prisoners. Time has been slashed, halved, quartered, and drawn. Aided by the scientific scalpel of time disembodiment, time is perceived in the minutest of units and like children, we experience life in the constant present. Reduced to small bits, time is seemingly managed and controlled, and the human being becomes habituated to living in the fractured moment. Over a lifetime, and rubbing shoulders in the mad dash with one's neighbor, the larger view is foreshortened to the immediate. Indeed, one can scarcely recall the long view of time, and, with habit, it is no longer considered— just as the stars themselves can scarcely be perceived due to the light reflections of thousands of city lights and thus are effectively obscured from sight.

There is a sense of control in dealing with small units of time; it seems time has not only been managed and controlled, but destiny has been secured. In fact, mastery of a type has been achieved. The measurement of time into smaller segments of milliseconds and microseconds, for instance, has been particularly useful to science and technology. Technologically speaking, the ultimate control has been achieved by escaping earth's gravity and blasting off into space. There, however, time has a quite different dimension, and the fracturing of time, as on earth, is quite useless. One considers space in terms of light years and time that flows beyond human life spans—huge blocks of time, planetary time. What is there to relate such expanses of time to terrestrial human experience, especially for those who have become accustomed to using the smallest bits of time?

Relationship and relevance must be established between the individual time experience, the collective experience, and the greater mass of time. Treated in minutiae, or perceived in limitless expanse, the medium is still the same. It appears that time is pervasively all of one piece. Only the perception, experience, and commitment are different. Nonperception does not mean nonexistence, however. Time is the essence; apparent or not, perceived or obscured, time is all about. The concept is mind-expanding, or mind-numbing, as the case may be. Whether by living with petite units of time, as westerners generally do, or by reaching back into the cosmos, as in the eastern mode—or however else—it is apparent that living with and by time may be variously experienced according to the particular cultural perception and commitment, contributing to different understandings and values in world views.

At the present time, with the extended view of time brought before our collective sights via space exploration, there is an opportunity to lift our heads, as it were, to contemplate the greater panorama, and, insofar as is possible, to absorb and assimilate the message. (One is momentarily above the scene, with unlimited 360-degree view all about. Standing upright and gazing thoughtfully forward into time, metaphorically speaking, the merest turn of the head enables one to perceive the path that humans have traveled. It is a long road, complicated and tortuous, disappearing at times into the mists....)

The road of human development is not of this moment only, it is seen, but of times past reaching into antiquity and beyond—a road on which all humans have come, those of apparent similarity of mind and those not. Our studious involvement in and concentration on the immediate moment usually blocks off thought and awareness of this traveled path, and it is effectively obscured from consciousness. But however it has happpened over time, and by whatever route, the fact is that humankind has arrived at this particular "pinnacle" and is collectively here. It is perceived that humanity is not merely a featherweight just now dropped into the sea of time to be quickly inundated, or a brittle organism to be easily snapped. The weight of history, of life and evolution, stretches flexibly backward into time. Human beings have sturdy roots of long duration.

At this exquisite moment of stock-taking and objective surveillance, of noting the possibly headlong rush into oblivion even as timeless survival lies before us, important events and flashpoints have connected and directed our past. The thread of human development extends unerringly backward into time, even as the road of peace has been (and is being) hammered and hewed over it. Have we deluded ourselves that peace is the desire of this moment only? Are we given to nonsensical musing that peace is our penchant alone? Life, survival, peace have been building through time, and they have been given impetus at strategic points throughout history.

Let us give honest credit where it is due and remind ourselves anew. Accumulating through human effort, peace has been building and collectively adhered to through centuries and millenia; armed with this awareness, there is strength, hope and clear direction for the future. But first, a reminder of some sentient times that have become milestones in humankind's ascension.

We have earlier mentioned and considered the founding of this country a little over two hundred years ago, but, of course, time goes further back than two hundred years. We are certainly aware of the earlier Old World ancestry of the settlers and of the native American tenancy of this land before 1776.

Chronologically, we continue to look further backward. Receding in time, past the eighteenth century's Industrial Revolution, past the sixteenth-century Copernicus's perception of the earth revolving around the sun (rather than the other way around, as previously thought), past the fifteenth century's invention of the printing press (bringing information and education to masses of people) and the date when Christopher Columbus is purported to have "discovered" America (and the same native American tenants), the Courts of Spain having been already well established, past the thirteenth century's Magna Carta (the beginning of democracy in England) and the time of great cathedral-building in Europe, we continue back in time, pausing momentarily in the sixth century. Here we take note of a startling change in the method of recording time, of *calendaring*. A change at that time in recording annual time has, over the centuries, been almost universally accepted, counting the present year as 1988.

Relevant to our subject matter, something as vital as the everyday use and acceptance of calendar time—something that is ordinarily utilized and daily observed (but perhaps little considered)—may need some further notation or gentle reminder of its place in the affairs of humankind and of how it came about. Accordingly, a short account of calendaring is in order, not only for clarification and its own interest in the matter of time, but for its specific significance to peace and the human story.

Today's calendar dates the present year from the birth of Jesus Christ. Previously, years or eras were variously identified by the names of dynasties, consuls, kings, and popes. The Roman calendar, for example, was based on the foundation of Rome, 753 years Before the Christian Era (B.C.E.).[52] In 46 B.C.E., Julius Caesar of Rome ordered another calendar to correct earlier time discrepancies—the Julian calendar. This was later reformed by Pope Gregory XIII in 1582—the Gregorian calendar, which is the calendar in use today and is still so named.[53]

The present system of dating of years was set in the sixth century by counting and recording the years from Christ's birth (off a few years, it seems) and dating events before and after that event.[54] Officially set by the Abbot of Rome *anno Domini* (A.D.) 523, this practice was upheld, gradually accepted, and in use in Christian countries by approximately 1400.[55] It has since been adopted almost globally as the standard for measuring calendar time.

There has been dedicated persistence and acumen demonstrated over the ages in understanding the globe's physical phenomena and in reckoning time in accordance with the related and observable universe. The calendar may appear to be a simple computation and quite taken for granted, but, in fact, it has absorbed human thinking, measurement, and imagination for millenia, representing, as it does, the all-embracing phenomenon of time.

Calendars and clocks are inextricably intertwined in our culture as measurements of time—calendars measuring the days, weeks, and months of the year and noting the larger units of time, such as the century and millenium, while the clock measures the hours, minutes, and seconds of the day. These mechanisms are useful in standardizing time and unifying it for general purposes. Such methods have seemingly become indispensable to the life-style of the twentieth century—to industry and the business world, travelers, students, etc. Activities are synchronized for general efficiency, and one is aware of the uniformity of time whether in Akron, Ohio; London, England; or Sydney, Australia. Planes and trains depart at certain standardized hours and minutes, and individuals fit and maintain schedules accordingly. There is a certain reassurance in this uniformity the world over.

Basically, acquiring a sense of time, recognizing its presence and passage, and developing the ability to utilize time to advantage has been a magnificent human achievement. All of human experience is embraced by time as it pervasively fills the world and universe,[56] and recognition of the time element has been a significant factor in the development of the species. The ability and need to plan accordingly, to prepare and project for contingencies, has assisted humans to survive throughout time. Cultural tools and education to aid and direct such efforts have been created, utilized, and refined.

There are many ways of telling time other than by popularly standardized measurements, and a moment's reflection will bring some to mind. For instance, the rotation of the earth on its axis brings us daytime (heralded by the cock's crow) and nighttime (suggested by the cows' gentle lowing as they thread back to the barn). The appearance of stars effectively tells time, as do the varied hues of the sky. The seasons of the year are revealed by the weather and by plant and tree flowering, and rings on their trunks effectively disclose the trees' ages. An hourglass spills out the sands of time even as the sundial shadows the sun's daily position. The thickness of geological deposits clearly reveals time's greater passage, as scientific carbon-dating determines aged time.

Time is observed as birds fly south from northern climes in winter time and by the bear's hibernation. Harvest time is a vital time of the year, following an earlier time for planting. The grunion run at a specific time, swallows return consistently, and whales migrate and sound in their own time. Nature plays out its repetitive fancy, and all existence heeds the tune.

Internal biological clocks are amazingly consistent, deriving their sense of timing from adjustment to the natural rhythm of the earth, sea, and atmosphere—whether to sunlight, temperature and moisture, tides, earth sense, or other phenomena. Time flows in and around and through us. From conception and birth through a lifetime of maturation, cycles and rhythms in humans are so definite that they could almost be used for measuring time.[57] Women's menstrual cycles are monthly occurrences. The heartbeat or pulse count is a measure of time. The most important unit of time to humankind, undoubtedly, is the individual life span. How long is the tenure on earth? How long is life? Consciously or not, human beings (and all living creatures) are adjusted to time and live their lives in accordance with its privileges and demands.

Religion, too, has had a hand-in-glove relationship with time. Early people observed the strange circumstances of the physical world and, since food and safety depended on factors due to sometimes capricious events, carefully safeguarded their lives and propitiated the gods by appropriate prayers, dances, and sacrifices. Specialists evolved to meticulously calculate the times and needs for sowing and planting, for instance, and they kept track of heavenly bodies, signs and stars, and star conformations. Later, some names of calendar months were named after Roman gods—Janus, Mars, and Juno, for example.[58]

People have been ordering their lives and calendaring their years for millennia, and the origin of the calendar may be a shared honor. It has been suggested that calendars were in use in Egypt's Pre-Dynastic period, 4500-3500 B.C.E.[59] The Egyptian division of the year into 365 days was brought to Rome by Julius Caesar.[60] Also, the Babylonians and the Jews were early engaged in grappling with the passage, effects, and meaning of time. Creating the concept of the seven-day week, the Jewish calendar is lunisolar; that is, its months are calculated according to the moon, and the year according to the sun.[61] The Jews count this year as 5748, its onset in the fall (not midwinter, as in the Christian calendar), reckoning retroactively from the Era of Creation, some 3760 years B.C.E.[62]

The Sumerians have been credited with early calendar recording, about five thousand years ago, using computations that were based on the moon.[63] Emanating much later (Islam emerged about the year A.D. 600, upon the life of Muhammed, founder and prophet), the Moslem religious calendar is also calculated according to the moon's phases.[64] Further East, the Chinese are reputed to have recorded time since at least the period of Emperor Yao, over four thousand years ago. And on this side of the globe, in our hemisphere, the Central American Maya people established 3113 B.C.E. as the beginning of time, their calendar and religion synonymous (priest-astronomers carefully calculated religious holidays based on the three major cycles: the earth's daily rotation, the lunar month, and the solar year).[65]

Measured time is based on astronomical observations. A year is counted as the length of time that it takes for the earth to revolve once about the sun (365 1/4 days); the month is calculated on the time the moon takes to orbit the earth; and the day is determined by the twenty-four hour cycle of the earth's rotation on its axis. (The western concept of the hour has had the effect of regulating the day as it is presently known—generally, office hours begin at nine in the morning and end at five in the afternoon.)

Modern science is quite dependent on exact time measurements, and physicists deal in nanoseconds (1/1,000 of a microsecond) and picoseconds (1/1,000 of a nanosecond).[66] Precise time measurement is provided by a special instrument in Washington, D.C., called the Photographic Zenith Tube (PZT) of the United States Naval Observatory. Photographs of star positions by the PZT show the rotation of the globe, and their pictures are used for the exact measurement of standard time in this country.[67] A phenomenal state of microtechnology has been facilitated as the lens has peered ever closer into the most petite units of minuscule time.

There is a surprise, however. In the apparent fascination with the minute, there has been near-oblivion of the whole. Incredibly, general attention seems to have bypassed accumulated time, greater time, time in the large. Acute attention has not been focused on the year, on the centuries. In careful observation, in meticulous calculation and correction of earth, motion, and time—in short, in scrupulous attention to the finest and most diminutive detail—it is almost inconceivable that the larger measurement, the overall time span, has been generally overlooked. But that seems to have been the case. Lack of attention, if not outright neglect, has been the accompaniment of extended time. Interest has been weighted on time minimizing. This fascination—obsession, perhaps—with the petite has blocked the larger view, the whole. In effect, time and humanity have been truncated and segmented and, in the mind's eye, disembodied from the past. This has led to apparent neglect of human continuity, and the implication is that the human tenure is of relatively short duration. Such is not the case. For instance, the numbering of the year is arbitrary.

Collective silence and common usage for centuries has implied a tacit consensus on the date and, although confusion is engendered by having to juggle centuries and millennia in the mind, by counting down then by counting up (B.C.E.-A.D.), the date of the year has apparently not been seriously challenged. Yet it is in error. The stated count or measurement of the year is, very simply, incorrect. It is not 1988. It is denied by the legion of humans who devised the very calendar it is recorded on, by the mathematicians, observers, participants, priests, astronomers, rulers, and dynasties of times long past. It is, in fact, denied by fact. Nevertheless, this obvious fact seems startling. And yet this simple (or startling) statement has the effect of taking scales off the eyes, of observing time more fully, time reaching further back and enlarging the human perspective.

Although this country is young in years of timed agreement of nationhood—212 years—and although the date claims this year as 1988, time and life and human development are far older than the current calendar and popular knowledge indicate. Our roots recede ever deeper into antiquity. We are an experienced people on the face of the earth and have been developing and refining ourselves for ages (wars and catastrophes notwithstanding). The calendar itself is concrete evidence of the human symbiosis with time. For purposes here, however, at a time of probing for roots and continuity in the human story, barriers must be set aside. The search goes where it will.

That the incorrect date of year has been generally accepted is acknowledgment of the impact and significance the birth and life of Jesus Christ has had upon people. Special individuals and events have left their mark on the human race. This must include Abraham and Moses, certainly—the former prophetically breaking with established thought, proclaiming a universal God over all humankind and the power of love (refraining from sacrificing his son, Isaac), and the latter, who upheld the concept of responsible human behavior (the Ten Commandments) after leading the Jews to freedom. Others elsewhere, and at different times, created their own followings and emphases.

As noted, religion and time have been intertwined for millennia, and the significance has impacted human beings. The call for social justice and for peace crosses races, religions, borders, and time. It has been taken to heart and transmitted through the ages. The collection of writings comprising the *Hebrew Bible* was set down over a period of hundreds of years before the Christian era.[68] These ideas transpired from thought and experience and conviction and were hammered out and refined over time. They represent the roots of three major religions, originating with Judaism and separating into Christianity and, later, Islam.

Comparative religions and many of the "ologies" (anthropology, archaeology, psychology, theology, ontology, teleology, cosmology, etc.) attest to the diversity with which humans have observed and arrived at conclusions about the universe, earth, and the human condition. Great tracts of time and energy have been invested in these perspectives, which add infinitely to the store of human knowledge. In the symbiotic relationship with time, men and women have had inspiring breakthroughs and sharp shifts in perceiving the world and their roles in it. Religions have given credence to our senses and concepts of existence and have attempted to add to humanness (some more successfully than others, and differently at times). Other means have also extended our development and added to human maturity.

World philosophies have extended reason, and human discourse has been upheld as a standard of growth and achievement. Skills and education and uses of natural resources have contributed to progressive development and mastery of self and environment, while science has focused and sought explanation of the natural elements. Thus religion and philosophy and mathematics and astronomy and skills and literacy and science, etc., have swept us into this latter twentieth century.

Have our ideas for peace originated in our time? Of course not. We are scarcely so self-enamored as to claim it. This refrain has been preserved in our hearts and minds and expressed in our teachings and learnings. It has been carried through the seasons and the ages and has been held constant. A tension, a living connection, has persisted and threaded through time, linking the common heritage and future of humankind. Each standing alone, but supported by a bulwark of humanity that reaches backward in time, almost every age has been instrumental in the erratic but ever upward thrust of human development. Moral lessons have been incorporated in the mind in approximating a human condition worthy of living. That condition, of course, decries war and promotes peace. It extols the virtues of peaceful living and manifests concern for life and the quality of life.

Certainly there is evidence affirmed over 2,500 years ago of the prophetic goal and ideal of universal peace and brotherhood, cited to this day and proclaimed again before the world in March, 1979, by the leaders of Israel, Egypt, and the United States:

> And they shall beat their swords into plowshares,
> And their spears into pruning-hooks;
> Nation shall not lift up sword against nation,
> Neither shall they learn war any more.
>
> *Isaiah 2:4*
> *740-700* B.C.E.[69]

CHAPTER FOUR

CHANGE AND PEACE IN THE DISTANT PAST

𝒫opular literature has portrayed the human image as being close to animal origins, ever ready to explode in bestiality, guarding territory jealously. A short rein on primitive emotions is inclined to let loose upon any provocation, and intruders are to be feared, warned, and/or vanquished. The jungle lies close, and the savage instinct is easily aroused. Small wonder, then, that the guard must be ever up, weapons at the ready, prepared to do battle. In this view, human progress has been at best a horizontal development, if not a regressive state at times.

When observed over the long range, however, humanity has advanced to an amazing degree. In foreshortening human development, the perspective of time is not utilized, and distortion in focus is the result. Humans are not newcomers to earth. If the spiral of evolutionary ascent is accepted, and if the scientific findings of the origin of the earth and developing life forms have validity, it is in the nature of things to take note of the vast amount of time that has been incorporated in the living progression. Human beings are a part of this panoply of time in evolution, a part of a still-evolving metamorphosis.

Wondrously, now, humanity is consciously aware of its continuous relationship with time and, in minuscule manner, now here, now there, has found a way to ride the change, if not actually to direct it. This would indicate a certain mobility and freedom of choice, a feeling of confidence and expectation in the natural order (if not in self). How, then, does this confidence, this freedom and buoyancy, equate with the popular image of the human being as but a step away from the animal world, mired in sloth and clinging to a morass of primitive and barbaric emotions? At a glance, the equation is uneven. Where is acknowledgment of growth achieved over time, of human development that has reached splendid heights, of the desire for greater humanness, not lesser? A deeper search is necessary to dispel the stubborn notion and to set adrift, once and for all, the demeaning interpretations that serve to keep the human spirit in chains.

To begin, one lifts the set focus from the breaks, disruptions, and problems of human behavior and from the plethora of daily events. Freed, the search is lightly mobile and far-reaching. The focus lifts, widens, and encompasses the larger circumference. What is the human story? Where does it go? Having recessed some few thousands of years, let us continue the journey back in time for a while longer.

At once we are setting foot into a time of great and catalytic import, a time that may have made demands within the human breast no less than our time is demanding of us now. Survival was again the urgent issue. Nomad existence was ending.

The nomadic pattern that had previously held the social units together since time immemorial, the prescribed manner of seasonal shiftings of tribe and livestock and equipment, was ending. The wandering pattern and life-style that had been followed for however long was drawing to a close. A new movement and pattern of life was being ushered in, with all the ramifications and changes that would entail.

What was the reason for the change? It is hard to say. Perhaps the wanderers were easy prey for marauders; perhaps the loss of some old or sick or weak or young members was finally too much; perhaps the food supply was deemed insufficient; perhaps resources were diminishing, water holes were drying up, lands were parched; perhaps the longing to settle was deepening; perhaps the competition for location was growing; perhaps the members took issue with authority; perhaps greater involvement and decision making was needed and demanded; perhaps certain sites were favored; perhaps a measure of control over destiny and environment was felt; perhaps questions of meaning and purpose arose; perhaps a sense of peoplehood began to manifest itself; perhaps a sense of the order of the universe was absorbed; perhaps a sense of the future was presaged.

THE GREAT TRANSITION

A great change was taking place. Whatever the reasons were, and surely there were many, a radical shift in the direction and life-style of human patterning was evolving. Fundamental to this change was the transitional step from being food hunters and gatherers, and loosely mobile wanderers, to becoming food producers in settled enclaves. The ability to grow food and to provide for physical sustenance was a tremendous step in furthering and safeguarding the human condition, indicating a great advancement in knowledge and skill, ensuring survival. (In our time, perhaps, a comparable situation would be achieved with the ability to produce and provide adequate fuel and energy needs, or in the change from a war system to a peace system.)

A certain mastery over the environment was gained. A measure of control over destiny was won with the ability to raise and provide one's food. Not just individual destiny was involved, however, since this change involved the community and continued the knitted social pact. What has been called "the great transition" took place at this juncture, the transition from precivilized to civilized society,[70] the change that became the springboard of civilization. The agricultural revolution, as it became known, was instrumental in establishing organized cooperative living in settled stationary towns and villages and was the basis of civilization.[71]

By some ten thousand years ago, when animals were being domesticated and plants cultivated, when village and city life was being established, this pattern of settled, organized bonding became the pattern of future societies—a pattern that would later mushroom and swell into nation-states. An overall observation of this pattern of unfolding human relations—a bird's-eye view of this system of human interaction—reveals a general similarity of peacefully structured behavior. The family and extended family, or kinship, spread to groups, villages, and towns and, depending on size and place, swelled into cities, states, and nations.[72] Progressively, over time, this general pattern of structured cohesion repeated itself across the earth and maintained or reinstated the pattern even when ruptures occurred. A permanent pattern of social interaction, of building communities and nations, naturally evolved—a pattern that must finally be acknowledged and seen as indicative of the human will to group together, to build, and to interrelate peacefully with one another.

PEACE BUILDING

The subjective view of each member of society may or may not appreciate the individual role in the overall scheme of things, although the individual is considered the bedrock of civilization.[73] Are there many who are fully cognizant of the interlacing structure and bonding of human patterning? Have many considered that such similarity of behavior is scarcely due to random chance and that, actually in opposition to the commonly held notion that humans are aggressively warlike, people want to live cohesively structured and actively peaceful lives? The model or paradigm for group behavior has been the family, forming the basic unit of cultural patterns and social integration.[74] This paradigm has successfully extended itself to the national level and now faces itself internationally in search of a future.

This structured organization has been too little considered by historians. Its import is greater than is realized. At the very least to be considered is that thousands of years ago human beings indicated a willingness and desire to live communally, to live in close proximity to one another, to pool labor and resources, and, generally, to live in an established, organized manner. The city has been considered the principal example of civilization[75] and, noting the growth of various cities of that period—the oldest of which is about ten thousand years old, purported to be Jericho (8-10,000 B.C.E.)[76]—the claim may reasonably be made that *the history of peace building is thousands of years old, at least ten thousand years old, in fact, as old as civilization is claimed to be.*

Civilization is the relative advancement from primitive living and behavior to organized cooperation and dependence, and its social culture is considered a growth in development. Distinguished from barbarism, civilized advancement manifests greater enlightenment and humanity. (Both are differentiated from savagery, which is the least advanced form of culture.) Established and spread over earth for at least ten thousand years, civilization is the legacy that has been bequeathed from those who went before, a mandate from the past. It is the world's human inheritance.

Acknowledgment of this legacy, and respect and acceptance of this living gift, is the job of present day world citizens, as is the need to protect it, preserve it, and pass it on to all who will follow. More than an idealized notion, peaceful cohabitation and interaction is a tried condition and actualization within and between nations by common consent and practice. Civilization is the form. Peace, then, is a continuation of civilization—of reaching forth to the world community, forging further links in international friendships, and of maintaining and strengthening existing bonds while extending the pattern around the globe. *Civilization is peace actualized.*

The style and pattern of civilization has successfully weathered the trials and vicissitudes of the intervening years, enlarging to nation-states the world over and continuing the species of homo sapiens. The understanding and recognition of human cooperation and the desire to live peacefully in a settled and neighborly style (a style that has been repeated worldwide) is of utmost importance to the subject at hand. Perhaps because we are all part of this style, participants in civilization, immersed in it, so to speak, it is scarcely realized or noted. Perhaps emphasis has been focused on the breaches of peace to such an extent that peace itself is obscured and well nigh invisible. Perhaps, as in the forest, we are too close to the trees.

A subtle mantle of myopic perversity persists in resisting any efforts to demonstrate peace as a viable option and, indeed, a *fait accompli*. What with wanting peace and deploring peace, suffering over peacelessness and anticipating dangers to peace, the *search* for peace has nearly become an end in itself, more important than its object. This circular path endlessly decries the possibility of peace in continuous self-denial, and all eruptions of conflict or potential conflict are loudly lamented (if not championed). Clarity of perception is urgently required.

We have gone far afield from the facts. The fact that peace has indeed been accomplished and has been in effect for ages in many places among countless peoples is resisted *ad absurdum*. The astigmatic insistence on perceiving only wars and clashes is nonsense and must now be completely put to rest, lest the holders of this view run the risk of schizophrenic split, denial of fact, and become subject to curious appraisal. It will do no longer. The refusal to admit human potential and the lack of faith in the human ability to act cooperatively and creatively are not tenable conclusions. A fresh viewpoint is essential, one that is not embroiled in the death throes of a waning life-style and perspective.

The above statements do not deny that peace in the world has been imperfectly maintained, unevenly distributed, ill-defined, and at risk. Nevertheless, continued misperception and misinterpretation of actual conditions cannot be condoned. There are pockets of peace, islands of peace, continents of peace. Peace exists, albeit not universally; it is steadfastly practiced and desperately requires acknowledgment, support, and extension for stability and growth. The crucial need now is for conscious and active efforts aimed at extending the system of peaceful cohesion. The goal should be clearly spelled out and conscientiously upheld—*world peace as a normative pattern for future interactions by a consenting world populace.* It is time to stand up boldly for peace.

Is there basis for common consent? Common concern has already been established by realization of the threat to civilization as a whole from the excesses of warfare. Common experience has been witness to the spread of civilization throughout the globe and has been a participant in the progress. Established over time—at least some ten thousand years of patient construction—tacit consent was demonstrated by those earlier people who, although less sophisticated than today's inhabitants, met the challenge of their time and turned to each other, thereby insuring survival for themselves and for later progeny (us). There is precedence in the survival crisis of this day to be garnered from the past. Although the issue then was mastery of the environment, whereas the issue now may be conservation, the crisis was and is the same—survival. As then, we must turn to each other.

At this turning point, however, mention of conflict is necessary. "War is as old as civilization" is an old and familiar refrain. Is there any explanation for this (self-inflicted) malady? In *The Ascent of Man* (1973), Jacob Bronowski has concluded that far from being a human instinct, warfare is planned thievery, having its beginning ten thousand years ago when the desert dwellers attacked the villages to plunder their accumulated stores of food.[77]

A deepening chasm developed between the settlers and the itinerants, a void that grew with time, the one negating the life-style of the other. Pillage and attack became periodic occurrences, the victor taking the spoils. Theft of stores of food and goods was lure enough to entice would-be attackers, and this undoubtedly contributed to the precarious condition of the time. However, it is suggested that a deeper, more fundamental reason was behind group warfare. Organized conflict was a violent response to that great and tremendous shift from an old order to a new one, from the roaming nomadic life-style to stationary village and community life, to civilization (and to peace).

As the ancient roving style of life had become unsatisfactory and was abandoned by those who now insisted on community life and involvement, the proponents of the old system may have been bitterly reluctant to permit a "changing of the guard", clinging to the established pattern, vehemently venting their anger against the settlers and the new way of life. The old order, the status quo, the entrenched system, was unwilling to accommodate the new movement, and they attacked it. That new movement, that shift in human perception and participation, was the beginning of civilization itself—the establishment of a settled and united people, a gathering together and a reaching forth at one and the same time.

Organized resistance was necessary to protect and sustain the communities (and food stocks). The villagers and townspeople necessarily formed their own protective units to safeguard their chosen way of life, meeting the threat from without. Effective, this method ballooned into standing armies for later landowners, noblemen and kings and, later still, for states and nations. It is apparent that matters progressed and became refined until warfare became the specific threat that is today confronting humankind.

At today's proportions, organized warfare has become an explicit and deadly threat to the world. Wars of present potential magnitude threaten all of civilization—friend and foe alike. Straining at the bounds, today's mechanized and sophisticated standing armies and automated weapons systems stand belligerently before humankind and the earth, threatening to consume each in cancerous abandon.

A juncture has been reached in human relations. Everywhere nations bristle with independent hostility, wary of any perceived incursions into their sovereign independence, but seeking alliances for group strength. Everywhere large and small enclaves of civilization are ready to protect their chosen way of life. And almost everywhere "protection" is in the form of military solutions. Yet if fully activated, as much harm would be received as tendered, omnidestruction being entirely possible. The means are inadequate for the need, and the cost is totally unacceptable to humanity.

A new perception is critically needed in viewing the state of the world and in safeguarding the future. A turning point in human affairs has been reached, as in the days of old. A crossroads in the evolutionary stretch has been arrived at and, as before, so long ago, survival, raw survival, is the common turning point—the point of departure, the destination and thrust into tomorrow's existence.

Precisely here is where there is common ground for consensus in the firm projection of *common humanity*, neither diminishing nor enhancing borders or boundaries. The common ground recognizes *common tenancy on the same earth, a common heritage and destiny*. The common ground recognizes that *the human species is one unit and must, first and foremost, assure its own survival.* The common ground is the *continuation of civilized living in peaceful interaction,* recognizing the desire to live and let live, while remaining interdependent within the greater world setting. The common ground recognizes *environmental demands and needs, and the attachment to earth.* The common ground is the continued formation of sturdy links between different cultures and customs, appreciating the multihued races, variety, and values of the diverse peoples of the world. The common ground, finally, is the *value of life and peace,* and the continuation of the species *in a manner and quality befitting the evolving human being.* It acknowledges both the past and the present and prepares the path for change into the future.

The change that is before us now is not so much an external change—peace and civilization being an established and experienced pattern on earth—as an internal change, a change in attitude. The new transition is one of fundamental refocus, of mental disposition and dedicated intent. The pattern is well set. What was started so long ago in the cradle of civilization and what has been developing for millennia, what is urgently the need and what shall safeguard the species and the environment, what shall propel us into the twenty-first century and beyond, is the extension of peaceful relationships and orderly transitions between disparate peoples and nations worldwide. Recognition of the peace process is necessary. The pattern need merely be continued. Peace is present in multiple places and is globally possible in the new age. Indeed, there may not be a new age without it.

Has our journey into time ended? Are we finished with this backward glance into the distant past? Not yet. Although this is the time where the marker of civilization and peace is placed and at which, for chronological clarity and global uniformity, calendars might well be set and synchronized to record the year as, say, 11,988—indicating that time of great human import, *the onset of civilization and of peace* (later manifested in that great religious outburst from which others emanated, and that has led to greater understanding and refinement of meaning and purpose in human existence)—there is still some unfinished work. Even civilization did not spring into form without its history, the history of time out of mind. One must recede yet into the mists....

CHAPTER FIVE

EARTH AND EARLY HUMANITY IN THE ANCIENT PAST

The entire globe is involved when the matter of peace is considered; the whole world is the issue. In recalling the scenario earlier upheld, the commonality between annihilation and survival is the totality of the situation. Extinction, annihilation, survival are all matters in toto. The narrowed viewpoint of the immediate, of this time and place only, is parochially insufficient to enter into the subject of peace. Enlarged perception and extended perspective sufficient to encompass the earth in its entirety, and humanity as a whole, is required. Existence, its future or its end, is in question. Such is the nature of the dichotomous problem that confronts humankind at this point in time.

In accommodating the need to enlarge the thinking and to consider the world globally, the recent experiences, image, and awareness of earth as a self-contained sphere in space may be recalled and kept in mind. This realization is brief in terms of human awareness, such knowledge being of relatively short duration. And, it can be argued, nothing has changed in the greater sense; that is, the earth is exactly where it has always been, as is the spatial expanse beyond it. However, although nothing has intrinsically changed in this greater sense, resultant human perception has been fundamentally influenced and unequivocally altered for all time. A basic shift in perspective has been involved, and it entails and heralds a change in understanding, adapting and coping with existence in the "new" reality.

This change is a core shift and enlargement of human perception and awareness of the nature of earth and living on it, and it is comparable to all such previous expansions of knowledge and understanding that have occurred during the course of human history, contributing to growth and evolutionary adaptation and, undoubtedly, permitting survival. This "nothing", this non-change, this change only in human knowledge and perception is, actually, everything. A long view of the physical universe, of time and of humanity, is engendered.

Biologically and fundamentally, each individual has roots in the cosmos, in veiled time, in the very beginning of life on earth. This extension of each man's and woman's attachment to earth and to the basic order from which all have evolved extends interminably the experience of life and the sensitivity that may be brought to the subject of peace. When and how did human beings evolve? What essentially human characteristics do we possess? How are humans different from animals?

A brief reminder of earth's and humankind's early development will serve to recall with respect the process and time it took for evolution to accomplish its handiwork. Within the global framework, humanity has experienced the dregs and the sublime of existence. Undaunted, humans have assumed magisterial qualities, daring even to reach beyond earth's bounds. Yet humankind is an earthling, a terrestrial being, spawned, as it were, out of earth's bowels. There is a kinship with earth (and, it is suggested, it would not be amiss to develop an ethnic sense of pride, responsibility, and proprietorship—perhaps stewardship is a better concept—towards earth, the homeland and base), and, until a later time when the stars may further beckon, it would be advisable to become comfortable with the roots of human blossoming for authenticity of being. Picking up the thread again, the journey backward through the ages will touch momentarily at some special developments along the way.

EARLY HUMAN DEVELOPMENT

The academic study of humankind's early history—anthropology, archaeology, ancient history, art, etc.—has opened up a store of knowledge attesting to the effects of time absorbed in human evolution. A very long time has been incorporated into human development. A minimum of *two million years* and possibly *fourteen or fifteen million years*, or more, separate the human from primate origin.

The belligerent and hostile aggressiveness so inculcated in our notions of human behavior as ineradicable parts of human nature, and as savage characteristics due to the line of animal descent, may be more myth than fact. The image of human antecedents as warlike "naked apes", so popularly presented, has been vigorously disputed.[78]

Discovered in this century, in 1925, a fossil named *Australopithecus africanus*, possibly female, was found in Olduvai Gorge, Tanzania, Africa. Thought to be about two million years old, theory has suggested that here is the antecedent of humanity, a being having more humanlike characteristics than apelike ones.[79] Another discovery and interpretation has suggested that human ancestry is even earlier, dating to *Ramapithecus*, precursor of *Australopithecus africanus*, who lived some ten to fifteen million years ago.[80] Yet other recent discoveries have placed the onset of the human race between these two dates, referring to another species, *Australopithecus afarensis*, a creature that existed three to four million years ago, suggested as ancestral to humankind.[81] Whichever theory and claim is correct, human roots are at the very least two million years old and possibly fifteen million years old or more. That is a very long time for humans to have been developing, to have refined their characteristics, and to have become special and unparalleled beings.

Unique in the living kingdom, admitting relationship but removed by millions of years from the nearest chimpanzee relative,[82] the human being has certain physical attributes completely lacking in animals. The ability to balance and walk on two legs in a permanent upright position was a major factor in divergence, contributing to the separation of the human from the apes.[83] This erect stance has altered certain other physical attributes as well: The foot formation is different, legs are longer in relation to body size, the backbone is not bowed, and because hands were freed in the upright position, they have contributed to the entire organism's development.[84] Of course, the head is balanced upright, with eyes and nose in different alignment than in animals, as can be readily observed. These and other physical attributes were set and utilized ages ago, and the vast expanse of time involved in human development cannot be longer ignored (nor can the self-defeating propensity for placing the human being immediately-to-back with the animal world be continued. It simply lacks veracity.)

There were other characteristics that differentiated early man and marked him for evolutionary survival. The ability to adapt to different environments was a lifesaving trait, as was the generalized digestive tract (and superior nervous system). Wide selection of plant and animal foods was permitted. The ability to gain food and energy is essential to life, as is the ability to withstand and adapt to climatic conditions. Specialized organisms are generally vulnerable to change; the species that best adapt to their environments are more likely to survive and proliferate.[85]

Physical development of the hand and, especially, the *thumb*, has enabled the great grasping power, efficient manipulation, and sensitive touch that are distinctly human features. This small member, a "masterpiece of nature", has been credited as a vital factor in human technological and artistic development.[86] Early man soon made use of the resources at hand, making tools from stone, rock, and wood, and, as time progressed, developing more efficient uses of the environment, ranging from weapons and clothes to shelter-making and advanced artifacts. "Man, the tool-maker" has been identified through the ages by the variety, artistry, and creative uses of devices made for using, changing, or storing energy.[87] It has been theorized that the technology developed for utilizing energy is directly related to the progress of a people's cultural and social development. A growing confidence and mastery of the environment was early evidenced, promising further control of destiny.

Human evolution produced a being ever moving far afield from the animal species; and, it has been emphasized, serious studies of human behavior should focus on humans, not animals.[88] Some vitally important evolutionary changes included complex brain enlargement and development, the ability to associate and conceptualize, finding and making meaning of life and conditions, and the creation of symbols, which were the basis of language and communication. All people speak, although languages differ, and there is an immense "freedom of learning". Whereas certain biological traits may be set or bonded, *learning* is not. Crediting the uniqueness of the human brain, learning has been considered a vital factor in distinguishing human beings from primates.

Widely diversified cultural characteristics are not found among the animals, notwithstanding remarkably developed instincts and patterns of behavior. It is the human family that possesses the rich variety of continuous yet ever novel cultural behaviors.[89] It is the cultural advancement and adaptations—the images, ideologies, and belief systems—that have created the vast and provocative diversity among humans.

A cultural system is learned behavior. It is neither predetermined nor an instinct, and it is subject to change and modification. Discarding old ways and/or inventing new ones are the continuous methods for introducing change into a people's culture to meet new and changing circumstances or information. Never occurring at the exact same time in society, change is a gradual phenomenon spurred by individual and collective rejection of customary norms, augmented by accumulated evidence and public involvement. At some critical point, the weight of the new knowledge, skill, or experience overtakes the old way, and the process of change is set in motion.

The world's cultures have not progressed at the same rate, nor are they the same—attesting to the variations of human imagination and interpretations. However, each sets the parameters of social mores and values in which individuals are born and live, indicating developed and complex thought systems and experiences within that specific social setting and natural environment. Responding to the needs and problems arising from individual and group living, cultures develop as answers and are evidence of the continuous growth and expansion of the human mind. Cultural evolution is an acquired knowledge and behavior and, once established, outstrips biological evolution a hundredfold.[90]

Over a million years ago human characteristics of speech and processes of thought permitted humans to communicate and express by word, dance and art, all the while inventing new behavior. Tools and artifacts attest to the development. Social action and communication that fostered planned cooperation in hunting, food procuring, and food sharing indicated processes of projection, preparation, and future planning. An important survival skill, cooperation was early implemented in human groupings and societies. Because hunting often involved group or communal planning and action,[91] enhancement of vital food supplies, for example, led to labor sharing. Early practices of division of labor were developed for ease of accomplishment. Humankind has always lived in groups; the human is a social being, and people early discovered the advantages of working together to accomplish what one individual was incapable of.

Cultural development and the progressive experience of living and working together would not have been possible without language and communication. Learned language was one of the prime characteristics of human cultural advancement, enabling direct and greater communication and improved cooperation in adapting to the common problems of the environment. The human ability to speak is universal.

Art further aided and transformed the spoken language in another mode of communication. Early humankind communicated emotions and belief systems through various epochal art forms, many of which have, fortunately, survived and accumulated through the ages. Art in early societies served not only to communicate and evoke responses in the members of respective cultures through expressions of religious and social views, but was (and is) a visible reminder of the ideas, experiences, and world notions held by those earlier practitioners. Universally expressed, but different in time and place, art has served to relate the human connection to and with the world at large. No less than now, early humankind tried to understand and cope with the environment and age into which each had been born. The cave paintings seen in Altamira, Spain, and in southern France are 20,000 years old and capture, through time, the images and environment of earlier human beings.[92] Representations of their exploits and perceptions, the artistic renditions have provided valuable insights to all future inhabitants.

Later, much later, as an outgrowth of visual art, writing became the abstract symbol of language. Improved communication, record keeping, and storage of information was afforded, as well as better transmission of knowledge and education. Culture is a cumulative phenomenon of human society, and generations of people have learned from the accumulated records of previous inhabitants. With the advent of writing and, later still, of printing, knowledge was more easily disseminated through the populace, quickening the pace of acculturation.

HOMO SAPIENS SAPIENS

The modern species, homo sapiens sapiens (contemporary modern man, from the Greek—homo, man, and Latin—sapiens, intelligent), was evident on the world scene approximately 100,000 to 150,000 years ago, the same species that has survived to the present time and of which we are all part.[93] Biologically, the human race is one species.

Those cultures that are now best recognized were formed as relatively recently as fifty to one hundred thousand year ago.[94] Whereas the law of genetics and biology may determine basic needs—the need for food, for instance—it does not account for the myriad ways human beings have devised for meeting that need. That is the part played by cultures and cultural methods.

The capacity to learn, to change, and to adapt has continually infused cultures and distinguished the human species from all others, and a variety of social systems, new behavior, and countless inventions have creatively resulted over time. (For example, fire was an invention that aided human survival, especially through the ice ages.) Because of speech, knowledge, and organization, human populations were able to adapt to varied situations that eventually led to technical skills and social progress. And it has been established through fossil records that *learning* was the major factor in behavioral changes 40,000 years ago or less, indicating that human nature had evolved by that time.[95]

But human development, as it is now perceived, took place within the last twelve thousand years.[96] It is during this time that the great cultural development occurred, changing humans into the burgeoning "masters" of the environment that they became. The agricultural revolution signified the end of the Ice Age mentality, the end of the ancient wandering pattern, and it ushered in a flowering of social life and civilization. The domestication of animals and the cultivation of plants eased the dreadful urgency of constantly foraging for food and released human potential to begin the long accumulation of skills and knowledge and technology that has grown and transcended the ages. The transition to a civilized and settled life-style was a forerunner to the growth of the cities, regions, and nation-states that have evolved all over the earth as they are now.

Humanity has been slowly spiraling in evolutionary cyclical growth for ages upon ages. Bitterly maligned, often self-deprecated, the evolving human has been walking indomitably through the corridors of time seeking exoneration and relief from some burden of the past, long gone. It cannot be but that the human species awaits that ennobling experiment that will accord its members the venerable respect due to age, and that will evoke the potential for greatness that is lying dormant within each human breast, trusting and waiting for recognition. It awaits only the *expectation* of ability to unfurl and authenticate the inner talent that has been imbued and invested with time. The long view of evolutionary time is latent within each human being; each one has successfully traveled through ancestry the same circuitous and hazardous route over eons of time; and each one potentially gazes untroubledly ahead to a similarly lengthy journey in time wherever the human creativity and adaptive ability will unerringly guide and direct life.

IN THE BEGINNING

Human history and evolutionary development reaches back engagingly into time millions of years, and recognition of this fact gives inordinately creditable status and pride to the human saga. It is a miraculous story, only partially told, and each person has a right to marvelously wonder at the innumerable bends, turns, and progressions that must have attended the elevation of human growth (so endlessly complicated that real comprehension is utterly defied).

In the eye of time, however—the greater time of global development—human growth is but another interesting phenomenon in the evolution of life forms, merely deserving of a slight niche in the developmental tale. What will matter, of course, is the durability of the species—the survival and continuity of the collective. Nevertheless, the human being has reason to take heart and be justifiably proud of the tenacity for survival and adaptive growth to environmental conditions that have been demonstrated for no less than two million years, if not for many times that span.

Recognition of the epochal nature of the time and circumstances required for development of *earth*, and all that has naturally evolved upon it (humans included), requires a most humble and awesome attitude. The matter must be seen in perspective. The earth itself is a living entity that has evolved from the mists of time, from time so primordially ancient that the concept must be reversed in the mind and termed, "In the Beginning..."

The structural concept of time far surpasses human timing, and in its contemplation, shades of planetary time hover on the periphery of our consciousness. After all, the earth itself is a planet, warming itself in prescribed revolution around the sun, and it has its own circling satellite, the moon. This visualization prepares the way to comparison with, and consideration of, space and galactic time, readying the mind to become intriguingly engaged in an entirely new dimension of seemingly infinite mystery and variety. But there is a prerequisite for all of this—we must survive!

An admonishment is in order. What has taken more than four billion years to develop was certainly not meant to be wantonly destroyed by some few megalomaniacal individuals of this day. This globe belongs to all its inhabitants (if it can "belong" to any at all). Past, present, and future, all have an investment and stake in its welfare. What has taken such vast amounts of time to unfold that it can only be reckoned in terms of epochs, eras, geologic figures and astronomical measurements, terms of such sweepingly inclusive nature, must fill the beholder with tremulous reverence, if not respectful fear. One stands on the mountaintop and surveys the panorama of earth in hushed awe. How did it happen? What began the formation? What balance of nature keeps the complex arrangement alive? What lies beyond? The grandeur of the spectacle enlarges the viewer even as it reduces him or her to the status of minute spectator, humbly giving thanks to one's God for the privilege of sharing in the living experience.

The lack of respect and barbaric temperament that ignore the timeless message are shameful disclosures, a blot on the species. Whatever else may have been learned, it is apparent that the value of life has been largely, and pitifully, underdeveloped. Blindness and irresponsibility to one's own habitat and environment (and everyone else's) is exhibited by the insane behavior that would place the very earth in jeopardy. Nuclear armaments and weapons of mass destruction have done just that, as has the mentality that would call such means into use. It cannot be condoned, nor silence continued, lest it be taken as tacit consent. The limit for compliance has been reached. *This is our home; this our planet; this is our life; and this promises our future!*

It is time to become better acquainted with our home base. Some greater facts about the globe are presented. In the diagram that follows, Figure 1, a circle denotes earth's developmental progress over time, touching on some specific ages and appearances of living forms. The total age of the earth as it is presently known is in the top (twelve o'clock) position—4.5 billion years old, approximately. A simple device, the "clock" portrays in chronological order the greater events that have unfolded on earth.

The process of photosynthesis, whereby bacteria convert sunlight and carbon dioxide into oxygen and food energy, is believed to have contributed to the early development of the earth. In time, this allowed for an atmosphere in which oxygen-breathing organisms evolved.[97] (A recent find of a large rock built up by layers of bacterialike organisms, a *stromatolite*, is said to date back about 3.5 billion years.)[98] Eons passed before more complicated life forms developed. Then, in relatively quickening tempo, various entities appeared, from marine life (550 million years ago) and dinosaurs (200 million years ago) to carnivorous and grazing animals (50 million years ago).[99] Untold variations that developed, struggled for existence, and changed or died out must simply be ignored or left to fertile imaginations, as must the physical upheavals of a developing earth.

Figure 2 is that relatively small segment of time wherein humanity made its appearance on earth, and it indicates the greater stages of human development. In these two simplified diagrams, it is noted that human origins on earth appeared only within the last moment of earth's existence, so

Figure 1: Greater Time Scale of Earth's Developing Life

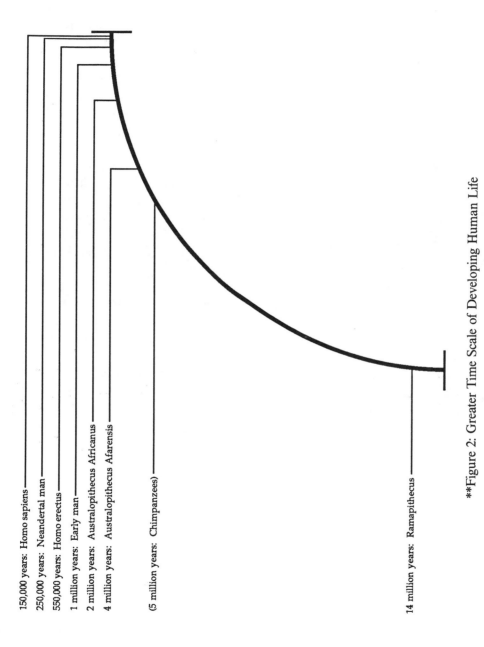

150,000 years: Homo sapiens

250,000 years: Neandertal man

550,000 years: Homo erectus

1 million years: Early man

2 million years: Australopithecus Africanus

4 million years: Australopithecus Afarensis

(5 million years: Chimpanzees)

14 million years: Ramapithecus

**Figure 2: Greater Time Scale of Developing Human Life

to speak, even if using the largest amount of time presently considered to encompass human development—fifteen million years. In other words, *earth existed for some 4,485,000,000 years of time, more than ninety-nine per cent of its existence, before evolution began to shape the human being.* On the one hand, the great tract of time invested and incorporated into human creation and development indicates unparalleled value. On the other hand, there are clearly some lessons to be learned yet from old Mother Earth. She has simply been around a lot longer than anyone or anything else, and she knows a great deal about development, survival, and evolution.

The message of life that earth has to tell has scarcely penetrated human consciousness, certainly not the minds of those who are hell-bent on war, destruction, annihilation, and extinction. These curious ones, possibly incomplete and errored beings, are living and pointing in exact opposition to earth's dictates and are best not heeded or attended to (if not clapped in irons). Those who would survive must reject or block out flawed messages from malfunctioning individuals opposed or indifferent to human and environmental life. Those who would survive must recognize and protect the earth that has spawned all life. Those who are destined to survive must primarily value life and know it for the mysteries that unfold in its wake. All else is chimerical glitter, shadows that envelop, shoals that impale....

Earth's message is clear and trumpeted across time: develop, adapt, create, survive! It would be less than "the peculiar glory of man" were it not diligently noted, taken to heart, and meticulously heeded!

PART II

THE MEANING AND PSYCHOLOGY

OF PEACE AND WAR

CHAPTER SIX

PEACE—WAR—SURVIVAL

$\mathcal{T}$he desire for peace, while laudable, is not enough for general implementation nor sufficient for its preservation and continuity. Naivete is revealed by nations, both by populace and leadership, in misunderstanding the psychology and dynamics involved. No matter how noble the intent, or even the universality of desire, greater understanding, sophistication, and respect for the entire peace process is required before it can be sufficiently established to become a globally accepted system and pattern of behavior in international relations and foreign affairs. A bona fide peace policy requires proclaimed intent bolstered by bold public action and broad public support, not sub voce secrecy or precarious standing.

Awareness is dawning that peace between nations is an active condition, a mutual arrangement of relationships, an agreement and process that require cooperative involvement, public education and stable support. Conscious identification of the principle, as well as the organization of plan, is needed. Ongoing peace is a living compact.

Activity on behalf of peace must be an openly declared effort, naturally and energetically engaged in, with general expectation of successful accomplishment and performance. Attitudinal and institutional support are necessary, involving the basic agreement or consensus of the world's citizens. This latter statement might cause some serious hesitation because of the sheer numbers of people residing all over the globe, more than four and a half billion. But inasmuch as the desire for peace seems to be a common thread among most cultures and peoples, sufficient agreement is anticipated to make of peace an accepted principle and working goal. People generally cooperate quite normally, or expect to do so, until militarism or war is decided for and thrust upon them. The greater rifts are usually between nations.

War between nations is generated as a rule by a military or political decision involving relatively few people—decision makers in power—that is buttressed and sanctioned by institutionalized systems of public support. There are more overtly established institutional supports for war between nations than there are for peace (commands, armies, weapons, and funds being readily available), a situation that is obviously unbalanced. The notion that war is *not* inevitable, or the realization that it can be loosed upon a hapless world by the decisions of some few people—decisions that are entirely arbitrary—is just beginning to sift through the public mind. No nation can decide to wage war in the world, for example, if there are no armies, no weapons, no budget, no citizen acceptance, and no public support to maintain the aggressively hostile act. The option to choose war and to sustain military operations can only be supported by the ready ability to do so. Trained manpower must be available, along with weapons and technology commensurate with the need and development of the times. These requirements must be kept in near-readiness and bolstered when needed through the active support of the people.

The people have become habituated to supporting the military pattern and presumably would continue to do so as long as the public need was served. As long as the situation and perception of means to accomplish the desired end was constant, it might be expected that the the pattern would remain unchanged. There would be no apparent reason to change a satisfactory method of protection.

It is the citizenry's perception of their security needs that is vital to the preparations made for them. *The responsibility and power for survival resides ultimately with the people.* Should the popular will decide that particularly *peaceful means* of international conduct are needed for security, and should the people be willing to support it actively, nothing can stop the implementation of such means. The time for peace will have come!

Waging peace in the world is a political decision without, as yet, a wide base of active public support (public sentiment, yes; public support, no—but the line dividing public sentiment from public support is a fine one and eminently bridgeable). The realization that peace itself can be waged has not yet penetrated far into the collective consciousness, although awakenings are occurring. As the idea of international peace becomes more conscious and more practicable, resort to war is increasingly seen as irrational, if not psychotic and suicidal. At the least, inadequate knowledge of options in behavioral control is demonstrated, and insufficient respect for the peace process is revealed.

CAUSES OF WAR

Although this book is primarily concerned with peace, the facts of war are long and insistent and cannot be denied. In researching the voluminous writings on war, some factors in the causes and conditions of war seem sufficiently pertinent to include here. The selection of these factors is necessarily arbitrary since reasons for war are many and varied. Nevertheless, in view of the fact that even as detailed a chronicler of war as Quincy Wright has stated that there is no one reason or cause of war,[100] the following selections are at least pertinent and relevant, and they attempt to cast some light on this area. Certain features must be kept in mind: the world overview, the overwhelming weight and habit of war, and the centuries and millennia of struggle in establishing and strengthening civilization.

The realization that war can be studied, analyzed, interpreted, and understood, reveals that war is not omnipotent, mythical or an immutable dispensation from a state of nature or higher level of universal order. War can be likened to humankind's struggle against death and disease and the medical search for cures, although war itself is now the greatest threat of all to life .[101]

Quite mundane reasons have been seen as direct or indirect causes of war. Will and Ariel Durant have stated in *The Lessons of History* (1968) that the reasons for war are similar to the reasons for competition between people—that is, belligerence, conceit, property, power, etc. Whereas individuals are generally restrained from mayhem by morals or convention, there are few, if any, restraints on the nation-state.[102]

In ancient days, war was considered a natural condition.[103] Quincy Wright in *A Study of War* (1942/1965) has acknowledged that group warfare was an accepted means for the acquisition of land, slaves, and stores of good.[104]

Noted earlier, reaching back into anthropological time, Jacob Bronowski, scientist, declared war to be organized and planned theft, its onset occurring in the springtime of human civilization, when the nomads spilled out of the desert to attack the settlements for their food supplies.

An army must be fed, of course, and the ability to produce food was an important factor in sustaining an armed force. The preparation of defense forces for the safety of the community required enough people and labor to maintain food production, supply, and surplus for the military as well as for the general need. Early civilization, with its neophyte town and city developments and growing agrarian capability, reinforced the might of kings and rulers by supplying surplus food to armies.[105] Whether through cooperation, duty, loyalty, or coercion, the stage was set for further group compliance. Threat and force, anxiety, and fear of attack may have been sufficiently compelling to reinforce and set the communal pattern of military support. Of course, additional energy then became required and generated for the satellite needs of military undertakings. Those needs have been amply evidenced from that time forward by all the accoutrements of this entire mode of reinforcing behavior—supplies, weapons, weapon makers, strategic planning, communications, forced conscription, taxation, etc.

Humans have refined their warmaking abilities through the ages, and warfare has been elevated to a great skill. One talks of the "rules of warfare", the "art of war", of "war games", and so on. Its dictates decide the fate of countries and peoples. Its demands and appetites are fed and acquiesced to religiously. This deadly contest has been socially sanctioned and raised within the social organization to an unprecedented (and ultimately debilitating) height. Now, in contemplating its reduction and eventual role change, there are many other conditions of war—some are beliefs—that should be discussed. Wars are also fought in the minds of men, and belief in the absence of war must have stable roots.

Since war has been planned and executed by a multitude of people over time, it has become deeply entrenched in the systems, habits, and thought patterns of individuals and nations. It has been taught, experienced, and expected. It is this *expectation* of war, the belief in its inevitability, that has led to feelings of helplessness and continued passive acquiescence. The author of *Why Nations Go To War* (1974), John G. Stoessinger, has declared that a feeling of the inevitability of war has been prevalent, and a fatalistic attitude has dominated. The result could be foreseen but not prevented; it seemed foreordained and beyond human control.[106] (And those who have been somnolently lulled into inertia have been swept into the lethal wake.)

Yet decisions for war were and are made by human beings, no matter what manner of oracle, deity, star conformation, social or national cause, etc., is invoked. There is no foreordained conclusion to the onset of armed conflict between opposing groups or nations. It was and is a matter of choice. And as with all choices, war may be rejected out of hand. No matter what reasons are cited for going to war, or how passively or actively stirred are the emotions, decisions for military fighting are made by quite mortal men. Human responsibility in this decision making cannot be evaded.

The personalities of the leaders, the decision makers, preempt the war-making arena, since so much depends on these few people. How the leader perceives or misperceives himself and his opponent's character, intentions, strength, or weakness is critical to decision making. Ego, power, avarice, economics, politics, and pressure all come to bear on the leader and press for decision. Typically, however, leaders delude themselves.[107] If they misperceive the other's power, strength, or intent, or feel overly optimistic or unacceptably threatened, war may become imminent. A psychology of power, testing, bluster and action is exercised. Innate characteristics and personalities are set off (while the lives and fates of countless people hang in the balance).

The weight and custom of war itself and its readiness to hand are not least of the pressures on the decision makers. Warfare has become embedded in social behavior, and many have grown accustomed to and dependent on this method of social "control" and "security". This forceful means has been invoked time and again throughout history. It is simple enough and excused by human societies to decide for war—a time-tested and "honored" method for resolving conflicts, for establishing supremacy, and for decimating the enemy. (Presently, of course, the enemy increasingly resembles the face in the mirror, and now retaliation is such that the face in the mirror is likely to be decimated as well.)

The pattern of war has been one of vanquishing the enemy, of establishing superiority by might, and of bringing the hated adversaries to their knees, thus signifying victory and identifying victor and vanquished. There is clearly established a winner and a loser, and perhaps the seeds of future war are scattered again in the fertile ground of smarting defeat and seething discontent (if not in the "successful" maneuver itself). Society must be rebuilt, leaders must again be thrust forward, and power must be regained. Decision making is again delegated to the few. The pattern is a hierarchical design, male-dominated, competitive, and repetitive in its nature.

Concern for life—concern for the quality of life or for life's perpetuation—is not the focus of the military. Such matters are the prerogative of the civilian, the public individual, the collective body whom the military serves. Civilian life is subject to unspeakable disruption in case of war, and it is now the public's duty and responsibility to be fully involved in decision making. Since the potential havoc from organized conflict is so vast, decisions for war should be totally reconsidered. Decisions for implementation of mechanical might that can cause possibly irreversible human and environmental damage should be ruled out of consideration. Shifting this decision making to the military machine, or leaving it in the hands of a few people representing that body, is an act of utmost irresponsibility and folly in light of current technological capabilities. The military might of the people is its tool, not its rule.

The result of continued warmaking worldwide may be the disembodiment of all civilization. Whereas the aim and intent of the military vehicle may have been to act in the service of the people by safeguarding its entity and life-style, the task has mushroomed beyond the capability of that body to perform. Incredibly, militarism itself has become an explicit danger to the people. It has become an ultimate source of potential annihilation (surely not its original intent). The mode of operation is dictatorial, in opposition to the society it defends. There is an increasingly wide division between military perception of the world and the public's need and viewpoint. Authoritatively and hierarchically established, most laws governing military behavior are jealously guarded under military, not civil, control. Rules and regulations are often in contradiction to societal laws and mores, and the laws of man and God are frequently flouted. (The consequence to humankind is not without its irony or, perhaps, supreme justification.)

As the nature of decision makers and of those influencing them has become apparent, and as the nature of power, of social pressure, and of the habit of war have been seen as the influencing factors they are in fostering and perpetuating war, knowledge and awareness are being gained in limiting and preventing its onset. Also, the more peace is strengthened and extended, the less war can be loosed. *Prevention of war, therefore, must be society's first watchword; simultaneously, peace must be nurtured, promoted, and extended.*

It has been noted that decisions for war have often been based on perfectly mundane reasons. Wars are not necessarily caused by special violations although, of course, that may occur. Nor are wars particularly due to the public's emotions, injustices, needs, etc., although they may well camouflage such conditions and divert energies accordingly. Wars may simply result from deteriorating conditions or worsening relations, nonstop irritations or combat readiness.

We have seen that wars may be dependent largely on decision makers liable to the full range of fallible human characteristics and explosive temperaments, of social habits and power-flexing, and of lack of viable options. They may be due to the necessity and pressure for the leader to make a decision (even a bad one) and the lack of peace options and peace commitment. The onset of war may be as much a predictable slide into the abyss, without proper safeguards and creative alternatives, as is the swing of a pendulum or the gravitational fall of a released ball.

This may not add to a sense of security in becoming aware of human limitations in leadership (leading, perhaps, to a sense of disillusionment and heightened anxiety). But the entire area of warfare, the military/industrial complex, authority and decision making, submission and passivity, etc., desperately needs demythologizing. Having placed critical areas of defense in specialized hands for so long has deprived the people of personal involvement and decision making. This has resulted in a huge near-dependency of the populace. And discovering that delegation alone does not guarantee needed results, or that those so trusted are not necessarily able to accomplish the task, requires courage, "fresh eyes", and a fierce determination to seek and establish new means of resolving disputes and conflicts, of safeguarding the people, and of peacekeeping. The entire war/peace system is in need of overhaul. We are talking of survival, after all.

SURVIVAL

The onus for survival must not be placed in impossible tenancy on a few individuals who may or may not recognize changed conditions in global circumstances, or who, although still admirably willing to serve, do not perceive that the change is so fundamental that an entirely new or different approach is needed. The circumstances and requirements for national and global security have radically changed, and this change must be acknowledged and heeded.

Habit clings long, however. Repetitive patterns of behavior and institutionalized systems that are now proving inimical to the public welfare and the world's health must be reversed or eliminated, and new modes must be established. The rattling of sabers is passé and bizarre, since peace is the desired condition between humans. Yet warmaking powers are an antiquated system that is still called into being, threatening the peace and survival of the group. Although survival in times past may have depended on defeating attacks on civilization by waging war, new means must now be found for the defense. A new set of controls—of taboos, as it were— must be set in motion in prohibition of war. Support must come from the world community in establishing new norms for international behavior; in essence, a mode of international etiquette must be established.

The undoubted desire and need of each nation for sovereignty and security is surely shared by member nations. It is precisely the need of the entire globe. The good and welfare of all must be respected and protected. And since all nations are integral parts of the world entity, the fate of the globe is central to each state. Survival of the whole is tantamount to survival of the membership.

Actualizing peace, civilization has been the survival mechanism of humanity, and its growth has been centrally instrumental in delivering its proteges to the present age. It has been noted that human social development has evolved from relatively small units in local areas to incrementally larger social enclaves. Civilization, "the culture of cities", has unfolded and spread discretely throughout the world and grown to nation-state size and status. Over millennia, the expansion of human contact in growing peaceful interaction has safeguarded civilization, permitting it to flourish and bequeathing it to today's heirs.

The growth of nation-states, however, is not so much overt civilization as the silent compact and the process that has involved each member of the human race in living cohesion. It is the linking of each person for individual group benefit that has forged civilization, and on each member the whole endeavor rests. The result and product of combined efforts, the creation of joint labors, the human connection has been as much for civilization as civilization has been for the individual and the group.

Human beings have formed a living web all over the world and in this manner have multiplied and gained some control of their fates. It is but simple deduction to note that survival and growth and evolution lie in continuing on the path of human cooperation as developed and experienced over time. Links need to be forged between nations even as individuals reached to each other through villages, cities, and states. The path is thus clear. The methods, however, depend on the difficulty encountered and the creative ingenuity mustered in achieving real community. The human qualities of learning, of conceptualizing the goal, and of communication—

using the skills, resources, and knowledge at hand to achieve the common intent, *survival into a new future*—can each and all form bridges upon which to cement relations between the disparate nations on earth.

The earth is one planet, one unit. It is also a community of nations, an international unit of human beings living in relationship with all the natural creatures and conditions of the land. It is one globe upon which the whole human race is one species.[108] And it is apparent that the survival of the species, the continuing saga of human growth and evolution, rests on the peaceful extension of human bonding—a path fully based on precedence and experience.

Continued human growth, then, remains each nation's, and each person's, express task. It is the direct assignment and immediate mandate. The process of linking nation to nation and people to people can be hastened and solidified if firmly decided upon. A species that can foresee its own possible extinction should also be able to preclude such an event.[109]

The responsibility for collective survival rests with the collective and cannot—dare not—be delegated away to a few individuals. Survival is the foremost dictate of the human organism and is secured by survival of the species. Species' survival is a matter for the discrete multitude, for each and every member of the group, encompassing the globe. And it is the fate of the globe, and of global humanity, that must be secured.

CHAPTER SEVEN

MILITARISM

$\mathcal{T}$he mammoth mechanistic weight and preponderance of the war machine is deeply entrenched in social affairs. Having precedence in history, roots in memory, and practice in actuality, the military is embedded in the system of governments and in the minds and conduct of people. There are chains of command, organized institutions, budgets for defense, weapons, research, employment, tradition, publicity, propaganda, inducements, etc. The military has branches in the most basic areas of socially organized and political life, reaching up to the presidency.

In the United States of America, the president of the nation is also the commander-in-chief of the entire military operation. He is the hierarchical leader of both civilian and military systems, even though they operate at times in diametrically opposed fashion—the social system being people- and peace-expansive, while the military system is authority- and war-intensive.

Highly organized and refined, war has been legitimately accepted by millions the world over and has been a recurring experience over time.[110] This recurrence has served to diminish questioning, criticism, and resistance to the military's nature and purpose. Further, its tentacled hold on the customs and policies of nations has entrenched it as a final means of problem solving.

The pattern of socially sanctioned militarism follows an old course that the collective individual has established and maintained for group protection. The structured organization was intended for the protection of life, land, and liberty, but the tremendous destructive powers now capable by man and missile have made this system perilously obsolete.[111] The former design for group protection is insufficient to the task. Since the plan and structure are incapable of safeguarding the populace, other means must be found to fill the need.

The relationship between the military and the people must be closely examined. Fundamental questions regarding the purpose and capability of the entire military composition must be asked and answered. The people have the right to know. How does it operate? Can it fulfill the intent and need? How, when, and where is the public involved? In the next few pages, some pertinent facts and concepts will be considered.

Militarism has been defined as the trust or belief in military means to keep one's country secure, a view which promotes a generally aggressive military policy or preparedness.[112] There is a high dependency on the use of force to "keep the peace". Military organizations have been described as grouped and armed individuals trained to act together for war's purposes, having a certain set of methods, rules, and regulations that guide the purpose. Resembling a huge weapon, a military system functions on command, the government deciding when and where to use it aggressively in foreign affairs instead of more peaceful means (e.g., diplomacy, trade, economics, international pressures, etc.). It is an arm of the government and subject to the country's policy.[113]

The military establishment is not only the method of defense, however; it is also increasingly becoming ensconced in positions of power that are by definition nonmilitary—that is, civilian—and closely aligned to the budget and economic affairs of state. Ruth Leger Sivard, in *World Military Expenditures 1982*, warned that the military network was spread throughout the topmost levels of power, the military dominating approximately fifty per cent of Third World countries.[114]

The year 1986 was named the International Year of Peace by the United Nations. Yet almost nine hundred billion dollars ($900,000,000,000) was spent on military weapons worldwide.[115] This amount greatly exceeded the sum of six hundred and nineteen billion dollars ($619,000,000,000) reported by the Stockholm International Peace Research Institute as having been spent on weapons just four years earlier (which was a substantial increase from the expenditure of two years before).[116] Military expenditures or competition translate into a race for guns and sophisticated weaponry and influence. It is an antiseptic euphemism for violent means planned and perpetrated against and upon people. This incredibly vast amount of public funds is well over two billion dollars a day. *Over two billion dollars a day.* Dollars, of course, represent the labor of people, the use of technology and scientific acumen, and the consumption of resources both natural and manmade. This grasp on the politics, resources, technology, education, and economics of a people is fearful; there are few contests more unequal than that between military costs and social needs.[117]

Involving an endless accumulation of arms and developments from a weapons-producing industry complete with sales, displays, and convention techniques, "creeping militarization" has created a substructure of power, prestige, and profits. Many jobs are dependent on the war system; silently, if not stealthily, a growing dependence has been fostered involving conformity, fear, economics, and power. Its influence may be even more insidious. We are warned that the weight of the military is felt increasingly in the public sector. It dominates the nation's goals the more security is linked with militarism. Fear of attack becomes paramount, and military means loom as the only solution.[118]

There is a growing imbalance that needs immediate redressing. Counterweights must be set in motion. It is axiomatic to state that the decision to go to war is the concern of the military, since war is its supreme function. However, this decision to go to war is now also the major concern of the people, for in this decision there is no less involvement of the people than of the military. In fact, it is the people's involvement that is more important, for war has increasingly involved the warring countries' populations and resources during the last four hundred years.[119]

The situation is now compounded by the nature of the destruction that would ensue from the types of weapons available. As noted earlier, any decision for war using nuclear weapons would be a form of genocide, the annihilation of vast numbers of people. Guaranteed retaliation—the MAD (Mutual Assured Destruction) pact in force between the two superpowers (U.S.A., U.S.S.R.)—would invite destruction in kind. Already of infinite danger, this insane plan has possibly been eclipsed by considerations of first strike potential, adding to the nervous tilt toward total nullification. Metaphorically speaking, the world is poised like a golf ball on a tee in increasing danger of being struck a fatal blow by one or more of a few players.

In December, 1979, a California congressman informed his constituents that within the next twenty-five minutes the United States and the

Soviet Union could destroy each other's nation and society, the United States having sufficient nuclear warheads to attack 450 major Russian cities twenty times over, while the Soviets could bombard the same number of United States cities ten times each. The people were advised that there was a global accumulation of nuclear weapons equal to one million bombs of the size that devastated Hiroshima, and that there was (is) no defense against the potential destruction, defying all rational sensibilities.[120]

No matter how many treaties are signed hereafter or what soothing words are intoned, the above arsenals already exist, are stockpiled, and even without proliferating (which is not the case, since the nuclear pie is burgeoning and spreading) there remains a terrible danger of instant catastrophe over the world. The time has come simply to step off the military merry-go-round. The game is finished (before it finishes us). In its terminal effects, war is the cancer of humankind, and the military is its carrier of deadly infection.

In the final analysis, the public is responsible for its own security and survival. It must look sharply about to secure its needs and its future. The military, after all, is *owned* by the people and is for the service of the people. Publicly funded, it is economically supported by the people; that is to say, the people are the outright purchasers and supporters of the whole enterprise. They employ it for a purpose. That express purpose is for the security and defense of the individual and the nation. Far from being used as pawns or feeling helpless and caught in an immutable system, the people are the actual owners of the entire military behemoth. As legitimate proprietors, the people have the right, responsibility, and obligation to inquire of its methods and purposes and to monitor its effectiveness. And since the military is subordinate to national policy and headed by the president of the United States (who is responsible to the people), the people have the right, responsibility, and obligation to make known their collective will.

Questions are brimming over in this critical area, and they demand answers. Is the worldwide sale of sophisticated armaments, their parts and technology, improving national security? What are the possible consequences? What restraints are there on the military presence in the national and international arena? Is the public involved in military matters and in decision making? Is power-with-gun the sole developed method and answer in maintaining security and retaining independence? What national body of influence comparable to the military—and equally funded—is established for overseeing the needs, conditions, maintenance, and furtherance of peace? Are defense and safety of the individual, nation, and world secured with all the armaments and all the monies expended in the present mode? What is the prognosis?

Mention was earlier made of the fact that the military system is in large part exempt from civil law and is guided by its own set of laws. What exactly are those laws? Where and how do they differ from the law of the land? Is the public better served by those who are not answerable to society's dictates, laws, and values? Since leaders of military "excursions" are attuned to the possible loss of personnel in battle or maneuver—planning for the potential loss or injury of its members (a "natural" attrition or shrinkage from risk and exposure under hazardous conditions)—is this same method of projected planning carried over to include the potential loss of the citizenry in event of war? Who decides who is expendable? And how many? Which of us is less valuable—You? Me? The president? The medic? The farmer? The child? The mother? The weapons maker? The banker?

It is superfluous to state that this mode of "rational" planning is a specific threat to the people. Consideration of the citizenry's demise, in whatever form or numbers, is not part of the original pact or plan. In its advancing stages this method of objective analysis borders on the inhuman, and it is detrimental to society at large. People may be susceptible to the military mentality that, taken to the near-extreme that is fast being approached, effectively anesthetizes them with a type of dehumanizing virulence that is paralytic in effect. Decisive action can stop the travesty.

Involvement and active responsibility of the public in matters of public welfare and concern (and certainly survival is the prime public concern) must be exercised during peacetime. The people must use their right to evaluate and decide the means for group safety during times of peace. This is in marked contrast to civilian involvement in the military business in either peacetime or times of conflict. The military is a sharply hierarchical organization with a closed inner chain of command that begins to operate authoritatively at maximum strength during critical periods or war.

The public cannot wait for war when decisions are taken out of its hands and control, indicating the breakdown and failure of peace. Since the president is elected by, and is answerable to, the people, and since he is also commander-in-chief of the entire military system which is subordinate to the national interest, it is obvious that the military is subject to the will, direction, and dictates of that same people. *The people are the boss.*

The time for unlimited independence and power is at an end for the military. The time for control and authoritarian hegemony over the source of its sustenance and support—the people—and the time for misplaced civilian dependence is at an end. The military was and is a system devised for the protection of the people. If its form and function now require change, that is entirely to be expected in a changing world with different perspectives and priorities. The old military order is shamefully out of date, an anachronism on the body civilian (for and by whom it was designed, and who is its mainstay). Further usage in the old autocratic manner will strain all bounds letting loose a possible disaster on the world.

CHAPTER EIGHT

NATIONAL RESTRAINT, CONFLICT RESOLUTION, AND POWER

$\mathcal{T}$here is little or no restraint and control on the warmaking powers of individual nations. The nation, so far, is the official top rung of the human bonding system that has evolved over time (with loose alliances in continents and hemispheres). Although the individual is subject to society's laws and restraints, there is no counter-restraint on the nation-state and its war machine. In essence, the world is at the mercy of each and every nation should any one, or any allied group, decide for war.

To date, people all over the world have joined together in groups, larger or smaller, to the topmost level of nation. On an infinite earth of limitless distance, such national groupings were, perhaps, bastions of security. However, on a finite earth with limited boundaries and resources, in an environment requiring symbiotic relationships and cohabitation, and on a fragile globe suspended in space, separate and discrete units are anomalies that keep bumping into each other as perimeters appear to shrink. The earth is one unit, and its human inhabitants are descendants of one biological group. Their cultures are varied, however. And their warmaking powers are multiple, threatening the whole.

Presently, as the process continues, there is ample evidence of human bonding stretching across national boundaries, establishing strong links and viable networks in life-affirming patterns. People weave their arts everywhere, and the word "world" appears ever more frequently as consciousness is raised to the realization that attention must be paid to conditions in the greater world beyond immediate and ethnic limits. The effects of events beyond national borders are felt in varying degrees; warfare and military incursions, of course, are destructive elements with disastrous effects upon a multitude.

The potential for harm to vulnerable peoples of the world from the warmaking policies of militant governments is gross. Until self-restraint is admirably evidenced, there must be world and regional restraints on military foraging by all nations. At the least, there must be *expectation of restraint*, since a *laissez-faire* attitude to unbridled militarism on earth is unacceptable. Certainly, the ability to annihilate human populations and lay waste the land is not to be condoned. Such "power" is pathetically misdirected and criminally constituted if applied. (The human is diminished even in the planning and preparatory stages, underscoring lack of foresight, responsibility for consequences and species' empathy, making the individual, even as the group or nation, an accessory to the fact of crimes against humanity.)

Restraints may be effected on two levels: by each individual nation's own population and laws, and by international rules and regulations. The state and all its retinue, the military machine in no less measure, must be expected to answer to its own constituents domestically and to the world body internationally. The world's inhabitants, local and global, must expect the military to be restrained and subservient to their needs, and such means as are necessary to accomplish this condition must be instituted. In the matter of species safety and survival, the people everywhere are one.

It has been severally suggested that an effective international body, or perhaps more than one, is essential for world stability. As a forum for and exercise of control over nation-states (and their military complexes), such an international organization is a natural extension of world societies and relationships. Historians Will and Ariel Durant recognized that the nation-state is sufficiently powerful to permit no interference with its imperial will, and since there is no effective international restraint, global law, or even basic protection, nation-states flaunt their own authority.[121]

Concern for human survival has given impetus to the urgent need for global cooperation and global perspectives, such needs finding focus and expression in a rededicated world body, such as the United Nations, or other world organizations as may be established. There are matters of comprehensive concern that must now take precedence in world affairs, matters that are common to all and that supersede local and national boundaries.

The question of sovereignty and perceived loss of power may be cited as reason for not entering more fully into global consolidation. It is spurious reasoning, however, since nations arose and grew from the combination of communities and states aligning themselves together not only for communal strength but also for a greater union and common good. Cultural identity is another issue. Love of home, language, life-style—all the essences of a culture—are ethnic attachments of a people and are highly valued. But the pressing problem is not sovereignty or identity. Ultimately, the safeguarding of the world has precedence, since all reside therein. Constraint on military power (the unchecked power to make war almost at will and to create world disruption) is the power that must now be instituted for the sake of all humanity.

Resort to overt force is public indication of the lack of ability to reduce or contain the problem or dispute and the inability to utilize all means to avoid the outbreak of armed hostilities. A serious indictment of leadership, outbreaks of warfare constitute a grave threat to all member nations of the world. Containment of violence and resolution of conflicts is of vital concern to the entire world body, which stands in mortal danger of being involved in an escalating conflagration. Responsible inner control must be expected and demanded of each nation-state, large or small, and censure applied to those who violate and jeopardize the public welfare.

Despots desiring to establish hegemony over others by making military inroads for their own gain, causing explosive anger in the world community and inciting possible retaliatory measures, must expect to bear the full weight of world censure and applied sanctions. Violations must be labeled and violators identified. It must become unprofitable to use military force for national ambitions. Exposure of national greed, extension of forced control, and blatant disregard for the rights and desires of others are patently revealed by the application of such armed might and must be clearly seen as contrary to world interest and world peace.

The nature of conflict is undergoing examination. Since unresolved conflicts have led to the widening disarray evident in the world, study and research are being invested in examining world problems and conflicts. The tendency to "fall into war" is no longer an acceptable option, the increasing potential for danger leading to destructive effects in the world at large. Efforts at containment, therefore, are essential both for the contenders and for the congregation of nations. Containment and reduction of conflicts and violence are entirely in the world's interests and, as such, must be considered as completely pragmatic in the greater sense. The lessening of tensions is everyone's business and is practical for all.

CONFLICT RESOLUTION

In researching violence and conflict, the phrase "conflict resolution" has been credited to two college educators who have claimed that the phenomenon of conflict was both repetitious and capable of amelioration. It was considered that conflict is almost a universal sociological, if not biological, condition, and that there are similarities in conflict situations, whether familial, organizational, or international.[122]

From abstract study in academic classrooms, the notion of conflict resolution has transited to the international arena, the realization surfacing that conflicts or potential conflicts can be impeded and averted without resort to force if attention is brought to bear before escalation of grievances has grown to unmanageable proportions. In broadening the understanding of global conflict, contending issues between nations are objectively observed and analyzed. Such analysis and consideration may be applied to international conflicts no less than to local labor disputes or legal contentions. As the practice becomes familiar, it is felt that successful deployment will be more frequently utilized and will come to be expected. The *expectation* of finding a solution—a sincerity of approach that considers that human resolutions are possible for human problems—is an important element in the entire proceeding. There must be a commitment to the peace-finding process.

Recent emphasis is being placed on deescalation of conflicts before potential violence is unleashed or unavoidable or, once started, before it is enlarged and prolonged. This containment of danger, or its actual reversal, is a recognition that although conflicts and disputes may be an inescapable part of human interaction, they are generally manageable. Escalation of tension is not inevitable and may be subject to diminution and even avoidance. In any event, conflict need not be elevated to its zenith, world war—the ultimate conflict. Such escalation indeed reflects immature control, lack of foresight, insufficient international understanding and concern, or inadequate safeguards at the highest levels of society.

Varied methods may be sought for effective control, for in an atmosphere of world concern there are many options open to the global community of nations, which, in turn, will generate more. An element of logical sequence introduced into areas of contention may cool the difficulties enough to introduce solutions. (It may even happen that a "snowball" effect will occur—a majority of nations may gladly join hands in supporting worldwide peaceful means of resolving conflicts in anticipation of living free of nuclear holocaust.)

Some methods for paving the way to problem solving involve a delicate balance of power. Basically, an airing of the problem begins, and arrangements for meetings are made (face-to-face or with third-party assistance). There is an attempt to reduce the problem into several smaller parts, and suggestions may ensue for handling or solving one or more of them. The intention is to diminish aggravations of seeming intractability, and intermediary assistance may be offered to world leaders.

Peacemaking assistance in the affairs of world governments is not as surprising as at first may be thought, precedent having been established long ago through the use of representatives, embassies, and other diplomatic channels. Relatively recently, the world has been witness to successful personal interventions in critical affairs of state by the "shuttle diplomacy" of the United States then-Secretary of State Henry Kissinger, and more recently via the direct personal involvement on behalf of peace by United States then-President Jimmy Carter. These dramatic intercessions have effectively and publicly underscored the possibilities, if not the necessity, for third-party assistance in the lessening of critical hot spots that threaten to erupt uncontrollably.

The extension of options to leaders, if diligently practiced, increases the chance of peaceful resolution until habit and expectation are formed, most urgently and beneficially reducing the impulse to threat or force. *Waging peace* is more than an option to quarreling nations. It is factual evidence to the world that there are available methods for dissipating or solving international disputes by reasonably diminishing potential danger areas or impasses. After all, nations, too, must have reasonable access to a forum or neutral source for airing grievances and disputes (of which there are many, such as displaced refugees, terrorist activities, hijackings, international kidnappings, pollution of land and seas, energy needs, economic disparities, etc.). It is clear that nation-states are part and parcel of the greater world, and that they must realistically and responsibly take heed of it, as well as be heeded. Growing daily more interdependent, nations need to be responsive to each other for the good of all.

Presently, difficult and intricate problems are being quietly researched to gain understanding and possible solutions for diffusing and diminishing aggravating national and international situations. Internationally, at the United Nations level, for example, professional training seminars are conducted by the International Peace Academy for diplomats, politicians and policy makers, military personnel, and others in the art of public mediation and negotiation.[123] Also, practical publications and teaching materials are produced for use of government officials and teachers at national and private educational institutes.

The intent to resolve crises and the firm attempt in an acceptable forum may be expected to further the peacekeeping process and strengthen it. The alliance of world nations in overtly seeking peaceful means of resolution of inter-nation problems would itself be a great restraint on the militaristic bent of warmaking states or on the excessive dependence on military solutions. Establishing the form, inviting world members to become a viable part of the experiment, and setting precedent, it would augur well for successful implementation and extension of peace if this country insisted on peaceful retention of focus while utilizing various means of conflict resolution (which are presently limited only by lack of their consideration and use.)

The rational approach to critical situations may act as a restraint in some instances, whereas others may prove more recalcitrant. Not all tensions can be soon ameliorated by logic and reasoned approaches, and the belligerent or festering factor may remain. However, the more reliance placed on boldly and actively waging peace in resolving inter-nation disputes, the more such reliance will come to be accepted and turned to. In the interest of world safety, understanding, tolerance, and time are needed for improving mutual relations and the extension of peace. In the process, notice is served that military options are depreciated, if not precluded.

Waging peace, "buying time", and keeping negotiations open and fluid are helpful in arriving at acceptable solutions in contentious cases. Whether used internationally, at the United Nations, or in expanding classroom discussions, conflict resolution techniques and interventions are being improved and enlarged. Appendix E describes some terminologies and avenues of action for waging peace.[124]

There is no wish to belabor the point, and another arena may prove more effective; still, another glance at the United Nations may be warranted. The fact that it is *there* speaks volumes. The United Nations is the one potentially unifying organization engaged in global dynamics presently on the world scene. It has been accepted by the peoples of the world as an *intended* peacemaking body. Established only some four decades ago, a stabilizing and heartening note in an unsteady world camp, the United Nations stands as a *potential* bastion of unification for the good of the globe. An arena for global affairs, composed of many varied interests and perspectives, it is as yet unfulfilled and far from complete as the central hub and hope of humanity.

Imperfect as it is, and fraught with manipulative factions, the United Nations has nevertheless been an educational and experiential lesson for its participants at the international and world level. An intensive examination has indicated that membership in this world body has necessitated development of some general standards of behavior and consensus in arriving at decisions of global import.[125] Whereas the goal of this body has not been assured, the framework and form for nations to come together has been established.

The intent and purpose of the United Nations would serve as a needed reminder of its *raison d'être* if upheld and championed before the eyes of the world, and if the means and manner were found for returning it to its original function and goal. Expanding and refocusing its design to serve the original purpose could better unite and bond individual nations in search of a sense of community in the world. There is great room for improvement and growth into the stature of a world forum, respected international court of law, and modifying voice for earth's populations—a role requiring the active involvement of many diverse peoples and viewpoints, not the least of which is equal representation of women. (One may no longer overlook women's presence, of course.) It would take time, dedicated involvement, and cooperation. But such effort is critical in stabilizing and curtailing the dangerous drift of individuated power states armed with deadly weapons and uninhibited ambitions.

The need for a central or overall world body is evidenced by the number of nations acting in semi-orphaned fashion, without real attachment or allegiance to the greater body of the world. Yet independent nations are adrift in name only, since it has become almost impossible to be unaffected by world events. The idea of a benignly functioning global entity may move closer to reality if the following concepts are kept in mind: (1) one earth and its natural laws, resources, and environment; (2) the essential unity of humankind, represented equally (and solely) by its two members, man and woman; (3) continuation of civilization worldwide, substituting social justice, cultural respect, creative change, and conflict resolution for social injustice, cultural ignorance, negativity, and violence (overt, covert, incidental); (4) institutionalizing of peace via organizations and public support, seeking its enlargement while diminishing the military-industrial complex and its effects and influence.

Before the United Nations (or another organization) can become a truly respected body that can act as a clearinghouse for the problems and projects of the world, certain elements are necessary. It must be *expected* to live up to its purpose and promise, and the people must *demand* that it fulfill the appropriate role and position. If enough individuals and nations decide to place further trust and energy in this relatively young experiment in world cooperation, enabling it to become a truly effective body and making of it a universal entity of truly humanitarian proportions, an entirely new era of proud human relations can ensue. (Several multi-purpose proposals to reform and strengthen the United Nations are being put forward—e.g., improved voting system, increased use of the International Court, suggested peacekeeping capabilities, etc.)[126]

The world's inhabitants have some distance to go in international cooperation. Nevertheless, the process has been initiated, and is overtly and covertly practiced. Realizing the speed with which cultural progress is effected, especially in this day of instant communication (and great need), defining international peace as a goal of first priority on all agendas is not an impossible aim to achieve. Whereas people generally may fervently desire and wish for peace, their antiquated systems of peacekeeping are weighted by centuries of warmaking habits that require attention and change before nearing or achieving the objective.

Bringing the war machines under control, declaring the intention of establishing peace as the basic human relations system in the world and utilizing all means of communication for rallying public support, citizens everywhere can be active conduits of peaceful change and effect. Popular opinion can be aligned and turned of its own accord in a relatively short period of time if proclaimed intent, information, and education on behalf of peace are widely disseminated. A publicity campaign would ripple throughout the entire world in quickening tempo if peace was proposed and actively promoted by serious world leaders. The effect would be quite electrifying, crossing borders and ideologies, uniting people in a hopeful and exciting display of singular focus and purpose.

At this critical juncture in human affairs, few persons would deny that peace is in humanity's interests of self-preservation and survival. It is also the general desire and, possibly, the common denominator across the global populace. It follows only that conviction must be followed in a courageous and confident manner.

POWER

Many forms rival military might for influence and power, and there are many assets that combine to make a nation powerful in its own right. Lack of confidence and poverty of dependence are revealed by the inordinate cling to brute force. Should the national sense of self be so shallow as to find nothing within itself of strength and fiber that cannot subsist without untoward reliance on bristling arms, there is ample evidence throughout history of similarly once mighty nations going down to defeat.

The notion of power by force has come round to attack the attackers, as it is now seen in its ultimately impoverished sense. Clearly, power is more than the manipulations of others, threat, or application of physically applied force—all of which are negative powers relying on direct or indirect violence, and none in nomination for awards. The concept of national power is being widened from its narrow definition of, and devotion to, "power-with-gun". (The club or gun is an extension of physical power that raises images of caveman tactics and mentality.) There are wider powers for humankind to utilize than savage force, such force having its limitations and excesses (as is now being fearfully contemplated). Whereas brawn is important in indicating a strong and healthy physical entity and may act as a deterrent on some with covetous ambitions and violent habits, it is a limited and self-conscious power. There are other powers for national claim of at least equal importance.

Power is defined variously as having the ability to act, producing an effect, having authority, using influence or strength among people, etc. Power is also that which is conceived in the mind, the idea of what power is, the concept that is held in common. If the concept of power is held to be a strong military machine, for instance, the investment will be in weapons, a militia, and all the trappings associated therewith. Gradually, as has happened, dependence will form, and the military will become the symbol for power. At the same time, other forms of power will appear of small consequence and go largely unrecognized. (Actually, expecting the military system to resolve the comprehensive problems of interaction with the international community—as it is now seen—puts a demand and strain on it that is beyond its capability to deliver and places undue citizen dependence on this single form of power, while, not incidentally, the nation remains at risk.)

The idea of power is in need of expansion. Like peace, there are many forms to be incorporated into the visibly acting structure of the country. Clearly, a great nation like the United States of America, with its pluralized population, its united cities and states and system of government, and its sense of purpose and mission in maintaining a free society of energetic citizens, is a powerhouse in its own right. That it is a land of natural resources, of lakes, valleys, and forests, capable of supplying not only an abundance of food and products to its own people but also a great surplus for others, is another power of tremendous proportion. This bounteous land is also empowered by a mobile and experienced citizenry whose abilities resound throughout educational, financial, industrial, and technological centers nationwide.

There is great power in an educated populace that has the desire and ability to govern itself, to strive to improve its standard of living, and to help others raise theirs. There is the strength of the written word, the transmission of knowledge and ideas, the educational, creative, and ideological bent of a people. It would be impossible to lay claim to all the forms of knowledge and education furthered by the written word and the numeral, other than, perhaps, to suggest the dictionary, the Bible, and the mathematical rule.

There are other powers, too. There is beauty, verbal power, emotional appeal, and the power of the creative arts. There is charismatic power, and there is love in all its manifestations. All these, and more, are strengths and powers that attract, bind, and unite. But over and above these forms of power is the force of an idea that transcends time and tempest, the ideology to which entire cultures and peoples subscribe, the reason for which humankind may have been formerly willing to die but for which, now, it is fiercely willing to live and strive, for nations, no less than individuals, have a common ethos, an image and goal.

This nation has strived for the freedom of the individual and the common good of the populace. From its inception, America has stood as a bulwark and haven of hope and liberty and, to this day, is sought by the world's peoples as a refuge and depository of dreams and human energy. Its failures do not come from the realization of its ideals, but from the neglect of them.

The goal of human freedom, of development, and of living a life that is meaningful and purposeful is the ideology and imaginative notion that fires the human brain—and is a powerful force of attraction. It is not necessary to club those who come of their own free will. A country that must have laws to limit the numbers of people trying to get into it obviously has an attraction and force that makes it desirable to others. And a country whose educational institutions are filled with the sons and daughters of distant nations is one that has much to teach and learn from.

Perceiving our world through the eyes of others clamoring to get in may have a slight tint of rosiness to it, but it serves as a reminder that powers of attraction far removed from military power radiate from this land to which others respond (and to which its own citizens, taking things for granted, may have closed their eyes). This country has an inner strength that permits its members to develop their human potential, to grow into full manhood and womanhood. This potential to develop, and the opportunity to do so, is a given, a right. It may be claimed. And it is projected by the nation as a whole. This strength, multiplied by each member, is a tower of fortitude that others in the world recognize in their diminished states, and it has nothing to do with weapons of destruction.

When individuals are permitted to grow into their full potential as human beings and choose to do so, the world will be peopled with citizens for whom wars will be an action far down the scale of human behavior, if not completely removed from it. This awareness coincides entirely with the stark realization that warfare is the inhuman use of mechanized and mindless power capable of destroying civilization and environment. (There are many who have long realized the danger to human survival and question why it has been necessary to arrive at this obscene condition when ordinary foresight could, and does, foresee it.)

The power of the mind and senses to discern, to accept responsibility, and to make plans is a human power of unlimited magnitude. To realize the cataclysmic threat from world war, with its potential for unleashing destructive forces of untold dimensions, is congruent with scientific information, the warnings of knowledgeable people, and the awareness of countless citizens. But that is only part of the picture. The other part is that this awareness must be heeded. The knowledge of possible catastrophe must be coupled with determined ways and means of both avoiding it and setting in motion plans to remove and eliminate the potential danger. The elimination of war from the annals of human experience should be—must be—grounds for agreement.

A warless world is the direction in which humanity must move if it is to survive and fulfill its destiny. In conceiving of a warless world, human empathy is enriched. Moving in the direction of greater humanness suggests inner growth, even as the world links arms in closer embrace. Our own individual humanity is enhanced in the reach to raise the human experience and level. Greater humanness is linked with *personal power*, the ability to achieve independent thought and skill in coping with life's vicissitudes.

This nation will project a force of unlimited power if it has the strength and simple sense of confidence to be authentic, to live up to its own ideals. The unity of ideology and effort, coupled with the common will for survival, adds up to a powerful effect that should see the group safely past present dangers. It must not permit itself to be led in blind abandon, contradicting its own basic and fundamental needs (survival being the primary need). No matter how worthy the leader or former pattern of behavior, the people's collective will for life and peace must be projected and indicated, giving direction to its representatives. To do otherwise is to disown group responsibility, target its agents for failure, and court disaster.

In politics, power is sought competitively by many who are covetous of the assumptions of its benefits, permitted by the consent of those who accede to and support the competition. The *direction* in which the leader (winner) moves should be designated by the group in order that the leader be subservient to the people's will, "ruling effortlessly". But this direction is frequently lacking, an indication of the aimlessness of the people who have forgotten or slackingly let go of their own motivation. Should the leader be equally aimless or follow an old bent, pretense of power may be effected by a show of force. There is no gainsaying the importance of political power, to which the military-industrial complex of powers is closely attached. It is a heady mixture and near-guarantee of instant puffery to even the most benign of leaders.

Should the ruling regime be faithful to the former method of group protection via warfare, there is the possibility of tragedy in the offing. Like the pied piper, the leader may direct the group to its demise. The trappings of the office and attenuated services may be buttressed and thrust forward to emulate the aura of power, giving the impression of super strength. Uniformed dress, stiff posture, tough talk, and large weapons reinforce the image (and may even comfort innocents). The authoritarian stance brooks little interference with established mode. It *knows* what it is doing and tolerates little dissent within its ranks. Conformity is praised, independence discouraged. As the authoritarian command grows, the independent mind does not fit into the unyielding stance and is seen as a threat to the rigid framework. Indeed, the creative mind is anathema to the authoritarian order, as the tightly bound rule is unhealthy for the freedom-loving mind. Emulating life, the mind must have movement and expression. But the more reinforced and the more tentacled the hold of authoritarianism, the more the tradeoff; the more mind is harnessed. It must not be permitted free rein; it must not have unlimited freedom.

Enthusiasm is diminished if the mind is stifled, and some eagerness of life is lost. In systematic suppression of the fertile mind, a great source of power is cut off from the group no less than from the individual. The more it is restricted, the less energy and ability there is to limit authoritarian growth, thereby entailing serious ramifications and consequences for all. Losing its own source of creativity and power, the group may place greater emphasis on positions that assume the rigidity of dogma (even while piously invoking some higher order). Stultified in its own further development, though some seemingly formidable level of achievement may be reached, the group arrives at the limits of growth. Frantic reaches, often by force, are made to simulate the appearance of growth or animation, but, in effect, the group is dying; dying, it can only project death.

The union of national goal with creative mind would seem a winning combination, but inexplicably, except for lip service and token appreciation of "the arts", there is still small outlet for its expression. Even in this powerful land, outside of the entertainment industry, creative thought and imaginative bent are relegated largely to a few safe avenues. The "aha" theory is spoken of reverently in scientific circles, and creative expression is safely channeled into lucrative advertising and business ventures. One may talk freely of creativity and emotionalism in, say, finance, advertising, or sports, but ordinary, normal, creative thought is considered somewhat unrealistic, naive, suspect.

It seems almost elementary to state that the mind, individual source of curiosity and creativity, is essential to the well-being of the organism, the state no less than the person. There is no substitute for an imaginative mind that has the power to grasp the abstract as well as the fact, to make connections, to intuitively grasp infinities yet adhere to the near and the finite. In an age dawning with expectation of technological marvels, the vigorous, creative, and humanistic mind is the probe and promise for directing the use of fantastic tools for the benefit of all humankind. *The creative mind, near-source of ultimate freedom, is the power behind the power.*

CHAPTER NINE

THE HABIT OF WAR AND AGGRESSION

The war system is tenaciously entrenched in the social and political systems of the people. The extent to which it is affixed can scarcely be comprehended, so deeply has it penetrated the social fabric. But, although the habit of war is admittedly of long duration and has become deeply ingrained in the behavior of nations, this is not to say that it is a biological or inherent condition programmed unerringly in the genes.

A habit is acquired by the frequent repetition of a pattern of behavior. Warfare has been a repetitive action in and between societies for centuries and, indeed, may even be embedded enough to be considered as more than a habit, an addiction. There is a psychological as well as a concrete grip on the populace, and the culture is riddled with evidence of its substance and structure—from inordinate dependence on arms and defense to the large budget that is annually expected and allotted to militarism.

Warfare is a cultural system, a human invention established and institutionalized over time, symbolizing group power and group protection. As such, its place in the affairs of society has become deep, deferred to (the iron fist brooks no argument), and confidently sure. However, it is not a given that warfare is impervious to change, control, or even elimination, should that now prove to be the need.

The purpose of war is generally cited as defensive, keeping the peace, guaranteeing the national way of life, etc. It is civilization that is safeguarded, the continuity and maintenance of a life-style that is synonymous with peace and that requires protection from enemies. Warfare has been condoned, supported, and advanced by the people as a tool for their preservation. However, since the scale of warfare has now surpassed even a hawk's desire (encompassing possible world destruction), this method has become incompatible with the need and the purpose, and the group must withdraw its support from such a nihilistic option. Yet nothing diminishes the need to preserve life and civilization. Other plans and means must be systematized for preserving peace and securing the survival of a global people without recourse to war.

The system of organized hostility and warfare can be superseded by another system less inimical to humankind and more vitally concerned with human needs and human survival. Indeed, instituting and utilizing peaceful ways and means for keeping the peace would seem to be a more natural path to take, holding the promise of greater success and authenticity in undertaking. It is apparent, as it was to Mahatma Gandhi, that there is a clear connection between the end and the means. He noted that, in overlooking this connection, even religious men have been guilty of gross crimes.[127] This does not mean or pretend, however, that the old habit is simple to overcome or change. After all, the pattern has been set for millennia, and habits cling tenaciously.

Conjecture for a moment on the nature of habit—for example, the habit formed by so small a vice as smoking. Consider its known disadvantages, its cost, and lack of grace. Consider its addictive hold once established, not to mention the economics of its agriculture, its production, promotion, sale, and purchase. Consider also the pecuniary windfall to government, one that is expected in the counting houses of the state. Consider the ramifications of this relatively small habit, a habit that befouls the air that is breathed, that is dismissed from certain areas and establishments, that carries a specific warning of injury to health on its face. Consider the difficulty in overcoming this obnoxious but relatively minor habit; the strength of will necessary to eliminate it; the intent, plans, and aids used in surmounting it. Reflect, then, upon the grip that the habit of war has upon humankind and the amount of effort and concentration it will take to be rid of it.

The military vehicle is part of the political and social environment, as well as part of the economic structure. The "art" of war is entwined in the art of politics, and there is scarcely awareness where one begins and the other ends. Politics is the highest form of social convention in which communal power and consensus has been invested. It is the people's representation, the public voice, the collective's choice for assuring national continuity. Under its domain, nestling snugly, rests the military command.

Whether subtly, stealthily, or overtly, warfare has frequently shifted from concern for and protection of the people to become a tool of the political structure. It is a condition highly visible in some countries of the world, where military leaders occupy the seat of power, and of not inconsequential status here. It is apparent that war is more frequent between political groups than between other organizations.[128] Since politics is at the zenith of political power, it would seem that the art of politics is where the disengagement process should begin—in diminishing the art of war in the affairs of humankind. This is in its power to do, the political system being subordinate to the national interest and the people's welfare, even as is the military structure itself.

In disengaging the military complex from the people (budgets, weapons, personnel, etc., as well as the psychological dependence), the *art of peace* must be introduced and gradually enlarged to fill the void. This art, the art of peace—or the art of humanity, as it may more properly be called—is in the national and international interest. Creating conditions for survival, cooperation, social justice, and equality is humanly sympathetic, whereas continued militarism and organized hostilities, especially on the scale now possible, are clearly contrary to human needs and interests.

The habit of war extends beyond politics, of course. It is also entrapped in the entrails of the economy, fed and grown to monstrous proportions. Whereas it may be uncomfortable to think that Americans are fostering war by pandering the weapons used by it, there is no retreat from the knowledge that American know-how and manufacture is producing some of the "best" products used to exterminate other human beings and is a leading sales source of them.

There is this indelicate matter of the business of arms research, production, and sales. Perceiving the world as a dangerous place, the message is projected that one must be fully armed for preservation's sake, and weapons for self and others are seen as utterly essential. (Yet there are many who abhor the primitive dependence on arms and the inhumanity of killing other humans.) Also, the fact that many are already armed "to the teeth", so to speak, while manufacture continues to turn out ever new and "better" models to an eager world market bespeaks an avarice in the field that is difficult to conceal. That there are purchasers of new equipment eager to try out their wares is also not difficult to know or imagine. And that there are nations competing with nations in the accumulation of either the latest in sophisticated weaponry or, better yet, the acquisition of our know-how in order to amply produce their own arsenals is common knowledge. There is the feeling that there is a game of sorts being engaged in, a glee at the cops-and-robbers aspect, a pretense. But it is no game.

The fact that sales and promotions of military hardware contribute to enlarging the weapons makers' and the nations' coffers is assiduously ignored, if not righteously rejected. That weapons production and sales are important to the gross national product is almost too gross to suggest. Yet even the promise of doing business in this field is enough to have some panting and has begun to dictate who our friends are or should be.

The measure of America is being taken by others who are willing to manipulate this country through its greed and immaturity. The United States of America appears to be willing to sell its soul for the sale of a gun—worse yet, for the sale of its knowledge in the manufacture of that gun. Is our integrity so weak that it is willing to be slid aside for the dollar? If so, can the security of such a hollow people be seen as difficult to undermine? Is the United States being led down the garden path of moral and economic seduction? Plain old horse sense shows that we are being led by the nose, and the military is holding the tether.

As noted earlier, the outlandish sum of well over nine hundred billion dollars worldwide in 1986 was spent on defense and security, while security in the world is more elusive than ever. This vast amount breaks down to more than *one million dollars a minute* spent on military equipment and related matters. America is a major supplier of military hardware, even as other countries vie competitively for the arms business. And many developing nations are themselves becoming producers as well as purchasers of weapons of destruction in the race to catch up on stockpiles and the necessary technology. Restraint of sales of arms and equipment is scarcely practiced, if not scorned, with sneers at the "do-gooders" who advocate responsibility, if not sanity. The world as a whole is becoming physically inundated with the goods of war. In cancerous proliferation, militarism is spreading its tentacles around the globe and around the practices of the people in and out of power, attempting to creep into the minds of the citizenry. (In its wake, of course, are the entrails of death.)

At a time when tensions are high, when energy sources are both tenuous and costly, and when the ethnic dollar is fluctuating unsteadily, military priorities are still sacrosanct and religiously subscribed to (and fast becoming an albatross around the necks of the people). Authoritative advice is emitted that intones that such extravagant military needs are for our "protection", our "defense", our "security". But how can this be, when outbreak of nuclear warfare promises to decapitate humanity?

At a time when widespread destruction is being predicted in the event of another war, and at a time when actions and promotions for peace were never more needed, military seduction of the public mind borders on criminality and delusion. Contrary rhetoric exhorting that "if you want peace, prepare for war" is both harmful and obsolete, since awareness and experience have revealed that most groups seem to get the war they prepare for.[129]

We are continuing an old habit in depending on militarism as the ultimate problem solver, rather like the lemmings who blindly follow an old bent toward the sea. The habit of war is weighing heavily. But the tolerance level has been reached. Continuation of this lethal habit in the face of current knowledge and practice is to continue the fatal bent of the lemmings and to suffer similar consequences.

The use and proliferation of current technological military means promises to boomerang—indeed, it is nearly guaranteed to do so. For instance, there is little talk of the consequences and possibilities extant in overloading an already volatile world with even more explosive materials. Such products contain the seeds of anger, suspicion, and irresponsibility and are fuel to the tinderbox of global military profiteering and hegemony. World militarization is taking place, and the United States cannot escape its active part in spreading it. America has come far afield from its vaunted ideals.

(The fact that, sooner or later, inhuman mechanizations may be turned against this country or strategic allies seems to be completely ignored. Yet it is a real possibility assiduously overlooked by the "realists". It would be quite ironic if the means used was of our own making.)

The lack of public involvement in the military-industrial complex may account for the increasing boldness of weapons makers who publicly hawk their wares. Advertised in local papers, items explicitly intended to maim and kill human beings—making murderers of the users and accomplices of the buyers, sellers, and makers—are openly displayed and promoted to potential customers in community convention centers in major cities.[130] The media matter-of-factly report the practice. A certain insensitivity to flagrant abuse of peaceful norms must account for the lack of public uproar. However, further infringements on the public's sensitivities may well serve to develop callousness and inability to distinguish or alertly note the creeping militarism.

Business is no area of delicate avoidance. The military and its industrial counterpart are certainly big business, and they have enjoyed immunity from public scrutiny overlong. All of it must now stand full exposure before intense public examination. Crucial questions must be asked and critical answers supplied. Is the war business acceptable to Americans? What image of this land is portrayed to the world? Is it good for the country and consistent with our basic ideals, policies, and goals? May a country literally litter the world with deadly war weapons with impunity? What moral and actual responsibilities for cause and consequence are implicit and/or explicit in the act? There are ethics and values to be considered, and it is time that we as a people begin to take stock. Dehumanization may not parade under the guise of economics.

Another factor has assisted the public in its habit and acceptance of the military role in its affairs. Along with business and politics, academia must share the honors. Education must accept its contributory share in deepening this perspective, which, of course, maintains the social viewpoint. The educational system has often enjoyed teaching history by focusing on wars, recounting dates and details of skirmishes, battles, strategies, treaties, etc. The subject of history has apparently been quite shallowly interpreted by historians and educators, who have chosen to accept the notion that wars and disruptions of peace fulfill the meaning of history. History. All that has gone before....

Warfare has apparently been deemed worthy of "prime time" knowledge, while peace education still brings a sardonic smile to most lips. Of course, having occurrence in the affairs of humankind assures warfare of mention in the annals of human experience and history. But surely the emphasis has been too great. Some schools have even permitted their grounds to become recruiting places for the military, while some fifty percent of research and development funds for scientists is for defense.[131] Also, that nuclear weapons produced in this country have been done so largely under the tutelage of the University of California is almost too much to note.[132] No wonder the popular expression "There have always been wars, and there'll always be wars" is maintained. For all the preaching of peace, we are still teaching war.

In general, the military experience has been puffed up in public affairs, fed insatiably by public funds, filled with a plethora of rigid rules, customs, and hierarchies—and fueled by habit. The habit is destructive, however, and has become a specific threat to the community—and, possibly to all humankind. Whether or not the intent is there, the old pattern is dragging a people toward an unfathomable abyss. A halt must be made. "The handwriting is on the wall." To continue on this path is to reach a predictably negative conclusion. The mad race to oblivion must stop, and the entire monstrous apparatus must be turned around. It is time to heed French existentialist Albert Camus' warning that the only hope left is to begin from the bottom up, to reshape a living society from a dying one.[133]

The imperative that must direct us now is not behavior suited to a cultural or earlier past, but behavior that is geared to the present and the future. Since the primary goal of all living beings is survival, it is posited that humans are at the critical stage where the stark issue is survival, and the means for achieving it have drastically and fundamentally changed. As matters stand, the enemy is not so much another country or another ideology as *war* itself.

Contemporary findings have been adding to this theme. In *The Meaning of the 20th Century: The Great Transition*, 1964, Dr. Kenneth Boulding stated that the great and unprecedented problem of our time was to rid the world of war.[134] This conclusion reinforced an earlier statement that the combination of deadly weapons and ongoing tensions portend the end of civilization and, possibly, the end of all life on earth.[135] And a researcher in the *Journal of Conflict Resolution* (1960) declared simply that the use of war may guarantee the eclipse of both user and enemy, leading to its utter uselessness as a means or tool of policy.[136]

This immediate reasoning is so fundamental that other considerations are almost incidental. Yet awareness is sharp that the Mutual Assured Destruction (MAD) pact between the two major powers, the United States of America and the Union of the Soviet Socialist Republics, is not only the current principle upon which the two countries rest their respective securities but, if allowed to progress to its naturally negative extension, could also prove prophetic in mutual annihilation (together with that of most of the world). It is a pact of hostility—hardly a peg upon which any peoples can hang their hopes and dreams for a better life in a living and creative environment. It is vividly apparent that Albert Einstein's belief in the avoidance of war as humankind's only hope[137] is eminently valid, and we must think and plan in a new way for securing survival.[138]

Whereas the above conclusions represent those of westerners, Mahendra Kumar, in *Current Peace Research and India*, 1968, observed similarly that awareness of the possible threat to all human life was causing a wide range of people to consider ways to avoid war and maintain peace. He noted that particular emphasis was being placed on developing viable peaceful techniques for resolving global conflicts, rather than involving the use of force, in order to firmly establish peace as a secure and stable condition.[139]

As noted, the scourge of war itself is the enemy, threatening not only individual life and property but also communal life and environment. Survival, therefore, depends on means other than war. Perhaps, it was suggested, natural selection is now operating internationally.[140] Although the Durants (Will and Ariel) have stated that a nation must be in readiness to defend itself in the absence of international law, and that the Ten Commandments cannot hold sway when life hangs in the balance,[141] the double bind that the world is presently in has added a new dimension of risk.

The very means of a nation's former method of self-preservation—war—promises now to be its own source of demise. It is apparent that aggressive militarism on the global scene has been rendered ineffective as a viable problem solver by its own scale of destructive possibilities, although it is by no means eliminated. The task now is to continue the process of diminishing war, as suggested by those mentioned above and many others. (Perhaps now is the time when the Ten Commandments should be shouted!) At the same time, there is urgent need to solidify and expand peace initiatives and processes to fill the vacuum created in the shrinkage of warfare and military solutions.

Although overt action must be taken to halt warmaking and to institutionalize peace, perhaps disengagement from war must begin in the mind. When realization of the insidious dependence on warfare that has wrapped itself around the people's psyche occurs and when understanding surfaces that it need not be that way—as noted, war is not a dispensation from heaven, mandated by a higher order of life, or programmed in the chromosomes or genes—the tentacles of habit will begin to loosen and drop of their own accord. In freeing the mind from its obsessive grip on war, energies frozen at the level of fear and anxiety can focus on the fundamental needs of humankind—that is, on life. Freshened viewpoints can sweep free the cobwebs of the past, affording an undistorted view and awareness of present and future living on this finite planet and begin to permit a healthier mode of adaptation to its conditions and possibilities.

Humanity is the collective creature that has absorbed the lessons of earth, and it stands now at the threshold of a new and endlessly curious adventure that beckons mysteriously through the space continuum. Focusing the popular will in the opposite direction from war, to peace, is likely to bring an explosion of creativity into being that can scarcely be imagined. The years ahead will be as different in experience as the twentieth century is to humankind's early beginnings. In this context, the added and remarkable goal of space exploration makes of peace not only a desire, but a necessity. Cooperation is essential. Resources need to be pooled, not squandered. Study, research, and experience must be life intensive, not divisive or war-expended. The recurring questions should be hallmarks: Is it good for humanity? Is it good for life?

There is no better incentive for united striving than to continue the human experience. Survival is mandatory. War must be declared an enemy of life and outlawed from human behavior. More than a gripping habit that reseeds itself continually anew and one that is contrary to the values of life, war is a direct and destructive threat to all that is future-oriented, and to earth itself. This globe is home to all that lives, and it is in the common interest to preserve and protect it and ourselves. War is obsolete. It is lethal. To safeguard the future, the art of peace must be accorded prime position on all agendas. To secure survival, the habit of war must be overcome.

AGGRESSION

Before further contemplation of a world in which warfare has been rejected or diminished as a tool for resolving human disputes, one must examine the persistent belief that seems to be prevalent about the inherent aggressiveness and hostility of mankind in the readiness and disposition to war, in some animal instinct that lies uneasily waiting to be momentarily aroused.

It has been noted that biological origins, cultural influences, and, possibly, environmental factors are determinants of behavior (in conjunction with will, of course). Since cultural patterning determines to a great extent whether cooperation or aggressive characteristics are socially prominent, the factor of social influence and conditioning deems further consideration necessary. War has been a recurring phenomenon throughout thousands of years, and its modeling role must not be overlooked. *War is the ultimate form of overt mass aggression. Hostile aggression is the business of war.*

War has served as a proving ground and model for man's developing and inculcating such tendencies as are usually associated with hostile definitions of aggression. The demand characteristics of the situation—that is, armies, conscription, training, war mentality, war behavior, weapons, etc.—have exacted, sanctioned, and rewarded the expansion of the aggressive role and aggressive conformity. In circular fashion, aggression has been drawn out, directed hostilely, expanded, taught, learned, expressed, and rewarded.

Some research findings have concluded that behavioral aggression may be learned and, if rewarded, may increase in occurrence.[142] One could also suggest that innate aggression originally may have selected itself for warfare, but this is too circular for clarity, too much in the style of questioning which came first, the chicken or the egg. Also, this is not to disclaim that aggression is part of the human character, but merely to point out that aggressively hostile characteristics have been excessively refined, strengthened, and brought to the fore where they have been socially and culturally expected and rewarded.

There are situational and psychological factors that involve hostility, of course, and that intensify or produce inimical feelings and behavior. Poor social environments or poor home conditions can produce inadequate settings for healthy human growth and development. Unequal treatment and social injustice are certainly grounds for frustration and hostility. The factor of sanctioned aggression, as typified by military and war situations, may tip these frustrations and increase by a large factor the susceptibility to channeled aggression.

Contrary to the popular notion that war is a ready-made outlet for personal hostility, however, it has been pointed out that warfare is a complicated and highly organized undertaking in which individual personalities are subdued or molded to the military perspective and needs. Except, perhaps, in immediate combat situations, personal aggressiveness and hostility is generally vicarious and sublimated to the group's ends and timing. Actually, there is sufficient reason to believe that such feelings can find expressive outlets in peaceful endeavors.[143]

Aggressive qualities are not always necessarily hostile, it must be mentioned. After all, determination, achievement, and pioneering qualities may also be perceived as aggressive, but with a *positive* connotation. Such dominant characteristics are frequently needed and displayed in sports, careers, art and music, adventure, space, etc. In achieving economic parity, for example, many women (like men) are using positive aggression—that is, drive, intent, achievement, and goal—to accomplish their aims. Society has definite rewards for such active and positively directed aggressive behavior.

Another aspect of aggression has been explored. Popular literature and some scientists have testified to the "territoriality" instinct and the extension of man's base nature from animal origins. One research conclusion in 1974 has clearly indicated that animals are poor comparisons for human social ills and conflicts.[144] It was further noted that territoriality in animals does not necessarily cause aggressive behavior but, rather, may actually reduce it. The acknowledgment of boundaries may serve as a natural means of spacing within a given area, leading to adequate sustenance and population control. In any event, it is doubted that such animal bounds apply to humans.[145]

The comparison of animal behavior with human behavior is a disparaging note heard with great frequency. It is a notion implying bestiality and portrays human beings as rooted and mired in base and animalistic actions. The comparison, of course, reduces the human image and potential. The science of ethology assumes that all living beings, humans included, have evolved ecologically over time in accordance with the laws of change and natural selection,[146] and it is presently concerned with developing a scientifically valid conception of human nature. However, criticism has been leveled at a scientific theory that humans have an aggressive instinct but no corresponding inhibiting instinct.[147] Many feel that this theory is faulty and, moreover, that it was wrong to apply the findings of animal studies to humans.

A consensus has been building that humans must be studied as humans.[148] In 1970 a Swiss psychologist and epistemologist was concerned about the danger of animalizing humankind by reducing human behavior from comparison with animal studies.[149] Concerned also, was another researcher in 1973 who claimed that some scientists were effectively reversing the error of humanizing animal actions by the animalization of human behavior.[150] As noted earlier, meaningful studies of complicated human behavior must start with humans, not animals.[151]

Opinion is building that comparison of human behavior with animals is faulty at best, erroneous and distorted, and, at worst, "animalization of human behavior". Findings are not yet complete, especially the study of "humans as humans", but it is reasonable to expect that as humans are so studied, their behavior will at least be classified as positive or negative to themselves, to the group, and to the environment. "Man's inhumanity to man" is subject to question and analysis, if not to judgment.

Conditions promoting hostile aggression among humankind, and the overt aggressive act itself, war, also cannot evade judgment. In no way can the mass murder of individuals or groups on command be considered a humane act. The planned group negation of life is in contradiction to biological purposes and cultural norms. Certainly, for example, nazi perpetrations of gross dehumanizing acts against the Jews and others fall into the nonhuman or subhuman category.

It is logical to conclude that diminishing the hostile influence of war and substituting the cooperative atmosphere of peace will at least reduce some maximal causes of negative behavior, while creating the opportunity for positive actions to develop. Man's relationship with man is of primary and continuing importance. It has been suggested that there is now a fundamental shift in the affairs of humankind. In *The Survival of the Wisest*, 1973, Dr. Jonas Salk, biologist, has found that the human struggle for survival that formerly was wrestled mainly with nature has shifted to itself, to the human species—between men, and in the individual.[152] Biologically, there is no blockage to peace and positive behavior.

Reducing organized warfare and aggression will remove some major barriers to human character building, it is safe to assume. Self-examination seems already to have begun, a surveillance that is almost as concerned with the quality of life as with life itself. On several planes, inner and outer, humans are eyeing themselves, their lives, and their behavior. Whereas technology, imagination, and creative exploits have been helpful in transcending early limitations, humanity must come to grips with itself on this plane, most immediately with the expanded powers of hostile aggression.

Dichotomous forms of aggression have riveted attention on the possible consequences of each. Where one is positive and life-extending, as exemplified by so many advances in the scientific, social, and medical fields, the other is negative and death-inducing, evidenced by unbridled militarism and hegemony. Ready to take near-miraculous flight into the universal expanse with experiences of entirely novel dimensions, or fearfully destined to drop into the abyss of eternal nothingness, the choice is still before us. But it must be made, and quickly, lest some awful mistake or chance tip the scale of life against the human species. Boldness, if not outright healthy fear, needs decide for life, in all its varied possibilities, and against death-inducing organized aggression.

CHAPTER TEN

ATTITUDES AND HUMAN NATURE

*H*ow humankind perceives itself determines to a great extent the behavioral role. Whether humans see themselves as warring, hostile creatures or as cooperative, friendly individuals is ultimately reflected in their behavior. And behavior, we have seen, is subject to analysis and interpretation.

In the social and psychological sciences, there seem to have been extraordinary attempts to find justification for and understanding of hostile aggression, an attempt that is undergoing refinement and redirection at the present time due to a wider definition of human behavior and the historical forces that have impacted on all. Lesser attention has seemingly been focused on communal positive behavior. A key to the map of social conditions and relationships is sought.

Innate processes have apparently been moving humanity toward peaceful cooperation via civilizing means, a process still continuing and now pointed in the direction of international cohesion. This latent force has been effected without strong conscious awareness and, at this tentative moment of extreme danger and infinite hope, has risen to a cognitive level where it stands tentatively poised, ready for further implementation. But an impasse has been reached. The innate forces for life have come up against a destructive habit that is antithetical to it—the lethal force of war—and at this moment of dramatic poignancy humankind has become aware that specific intervention is required to redirect the course of human affairs in order that life may proceed.

What is to be done? To begin, it is essential to examine the individual attitude of the self, and that of the collective, to global humanity and world affairs as they pertain to peace. What is the general attitude toward peace? Is it considered within the realm of possibility? What of the concession, grudgingly made, that peace is a pleasantly utopian ideal that may be realized in some distant age, but certainly "not in our time"? Or is peace thought to be an impossible dream, an impossibility resting on "human nature", on an erstwhile savagery and hostility in man? Perhaps there is even felt to be an irrationality that blindly and periodically erupts. Is humankind ever ready to burst the bounds of reason in snarling attack, and are we therefore doomed to perdition? And what of the nagging notion that perceives peace as "passive", an eviction of "excitement" from life, a surrender of sorts?

Questions of attitudes on peace must be considered in context of the human condition, and an apparent imbalance in perception needs correction. There must be evenhandedness in acknowledging the great human effort that has gone into building world cultures, religions, and societies. Notice must be taken and assimilated of the persistent, if often painful, ascent of human development throughout the ages. The peculiar readiness to casually dismiss the accomplishments of humanity as if of little importance or value will not do. Shrill trumpeting of failures to the exclusion of meaningful successes has contributed to skewed judgment of human behavior and may have robbed the individual and the group of confidence in human associations.

Little note, apparently, is taken of daily life, that which is relatively calm and socially structured, ordered by concern for sustenance and meaningful work, and bounded by relations with family and friends. Is the work of millennia—the building of communities, states, and nations—to be ignored and dismissed as non-event and non-history? Are the fruits of human ingenuity and skill to be treated as nonexistent and unreal? And what of love? Are love, cooperation, and greater humanness figments of the imagination? The willingness to dredge up and concentrate on the failures and frailties of existence must be offset, at the least, with the marvels and accomplishments that have been evidenced over time. Opinions and attitudes have been negatively influenced and are in need of correction.

Whatever are the thoughts and concerns about peace, those mentioned above or entirely different ones—there is a vanguard of attitudes behind them where the greater concepts of opinions, attitudes, and beliefs regarding humans and their relationships have been accumulating. It has been stated before that the fundamental biological concern of the organism is survival. It is to be expected that the underlying purpose in formulating attitudinal systems of thought, and all manner of ethnic and cultural understandings, is for allied cause—to further the progress of survival and the enhancement of life. Cultural means are decidedly human methods for assisting biological givens. Culture enhances biology. The one aids and abets the other, refining both the human being and the relationship in the process, and keeping life fluid and changing to meet the need.

Willingness to examine or challenge existing patterns of thought implies an inclination to entertain new concepts, which, of course, implies the possibility of change. And continued change seems inevitable. To realize that change in perspective is occurring at the healthy bidding of the individual's sensibilities is to acknowledge the ability to recognize new facts, new viewpoints, and new directions. Also, understanding change and its direction aids in opening new avenues and new levels of approach in changing course for the future. It helps in overcoming the confusion of change and in the successful navigation of options chosen. An understanding of the human organism and conditions for life may be the ingredient that will unlock the map of our social behavior and serve as a basis for meaningful change.

There is ample reason for confusion at the present time, however. Given the dichotomous circumstances extant in the world, divergent messages are being received, causing not a little consternation and bewilderment. For example, a military system is employed ostensibly to provide safety and security to the people, but the weapons and conditions of modern warfare are such that an outbreak of war threatens the very existence of the people. That which was and is meant to secure the future explicitly promises to end it. The situation is fragile, and pressures are building. Steps must be taken away from the military quicksand of confrontation to the higher ground of cooperative peace building. Ways must be found to build alliances and create firm footholds of national and international networking.

At this critical juncture, old myths, outdated attitudes, and irrelevant thinking must be sloughed off. We must be prepared to cast off outworn notions preparatory to a new direction in human experience. If necessary, in the manner of Ulysses, we may need to "bind ourselves to the mast" in order to pass the sirens and rocky projections of outworn habits and anachronistic behavior that promise an untimely end to humanity's habitance on earth.

Challenging possibilities rise before humankind, setting in motion a variety of actions requiring contemplation and decision making, all attributes of choice. The specifically human proclivity for observing and/or introducing elements of change into the life process is distinctly in operation and is manifesting itself on an international scale. But how are we to proceed? What are our real attitudes on human relationships, on peace and on war? We must analyze and understand ourselves. Such awareness of thoughts and attitudes may now be vital to our lives and to the lives of all that live on this planet.

ATTITUDES, OPINIONS, BELIEFS

Ideas, if held in common, bind a people together. They are enveloped in the combined attitudes and opinions about the world that, over time, have become experienced and valued guidelines in understanding and navigating through the often convoluted passageways of human relationships. It is the opinions, beliefs, and attitudes about self and others with which the idea of peace in the world has largely to contend. Based on the growth of learning and experience, much of it stored wisdom and not of one's own actual experience or knowledge, opinions have been held and forged, solidifying into attitudes.

An *attitude* is an opinion writ large, a firmly held conviction that has been tested through experience. It is an inclination to react positively or negatively to a variety of objects,[153] such as situational changes, new and old information, people, conditions, etc. It is the internal posture that may give rise to external behavior under various circumstances.

Opinions test and confirm or change in accordance with available information and may be short- or long-term. Of course, it is the organism's intent to form and keep relatively stable opinions for efficiency in its own operation, but opinions can and do change to accommodate new facts and conditions. They are the mediating antennae for testing and validating inner beliefs and for confirming attitudes that are more firmly held (than opinions) and resistant to change. Although behavior can lead to opinion change and attitude formation—say, in the case of youths, who are still in the process of growth—developed and strongly held attitudes are generally the forerunners of action, motivating behavior. Opinions and attitudes may be seen as different sides of the same coin, the one validating (or disconfirming) the position of the other.

Beliefs, on the other hand, are based on understandings of the nature of the world and universe. Allied to faith, belief is the mind's agreement as to the truth of a statement, proposition, or supposed fact, from evidence separate from one's general knowledge.[154] Held individually or in common, a belief may amount to a creed or body of faith supporting, for example, religious tenets.

What is perceived, and the attitude toward it, creates the immediate environment of behavior. The cultural or societal image held in human minds is largely effective in determining human behavior and shaping the direction of social attitudes.[155] Awareness of both the self in the world and of operational processes (manmade or natural) creates the opportunity to make meaningful changes in the human social system.

Much depends on the basic attitudes, ideas, and ideals of an individual and of a community. Humanity's "peculiar glory" has been credited with developing awareness of both the immediate environment and the larger picture of which it is a part. This mental picture of the world is an essential part of the world's process itself.[156] The actions of a people are not far removed from the notions of behavior and relationships. Expectations are largely fulfilled.

If, as noted, the common perception of strangers is that they are to be feared, and if the common belief in human nature is pessimistic, there is every likelihood that attitudes will influence the community's actions in a negative manner (in order to protect oneself and one's family and homeland from danger). Preparations will be made for sturdy defense against the common threat, and conflict and war will be seen as, or will become, inevitable. If, additionally, there is a dependence on authoritarian command to control the situation, as well as self-perception of untoward vulnerability, a situation of leader and led will be erected. (It does not take a Sigmund Freud to analyze the father-child syndrome.)

What happens when discrepant messages or images of the world occupy attention? When people are faced with information different from the attitudes or beliefs they hold, there is a resulting inner disquietude. This usually causes an informational search for clarification, verification, and understanding, in order that adjustment and balance are again achieved. This inner tension motivates behavior until urges for balance between divergent attitudes and information become stabilized. We are advised that mental processes always aim for balance,[157] between perception or the idea of the world in one's mind and the responses that are shaped by how it appears.

The complexity of the human mind and of the world does not make absolute consistency possible at all times, of course, a wide spectrum of possibilities pertaining. There is a vast range of choices in the realm of human behavior to accommodate myriad variations in actions, and, correspondingly, there is a wide panoply of variation within the mind, thought and creativity causing ever-novel images and situations. There is the ultimate freedom to choose, change, and transcend.

The present moment of danger, however, has little room for accommodation, the leeway having been absorbed by the mushrooming threat of the species' devastation. The nuclear capability can close out all human options. The fundamental danger is forcing close attention to the threatening situation, crowding out less vital matters. Search for alternative solutions (to warfare) leads unerringly to peaceful coexistence, and, in true human style, the sharp shift in perspective is ready to set aside outworn notions and attitudes as hindrances to future goals. But time-tested ideas are not easily discarded. Humans are not dilettantes in opinion setting and attitude formation.

There is a great unease in the public mind. The facts no longer fit the old mold. Can it be that the social pattern is flawed? Attitudes of long duration on peace and war need careful reexamination in the light of the new situation and information. Data must be properly assembled and assimilated. The subject matter of survival is of deep content, and the scrutiny must include the biological level, below the cultural plane. It is not a matter to be taken lightly. Also, it is not a matter for overlong contemplation. Survival is at stake.

STEREOTYPES—DISSONANCE—AWARENESS

Whereas attitudes are deeply held convictions that have been invested with time and experience and formulated to succinctly represent some measure of the world, *stereotypes* are generalized concepts—loose ties—around a bundle of similar groups. An efficient thought-saving and categorizing device, stereotypes reduce complex issues to neat generalizations. A simplified means of handling a complicated and repetitive concept, group, or event, stereotypical thinking is usually incorporated in arriving at attitude formation.

In attitude shaping and retention, new information may generate another look at the set belief or attitude. In most cases, the held attitude will stand up against the recently acquired fact, having previously weathered many such expositions. A stereotype, by comparison, is only a generalization of a condition or issue—an assistant, as it were, in formulating opinions and attitudes. It is not an exact or specific fact and is subject to change. Though it serves an efficient function in shaping attitudes—a short cut, so to speak—a stereotype is merely a reasonable facsimile of some part. There is not much emotional investment in stereotypes (which may be different for the stereotypee).

Consistently contradictory information may serve to invalidate the stereotype, and it will then no longer satisfactorily represent the complex issue. Evaluation of stimuli, issue, and attitude will ensue. If the present experience and new information are sufficiently strong and valid and defy denial, stereotype (as well as opinion and attitude) change can and probably will occur. But time is a factor.

The longer held the attitude, opinion, and belief, the more difficult they usually are to dislodge. An investment over time has been made, and, depending on the issue or situation, attitudes become entrenched. Change becomes more difficult to elicit. However, if materials presented are as valid, as deep, and as valued, movement will begin that, if unchecked, can unseat the now invalid concept. But it is not given up lightly.

While it is true that holders of a set of beliefs and opinions tend to reinforce the stronger attitude and search for information and experiences that continually validate it, stimuli that negate the belief or notion will cause a certain amount of psychological discomfort. As noted, the human organism desires consistency between internal cognitions and external reality, between thought and feelings and "the world". Inconsistencies between attitudes and facts cause what has been referred to as *dissonance* within the person. There is a desire for consonance—to have the contradictory messages harmonize. Dissonance produces pressure to decrease or eliminate the discord.[158]

The behavioral element may change to conform with the (new) reality, or the environmental condition may be changed. Of course, changing the social environment in order to decrease dissonance is more likely than, say, changing the physical environment.[159] In the matter at hand, the present social environment is indeed in need of change, and it is a possible condition. There is the need to change from a war system to a system of peace. *Desire* for peace is consistent with the *need* for peace. But the existing socially sanctioned war system militates against it. It is this obsolete and death-inducing mechanism and system that now must be confronted and changed to conform to the need and human desire to live harmoniously in a nurturing and non-life-threatening environment.

The problem is scarcely easy, as conflicting messages collide within the human breast. One may be torn with the experience, custom, and belief in the past method of national security through armed might versus the startlingly new awareness that today's sophisticated weaponry can cause a catastrophe destructive to ourselves, our nation, and all humankind. Specifically, the nature of war is now such that it can cause disintegration of the very society that relies on it and calls it into being. Danger has been additionally intensified because decisions for the onset of war are in few hands. (We learned earlier that it is a myth that an entire nation is involved in the *decision* to go to war, such decision making being highly concentrated.) A great uncertainty is spreading throughout the world.

A critical dilemma is thus starkly portrayed before the human mind, and regardless of the former immutability of an idea, conflict is now present within human cognitions, forcing comparison and new evaluation. Awareness forces acknowledgment that some former staunch beliefs are no longer valid. There is no escaping the fact that inordinate amounts of funds and resources are being consumed in production of material deadly to the human race, the whole of it. Security has diminished, if not dissipated. Warfare constitutes an unparalleled danger to humanity and the environment, undifferentiating between friend and foe, guaranteeing destruction to all. (And incredibly, there is a host of people apparently committed to continuing the debacle to the bitter end, defying rational consideration, honest appraisal, or responsible concern.)

A decision must be made. Shall the former attitude and pattern of group protection be retained? If not, what is the new one? How does one secure survival and maintain continuity and progress? Generally, when pressures to change are growing, a major method for achieving a social objective is to generate active public awareness and support.[160] Correction and change now must emanate most emphatically from the people who, as a whole, have the power to offset and overturn the weight of the entrenched system of military hegemony and fostered dependence. The people, collectively, must have the courage, foresight, and will—as they have the power—to do just that. The group must forge a new direction in human affairs, one that will ensure perpetuation of the species. And, it is expected, a strong position for peace from a strong nation will find friends and nations eager to join the common stretch for survival which is, after all, in the interest of the total human community.

Rendered obsolete by current technology and events, although long decried by humanists, warfare must be banned and eliminated from the roster of human behavior. It must go the way of other cultural taboos and prohibitions, those ways of behavior that are not socially condoned or permitted in human societies (e.g., witch hunting, debt imprisonment and pillorying, public hangings, etc.). Survival brooks no permanent hold on a method or system that no longer serves the need and purpose of human preservation.

Concern for collective survival must stimulate behavior to substitute a system of cooperation and responsibility for the ancient—now obsolete—"art" of warfare. To some, it is recognition of human behavior tragically overdue. To others, a formerly tested means is being found wanting, calling for abandonment. But it is action that surely finds consent within the human breast, awareness growing that civilized means for resolving human conflicts are compatible with feelings of justice, equality, and creative human potential. Conversely, organized and planned methods for killing one's fellow being are shabby evidence of the human turned against himself. It is a sadly unloving revelation, and unlovely spectacle.

Still, beliefs based on experience and education over a long period of time, and shared with the group, may prove resistant to dispelling. But this is not to say that attitudes and customs cannot be changed, though they have been formerly firmly held convictions upon which behavior and social customs were fixed. The cliche that "you can't change human nature" gives the impression of permanency and inflexibility. However, bearing in mind that life reserves to itself the ability to move, total rigidity in outlook would negate the living influences of choice, change, and evolution.

The realization that attitudes can indeed be changed is not to infer an instability in outlook or ficklemindedness in human tenets. Consider the magnitude of the dilemma facing humankind that is necessitating a possible change in attitude and a shift in directing human affairs. It is no small matter that is under consideration.

The fact that attitudes play the part of anchor in stabilizing human behavior and influencing social structures is an amazing human accomplishment. It is a marvelous technique when used in the large, since it assumes commonly held assumptions about the world. People pool their social behavior based on a common outlook—a most cooperative venture. In the situation under advisement, a war system was devised to protect the people from harm, to safeguard life. (Imagining the ancient past, it was no mean feat to protect a clan or tribe from marauders, and a host of ready warriors was undoubtedly a protective and reassuring necessity.) As time went along and warfare became more sophisticated due to improved and clever means of slaughter—say, from the bow and arrow to mechanized rifle power—strategies, too, became sophisticated, involving high-level thinking and planning. Matters specialized further, and the hierarchical group became a vertical command. In all of this, little rocked the anchor or attitude about armed force, since warfare was waged against an enemy of the people. How else could succeeding generations live with the scourge of war, if not by believing that it was for a good and just cause? Myths and romanticism were woven about the hero in uniform who was the savior of hearth and home. It was a man's world, and little dissent was heard. Things were as they were supposed to be.

Who can say when attitudes changed and the great disillusionment with war set in? It has been building over time, of course. But in the relative near, perhaps it was when, less than one hundred years after the United States was formed, a great civil war in America broke out. War between the states found the North pitted against the South, neighbors split, families torn apart—and over half a million were killed or maimed. It took many years for the hatred, hardships, and wounds of war to heal.

Or perhaps World War I, the war to end all wars, rudely awakened the population from the reverie of war as romantic when one-legged and sightless men emerged as veterans of the foxholes. World War II brought us the dementia of Hitler and the fanaticism of "aryan superiority", visiting the holocaust of nazism on a primarily Jewish sector. We observed the insanity and inhumanity of planned genocidal murder.

The United States was attacked in Pearl Harbor, a mission that later earned the Japanese the horror of our A-bombs, decimating Hiroshima and Nagaski. The *hibak-shi* (survivors) of that holocaust have traveled the world to publicize the tragic consequences of war and to cry out that, indeed, war is hell. Certainly the Vietnam fiasco caused a great upwelling of resistance, and a cry resounded against that war, if not all wars.

Awareness has come from other directions as well. Has the ongoing development and "emergence" of half the world's population been formative in crystallizing emotions and attitudes against war? Have women observed that warring is not so much a protection of home, women, and children as it is a "sport of kings"? Have they decried the uselessness of living with the debacle of ruined lives in favor of life purposes?

And what of the lessons of religion? After centuries of incorporating religious principles, ethics, and guidelines into human thought and practices, is it not to be expected that "graduates" would absorb the lessons and attempt to utilize the knowledge in daily life? Also, perhaps our attitudes against war have been formulating ever since the printing press made it possible to distribute information to the masses of people and we became educated to matters of public policies and events.

Learning is cumulative. Probably all these events, and more, have played and are playing their parts in forming our attitudes. Perhaps the experience of this century, especially, in learning of the ruin and devastation, waste of resources, economic upheaval, and the maimed and dead victims of pockets of war has forever dispelled any aura of respectability to war as solution for human problems. The ability to read millions of words on the subject, to have viewed countless films, to flick on a button and bring pictures (in living color) of suffering, battered, and mutilated humans into the family room has embedded a message of the travesty of mechanized and inhuman warfare. It is simply an untenable notion and pattern of behavior to sustain any longer in civilized society.

Combining the above awarenesses with relatively recent information about the finiteness of earth, common origins and tenancy on this globe, the natural environmental factors, and life's dependence on all of it, is to present an entirely new set of information to the public mind for careful evaluation. To realize, as well, that struggling humanity has created a civilizing process for centuries upon centuries is to begin to perceive with awesome respect the meaning of survival and the great privilege of life— that innate sense that unerringly guided our ancestors and that is still operative in us.

All of the above have impacted upon our sensibilities and await the coordination and synthesis of our consideration and creative abilities. Like a pot at boiling point, the lid has come off. The contents cannot be contained, and it will never be the same again. Nor should it be. What must happen now is for an enlightened people to look at the facts, condense and clarify them, and begin plans for the new direction. Since survival and civilization have propelled us here, the direction is merely a continuation of the path trod heretofore, a path of familiarity and precedence. To expect that an aware citizenry would not examine its attitudes and behavior in this respect—and wholeheartedly move in a healthier direction—would be to diminish human potential and creative resolution of problems.

Humans have adapted to change throughout all lifetimes (perhaps more enthusiastically by some than others). There have long been change-producing agents at work. Artists, educators, leaders, politicians, and others have been interested in ideas and conditions that may influence people to discard old habits of thought or behavior.[161] This century particularly has seen dramatic change effected throughout the world, from the automobile to space exploration, and from the A-bomb to genetic engineering. Presently computerization is unfurling its change-producing effects, and the fallout has wide ramifications, promising an entirely new era in knowledge use and storage. Especially since the advent of Apollo and Soyuz in space, a sense of change has hung pregnantly in the air, suggesting processes of assimilation, adjustment, and adaptation.

The critical factors of desire, instinct, and human will are motivating tools for instituting change, notwithstanding the tremendous influence exerted by attitudes and patterns of long standing and the energy needed to overcome and change the status quo. Recall, too, that survival needs are adamant in the struggle for life. Combined, the force is compellingly irresistible when taken up by the community. Concentrating on peace and bringing its collective mind and enlightened attitude to bear on the matter, a determined people could scarcely be stopped from making the necessary changes, if it should so decide.

The possibility of actual attitude and social change exists through the combined efforts of a multitude of individuals in various fields of endeavor and with varied perspectives who agree on the issue of life and survival. If the promise of peace is considered, in whatever part, there is reason to believe that cooperative efforts expended in its behalf would give hope and direction to a sagging and demoralized world. The fact that efforts would be made toward valued moral and ethical ground should substantially bolster the action and assist in overcoming some panic or fear, dissipating the possibility, if not the incidence, of antisocial and discrepant behavior. Expectedly, this positive behavior would fold back on itself and strengthen the tentative outreach (further lessening fear and gaining confidence and experience, creating energy and support, etc.). After all, circular self-fulfilling actions can work for good, too.

This tentative moment is also one of expectancy. Although apprehensive, it is tremulous with hope and responsive to the need for meaningful action. It is a moment when the ills of the past may be wiped clean, when willing people may make a difference, when the future may be both secured and filled with the excitement generated by energetic striving. And, most splendidly, it is a moment in time when those who were derogated as dreamers and utopians may hold forth the vision of a better world for humankind, one in which the creative arts will have equal time with the pragmatic. Adding this greater dimension of expectant fulfillment to the specialized experts of customary pattern—those who think in the large and those who think in specifics—creates an entirely new partnership. Together they are whole in perception of the world. United, they are a powerhouse.

History has swirled into a great pivotal point, and a swell of gigantic energy is gathering to surge and shift the direction of human affairs. The knowledge explosion, the scientific leap in unveiling marvelous space possibilities, and the newly self-conscious reappraisal of human strivings have all combined into a great tide sweeping the rock of attitudes from its moorings. It requires only our combined efforts to ride out the waves, to chart the new course, and to set sail in the new direction. What is fueling the drive is the active ingredient of survival. The events over time—those few mentioned herein and countless others—are feeding into this current of energy, and all of it is a movement that has its own momentum. It must be heeded. *Life is demanding action in its behalf!*

HUMAN NATURE

It is vital to the task at hand that people have sufficient confidence and energy to accept the challenge of turning around the deplorable state of affairs that threaten all lives. Confidence to accomplish this seemingly herculean undertaking is essential, and the matter of human nature may be of concern. Peace may be desired, but is it contrary to human nature?

A profound restriction on a people's psychological and human development surely has operated in tandem with warfare. A disastrous residue of distrust, fear, anger, guilt, sorrow, and diminished personal goals has neighbored the growth of the war system. People have been pitted against people, and divisiveness has become endemic. This has been in addition to the usual great and tragic consequences of war itself—of multitudes killed, maimed, and orphaned and the dreadful misuse of talent, resources, funds, etc. This vicious syndrome has trickled down through the ages and left its discoloring effects. The concept of human nature may have been victimized in the process.

Vapid self-demeaning phrases proliferate about human nature that denigrate self-worth and reduce confidence and sense of independent capability—for example, humans are untrustworthy, steeped in evil, just a step away from the animal world, etc. Yet how human nature is expected to be, how one sees oneself and others, and how attitudes and beliefs of human aggression and compassion are presented and internalized are vital to development of self and relationships.

"Human nature" is a descriptive phrase referring to all humans in enlarged and stereotypical fashion. The popular viewpoint that cites human nature as rooted in evil and hopelessly savage ("man is a warlike animal", "the world is a jungle", "man is basically evil", "you can't change human nature", and so on) is a blanket indictment of character. But as long as there are any examples to the contrary, the apparent condemnation may be questioned, if not categorically dismissed. In merely contemplating and observing one's own experiences—with family, friends, neighbors, and acquaintances—there are obviously many instances to the contrary. The negative descriptions of human nature are not valid in toto. Not at all. As a stereotype, therefore, it is invalid. Yet it persists.

Ample negative news abounds into which the outworn cliches are plugged, and in circular fashion they tend to reinforce the old shibboleths. Decrying any possibility of change continues, and since one is part and parcel of the lot and does not dissent, character self-defamation is implicit therein (a predictive approach and boomerang effect, like kicking the dog and then kicking it again for barking or biting). This defeatist syndrome paves the way for concluding that change is impossible and that unworthy humankind is out of control and, of course, doomed.

The notion that change is impossible at a time of great change is an idea that is startlingly out of touch with reality. There are few persons today who would consider the present age as a time without change. In this century alone, and in living memory, change has swirled over humankind almost everywhere. The hackneyed concept is an incorrect assumption, and the matter should be easily laid to rest. (Indeed, people should be realizing their admirable qualities and finally be willing to consider that they have grown immensely in stature and that standards of self-appraisal require new molds.) However, present implications have pervasively negative undertones. Since each person is included in the widely accepted unsavory perceptions and definitions of "flawed" human nature, all are defamed alike. Without contradiction, tacit consent is implied, and the debasing descriptions stand as standards of truth. Actually, all are robbed of some personal strength thereby, and support is weakened in counteracting the baleful indictment.

Is human nature basically faulty? (The subject is scarcely considered outside of religious or psychological circles.) If it is not faulty, what is it? Can it be perfect? But the state of perfection implies a finished or static case, untenable for a living organism. Are humans doomed to a permanent search for personal perfection only to slide down the greased pole of permanent imperfection? Is there confusion in outreach? Has humanity been sidetracked in search of perfect being rather than, say, healthy being? Is this search fueled somehow by the need to escape some negatively inspired basic notion of human nature?

But perhaps there is too much concern with these catch-phrases that may demean self-worth. Are negative concepts of human nature sincerely believed? Is anyone really injured? It depends on whom such standards impress. Is it not reasonable to expect that if a child or youth hears it from important others, and often, the negative message may well be taken to heart? It may lay there like a stone, heavily, an invisible burden that diminishes some joy in life, some satisfaction with self. Matured, one may dismiss such slogans in moments of optimism, but at other times they may be used as reasons, excuses, condemnation, self-hatred, etc. Unexpurgated, negative self-concepts remain within, weighting the spirit, sapping energy. Although personal salvation may be heroically attempted, the overall effect tends to lead to loss of confidence in self and others, diminishing expectation.

The reductionist viewpoint of human nature is widely maintained. Feelings of impotence, rage, depression, etc. may be reinforced, if not kindled, and an entire defeatist syndrome retained or set in motion to the detriment of the individual and the society, which is only as good, perhaps, as the (self) appraisal and expectation. (If human nature is basically faulty, any manner of evil or deviate behavior may be expected and excused. After all, it's only human nature....)

Labels and expectations very often produce the results named. Negative social expectations, misnomers, and stereotyped images reinforce demeaning human characteristics and conditions, thereby helping some to grow into the squalid descriptions of themselves. The expectation is thus fulfilled, giving rise to reinforced opinion, and the cycle is perpetuated. The belief in human nature as debased may be partial cause for the seeming insistence on continually citing and publicizing examples of human failures, crimes, and the bizarre. Exclaiming again and again about the perfidy of human nature serves as both a reminder and a lesson of basically flawed humanity. The pattern follows the path of seeking ruptures, and the message reinforces the negative belief.

The apparent need to be constantly reminded of shabby human behavior may border on the compulsive. Rooting out the ills of the world without careful compensatory balance of the good suggests, at the least, a (morbid) fascination for the negative and may be a cause and effect in actually creating more of the same. It may be expected that much energy is expended in relieving oneself of these (self-) applied labels—an untenable load that, try as one may, can scarcely be lifted, so reinforced is it by social and cultural norms and expectations. The personal attempt to escape vilification of the self is an exhausting effort consuming vital energy. How much energy is left with which to aid the world? It is to our eternal credit that any efforts whatsoever are undertaken to improve the human lot in spite of personal loss of confidence and energy.

Incredibly, many are bent on teaching themselves how deplorable human nature is in actual contradiction to their own virtuous strivings. It is a great pity and a huge waste of human potential. Courage and honesty dictate that the underlying belief about human nature itself must be reconsidered and upgraded to accommodate a healthier opinion and attitude of humankind in general, and of self in particular.

Some basic work was covered in this area by psychoanalyst Abraham Maslow, who affirmed that human nature was not as bad as usually considered and, in fact, that it has generally been given short shrift.[162] He observed that there is an instinct for goodness that strives to actualize itself and, if permitted to develop and flourish, aims to guide life in healthy and fruitful ways. Dr. Maslow, who made studies of well people, [163] suggested that healthy persons passed through growth stages that fulfilled fundamental needs and helped them to realize their potential (self-actualization). This theory is incorporated in his early "Theory of Human Motivation", [164] a pattern of growth or "hierarchy of human development" that he continued to refine, and to which many others have referred. Physiological, psychological, spiritual, and material needs are all involved.

Satisfaction of basic growth requirements permits fuller personal development, an ongoing process that finds greater belief in oneself and in the sense of control and responsibility manifested in one's life, in Dr. Maslow's findings. Such persons strive to incorporate the "being" values, values that transcend ordinary concerns and reach for universal truths and ways of being.[165] Interests and causes beyond the self are sought, and there is a deeper sense of harmony with all of life. The desires for beauty, truth, goodness, etc. are the greater needs—meta needs—far removed from the materialism one constantly hears western man accused of.

The fact that such values are sought after augurs well for the possibility of establishing a peace system in the world. The most elemental human needs are mirrored in the need for a world at peace. Yet basic physical and security needs—food, shelter, health care—are diverted and denied multitudes of people, due, in many places, to social and political manipulations as vast pools of energies and funds are diverted elsewhere. We are advised that whereas, globally, a minority is overindulged, over fifty percent of humankind is underfed and malnourished, and almost that many are completely without any health care at all, an inequity that is a festering source of international stress.[166] Yet worldwide, the insatiable needs of the military and the fear to which it caters demand constant satisfaction.

Our most basic security is threatened by war, its promised residue of death possibly affecting all of humanity. The divisive atmosphere fomented by the hostile forces of militarism is a wedge between people causing hatred and violence, while normal developmental concerns are shunted aside or backtracked. And a fundamental element is also denied—that we are all of one biological species, the human race. Espousing peace and love, but planning and arming for war and death, is a twisted perversion of the cause and is completely unstable and unreliable in effect.

It is sufficiently evident that ending widespread support for warfare and the active hate and violence it spawns—at last viewing it as the uncivilized and prohibitive behavior it is—would permit an atmosphere conducive to cooperation, respect, and self-respect to grow. Desires for truth, justice, goodness, aliveness, etc. are natural extensions of human values and human nature and are worthy ends in themselves. Positive expectations of human nature would ensure healthier human beings and go a long way toward correcting abuses in the social sphere.

In searching for root causes of inimical behavior, however, limited self-appraisals seem to have kept the search incredibly narrowed, if not short-circuited. For example, comparisons of humans with animals have been made; human nature has been derogated; irrationality has been cited; diminished sights have concluded that humankind is unworthy and doomed. Have these and other negative, possibly self-hate, notions effectively curtailed deeper probing of systems and institutionalized supports that invoke, sustain, and reward hostile behavior?

The often demonstrated need to search for behavioral cause of overtly errant behavior indicates, at the least, an attempt to find understanding and balance between actions, feelings, and cognitions. Although most findings have been deficient in perceiving the broader issues that have served to keep human nature in chains, so to speak, there is uneasiness and dissonance between inner feelings of human sympathies and overt manifestations of unbridled hostility. Obviously there is a discrepancy, if not a dichotomy, and it must be reconciled and bridged. Explanations of individual and communal behavior demand deeper probing into effects of social conditioning and control than has generally been the case.

The needs that give rise to the particular social institutions that have evolved must be analyzed. Uncomfortable ground may be unearthed as dearly held notions and convictions are held up to bright and public scrutiny. It is not without risk, at times, to delve into areas of private perspective and automatic response. The possibility that such penetration may cast its gaze upon ground hardened (or hallowed) by practices and traditions presupposes the possibility of finding errored, unhealthy, or outmoded notions and habits. Vested interests may be threatened.

Clinging to antiquated notions of human nature retains the status quo, of course. Retention of negative stereotypes and practices may sustain feelings of inadequacy and continue dependence on authority. Presumably, too, "authority" will be inhospitable to stirrings of independence. However, perceiving human nature and strivings in a new light may be all that is keeping us from moving firmly ahead in a healthier direction, away from the spreading morass into which we have been sinking.

Lack of conscious awareness of the human desire to live cooperatively and peacefully has closed our eyes to creative possibilities for improved human interaction. Clearly, adherence to the outmoded and destructive system of meeting problems with violence has brought the state of the world to the condition it is in. It is primitively inept. In "protecting" themselves, supernations have literally encased themselves and peppered the world with arsenals of vast destructive power. All the while, human nature is decried, and the lack of peace is lamented. Toe to toe and head to head, the game of armaments continues while responsibility for consequences has been almost totally abdicated.

Common sense, and even the most limited appraisal, can foresee the disastrous possibilities in store. Common sense would refrain from filling potential powder-keg areas with the ability to inflict grievous harm; common sense would keep sophisticated weapons from factions fanatically committed to terrorism, violence, guerrilla warfare, and the like; common sense, love, and responsibility would protect family, friends, and law-abiding citizens of the world by withholding such caches of potential

destruction; common sense would demand public explanation of the purpose of burgeoning manufacture and sales of such explosive materials in
the face of unspeakable danger; indeed, common sense would reconsider
the whole irresponsible syndrome and call a halt to it! Reiteration of common sense reasoning is a reminder that, instead, powerful interests have
circumvented common sense and spread their tentacles over the earth and
the people, producing the situation that holds the whole world near-captive.
Can there be any who do not realize that this pattern of inhuman rationale
and behavior is responsible for some of the disastrous turn of events?

The military habit needs to be drastically reduced, and simultaneously
peace needs further specific urging and implementation. Acknowledging
that the military presence is a method of protection, a weapon of control,
a measure of physical strength, it is not conceded to be the nation. It is not
the government. It is not the people. Above all, the military is not "human
nature". The whole military conglomeration is employed and funded by the
public and is subordinate to the national interest. It is subject to the
people's control, and it may be wielded, diminished, or dismissed at the
people's discretion.

It has been noted that there is an opposed fixity of purpose between
military and civilian modes of thought. To which school is the concept of
human nature affixed? Has the military mentality permeated society to
such extent that its manner of perceiving the world has been absorbed into
the thought processes of the people?

Power has been invested in specialized experts and authorities in a
social environment that has birthed a population holding a largely negative
view of human nature. To a great degree, personal power has been
displaced outside the individual, and, it is suggested, power in large part
has been deflected, invested, and/or usurped by the mighty and powerful
military organization of the nation. Rendered somewhat chastened and
unsure, effectively dampened individuals fit neatly into the needs of the
military framework and mentality. Under the banner of rigid authoritarianism, control is more easily exercised over meek and powerless individuals-
turned-soldiers. Power is readily assumed over weakened individuals who
have given up their own power, or who may have no conception of it,
having little developed it and having placed excessive reliance in others,
especially in power-with-fist.

The metamorphosis from independent citizen to dependent recruit is
more easily accomplished if society is primed for the transition by accepting the notion of the military as omnipotent and authoritarian champion

and defender of life, liberty, and property. Obligingly, a paternalistic and autocratic command demands and expects complete obedience, if not servitude. Conformity is expected and praised; dependence is fostered. Agreeing with and absorbing this line of thought and behavior demands the release of individuality and creative expression (both of which are anathema to the military format).

Working hand-in-glove, dovetailing neatly, the varied negative social, religious, and philosophical viewpoints that adhere to the notion of human ineptitude, if not human nature rooted in evil, harmonize beautifully with the needs and desires of those who would establish hegemony over others. And inevitably, these inhibiting factors have become part of the social milieu.

Polarized messages are thus simultaneously projected to society at large. Whereas family life, education, and social conditioning attempt to impart moral values and noble human standards (upholding creativity, rewarding independence and achievement), warfare and its military following demands obeisance to authoritarian and hierarchical roles and commands, and impersonalized, if not dehumanized, behavior. There is a vivid dichotomy of expectation and practice. Small wonder that many (perhaps the finest, the most sensitive) become disoriented, even schizophrenically split. They reflect no more, perhaps, than the actual societal split.

Spurious reasoning has even burdened many in affixing the *need* to war on beleaguered human nature. There are some who have managed to convince themselves that warfare is equated with life and excitement, desirable change and power. Conversely, peace is perceived as the epitome of passivity, inertia, weakness, and disorder. Some wonder if a world freed from the habit of war will produce a boredom tantamount to death, an environment wherein passivity and laxity will diminish creativity and dissipate energies, a world in which the human spirit will cease to strive. Not a few hold these views.

Some require the overt threat, the actual flight from danger, the flexing of muscles in panic, to remind themselves of life's value. Imperfectly conceived, the value of life has been confused or equated with a race from danger. There is a distorted perception of the meaning of life. Some even require the specter of death before beginning the flow of adrenalin signaling flight therefrom. For those with such delayed reactions, the present scenario offers plenty of motivation.

These perceptions may indicate an unsuccessful search for meaning in life, blanketing a fear, perhaps, that it is all meaningless. This notion will be more fully addressed later. The viewpoint that finds "excitement" in war, however, is a strangely shallow and self-defeating perspective. Whereas escape from death may indeed remind one of life's value, it need not be pursued for reminder's sake (as one does not need to have a broken arm to know it hurts).

The myth that warfare is inherent and endemic in human nature is a blight of highest proportions. It predicts that humankind is forever doomed to brutality and self-inflicted violence. This raises the specter of negative predetermination, diminished human options, and lack of choice and will. It is a stunted opinion, negating optimism about the future of humankind. Besides providing support for allegedly hostile human nature, it twists reasoning to adapt to the tragedy of war and attempts to make of it a positive event. In this it fails, but sadly, those who are certain that humankind is inherently evil are most susceptible to this perverted logic.

The concept of human nature is in flux. In lifting the stigma of evil and warmongering from the human back, in recognizing that it is a burden that can be lifted or ejected, the spirit is immeasurably lightened. The weight need not be carried. Human nature may lay claim to a more wholesome definition at last. Individually and collectively, it has long awaited the chance for growth and is more than ready. This growth of human character development, so long withheld, can at last be permitted a thirsting people.

The twenty-first century looms just ahead and promises to depend on the peaceful arts—on cooperation, persuasion, communication, education, skills, symbiosis with the environment, husbanding of resources, creativity, imagination, futuristic bent, etc. Hostilely sharpened aggressive faculties are of diminishing usefulness. Similar to the problem of converting military weapons to peacetime needs, assistance may be needed in diverting and redirecting negative tendencies into socially acceptable and reconstructed avenues, the better to direct destructive behavior and energies to positive channels for the good of the individual and society.

It is to be expected that the development of a nation's psyche will rise and progress to the degree to which it has been subdued and stymied, and a quantum leap in the national character can be expected. If it matches the achievement for cooperation, skill, and imaginative daring that has resulted in the magnificent explorations and sorties into space, a human being of incomparable nature and potential is possible—perhaps inevitable.

CHAPTER ELEVEN

CHARACTERISTICS OF MEANING AND PURPOSE

*I*t is not novel to state that the present time is a period of great change and uncertainty. In this uncertain state, the search for meaning and purpose in life is more necessary than ever to provide stable ballast to behavior and to point the direction of action. Whereas many lessons can be gleaned from the past—indeed, they should be, experience having been hard won—they are almost worthless unless there is continuity bridging yesterday's knowledge with today's certainty and tomorrow's promise. And that is precisely the problem—continuity is lacking. The bridge is incomplete and unstable. Something is missing.

Meaning in living is an ingredient that is essential to living purposefully. When missing, it cannot seem to be satisfactorily filled by anything else. A so-called "soft" subject, its absence in life is alarming, giving rise to a sense of aimlessness and floundering. Ranging widely from material to metaphysical inquiry, the search for meaning continues, yet seems to elude the desperate majority. While material riches may raise the physical standard of living, the paucity of life is felt by those who have not determined the purpose of it or, worse, who decry *any* purpose at all. A gap is felt, a hole or pit that no amount of substitution seems to fill. The need remains gnawingly unfulfilled.

At the point of development where the individual seeks to understand the meaning of life, and especially the particular purpose of one's own life, the perspective and guidance is expectedly from the cultural vantage point. Cultures represent the viewpoints and patterns of living that have developed over time. Of all the functions of a culture, the most human is to define the meaning of life.[167]

Culturally, the ways of a people are expressed through its thought systems, its philosophical, historical, religious, artistic, and scientific interpretations, its customs and habits, skills and actions. These are passed on and imbibed by the young, who, in turn, accept or make changes and carry on the cultural teachings in continuous renewal. Besides indicating ways and means for providing and securing the physical necessities of life, cultural settings also portray the motivation and tenacity for survival. Institutionalized over time, patterns become set, and the effect is cumulative.

Answers are naturally sought from one's own setting, one turning trustingly to experienced elders, that will, hopefully, knit together the outer and inner aspects of societal and personal life. Wholeness and direction are sought. A sense of authenticity is strived for, and a serious attempt is made at unity and synchronization of self within the framework of life and environment. What is expected of the individual and of the group? What do the individual and the group ask of life? What is it all about? The mind probes the living universe and presses for answers.

Presently, as inquiry deepens, an unpleasant surprise is often encountered. There doesn't seem to be sureness of purpose and meaning at all. Anger and dejection are rife at one and the same time, and the questions are sought after fruitlessly, shunted aside, or despaired of. Somehow there seems to be open ground that has not been covered. Still, the questions pour forth hungrily: Are we an accident of evolution, a chance on the face of the earth? Do we live only to die? What is the meaning of (my) life? Although philosophies and religions are concerned with the same questions, the answers seem to be unsatisfactory, and cognitions are separated from feelings. There are unconvincing suggestions, incomplete notions or none at all, and the searchers are left hollow-eyed and empty-handed. Discouraging notions increasingly intrude, and amidst a plethora of negativity and defeatism, some are suggesting there is little or no meaning left in carrying on against the (insufferable) odds.

Something has gone seriously wrong. At precisely the age when eagerness and youth are ready to enter into life's vast arena, there is perceived disarray, frustration, and lack of direction. At the very time that optimism and daring hope are needed more than ever, some certainties of life are glaringly absent. What is the goal? What are the guidelines? Where are we going? Why? A great confusion overlies society, and there are innumerable eddies and swirls of disconcerting thought and behavior.

MEANINGLESSNESS

Meaninglessness evidences the person's or group's lack of purpose in living. Nothing seems worthwhile. Lack of self-direction and self-confidence, if not control, may be accompanied by passivity, defeatism or, conversely, by easily aroused anger. But without adequate self-management, the stage is set for easy manipulation or rudderless action. Commitment and responsibility are weak, if present, and actions may range widely, disconnectedly, and meaninglessly. Cohesiveness and bonding to others is lessened. Any sharp current or unexpected squall, so to speak, may sway the craft erratically or swamp it entirely. One's life may be deflected capriciously or tossed overboard. It is as if the inner anchor is insufficient to stay or ride out the tempest.

A life devoid of meaning may be filled with sharp excesses or sunken depression—the vacancy is endless to occupy. The effects of meaninglessness lie in shattering evidence all about. Daily accounts may be read of attempts at avoiding or misreading reality, of the use of synthetic means for elevating or depressing emotions, and of growing criminal tendencies. The pervasiveness of the problem is increasingly extensive, having little regard for age levels or socio-economic factors. Dissatisfaction is endemic. The inner core of life is destitute, and a feeling of emptiness and bitterness persists, leaving only the shell of existence, which, in time, becomes consistently more brittle.

Whereas there may be many causes sifting into the general pool of meaninglessness, there is overall indicated a failure of social and personal integration. Generally it is considered the individual's failure, rather than the culture's, to be unable to find satisfactory meaning and purpose in life and to be unable to fit oneself meaningfully into the prevailing milieu. But can it be that cultural teachings are now out of synchronization with personal and group psychological and biological needs?

It is hard to believe that basic and fundamental systems of society are inimical and detrimental to growth and development. It is usually easier to believe the self is faulty (God knowing of one's imperfections) and to make the self conform to the prevailing mode. Yet surely a culture must also be held up for examination. It cannot be immune from flaw-finding and correction, especially if its adherents are suffering in large measure, and if various vital signs are showing distress (e.g., general purposelessness and directionless living, over-great suffering, destructiveness, criminality, inhumanity, suicidal tendencies, threat to survival, etc.).

The fact that the present time is characterized by many changes may be reason enough for some to feel uneasy and hesitant. Change in and of itself is not a new phenomenon, however, and it would be expected to be a transitory condition, with the individual and the group growing out of it together. But overlying this unsteady time there is the added real threat and possibility of widespread devastation and potential annihilation. That is a totally different matter that cannot—dare not—be shut out from mind and heart. What manner of (irresponsible) behavior has brought about this terrifying situation? What will overcome it? And what kind of change is needed in order to guarantee the future? Indeed, without this change, without certainty of a future, what meaning and purpose is there at all?

Without meaning and purpose, there is a rash of false goals that pretend to value. There may even be the tendency to fall back on former experiences in order to effect a sense of familiarity and possible mastery. Problems, conflicts, suffering, etc. may be enlarged, if not (re)created, to bring a sense of purposeful direction to a people. History may well repeat itself. A common enemy, a common disaster, a common threat will overshadow more mundane matters—especially floundering resolve—and promote a sense of united purpose in the common effort to overcome. Here, at least, the group knows what to do.

In the current general milieu, meaninglessness is a quagmire of uncertain direction. It is a swamp in which many are caught and into which many are falling. As it widens and deepens, not only is it increasingly easy to be caught in it; the struggle to find life's firm footing may be compounded by the fact that there are unfriendly others who perceive the situation and take it as a sign of vulnerability and weakness. (In truth, it is not a sign of strength. It is indication of inner instability, confused resolve, and lack of direction. Wavering decision and indecisive actions are signposts of uncertain course, and it would be well to overcome the general malaise quickly.)

Globally, of course, this is many times intensified. There is no clear indication of where the people are going or what they stand for. Friends and supporters may be very much confused as signals clash and counterclash. Certainly, it is not a rock of stability to which others can cling (in an already unstable world), and fear may be struck in many hearts. To many others, if not ourselves, *we* are their bastion of hope and security. After all, if this promising people is indecisive, confused, and directionless, what hope is there for floundering humanity elsewhere?

In the course of the current shifting ground, the need for meaning, purpose, and direction is more crucial than ever. Meaninglessness deflects vital energy, sapping strength and the clearsightedness needed to chart life's direction. It is a splitting wedge at a time when united purpose and resolve are critically required. But how will this come about? What will stabilize the community? Are wars needed to unite people and give meaning to their lives? Must there be suffering to live? Is that what it is all about? Is life one great barrel of pain that must be clambered out of?

Were the pain theory of life the final word—the whole of life's purpose and meaning—it would seem that there would be little sense or real desire to overcome it; that growth comes *only* from overcoming and/or becoming inured or accustomed to suffering. (Shades of masochism hover uneasily about this notion.) Were disorder entirely prevalent, entropy would enlarge, putting an eventual halt to growth, change, and evolution, and the natural order would indicate that disarray prevails. Creativity would cease.

But such does not seem to be the case. Rather, the natural order appears to be precisely that—orderly. Furthermore, it is exquisitely timed, both in the minuscule and in the large. There is a growth and flowering in nature that is entirely evident, an evolutionary design that is extant, an endless array of variations. And in the greater universe there is a panoramic pattern that sweeps earth within the larger design of the spatial sphere. The globe, our habitat, is a small "dot" within a region of other "spots" centering about the sun. Our place in the celestial firmament is within a neighborhood, itself in a span of profuse regions and vast galaxies. The expanse is magnificently immense, dotted and patterned in myriad profusion and, at least in the relatively near, accessible to human exploration. One *can* leave this world alive.

It has taken earth eons of time to have reached its present development, and ages for humans to have reached this time. The sense of human meaning must undoubtedly incorporate the experience of time. However, before pursuing this line of thought further, the pain-and-suffering theory must be examined more closely, since it seems to have a pervasive hold on the people's sensitivities. It is intricately entwined in notions of life and death and is pertinent to the subject and psychology of peace and war. After all, if one is to embrace the theory that peace is possible, some established ideas of life and death may need readjustment.

PHILOSOPHY OF LIFE AND DEATH

There is a certain high drama in the phrase "life and death". A starkness is evoked, the contrast of brightness and darkness portrayed, and perhaps some trepidation felt in treading on unfamiliar ground. A sense of mystery is implied, even danger felt. Is it hallowed or haunted ground? What is the unknown quantity? One steps cautiously, if not respectfully, for there is uncertain footing. Yet it is not an unfamiliar phrase to the mind and ear.

Equally highlighted and in frequent linkage, the two events appear evenly matched. Two-sidedness is enhanced by the combination, as if on one coin, and a sense of balance is neatly projected. Life and death. Hand in hand, referred to and considered factually and symbolically in unison and repeated constantly, one is lulled into passive acceptance of this dichotomous duet. Life and death. Continually called forth, the message is reinforced manifold in custom, thought, and speech; the seeming alliance is virtually drummed into consciousness. Although it is life only that is lived, death is accorded an extraordinary share of interest and consideration and occupies a strategic location in awareness. There is ready belief that each is of equal importance and meaning.

The prominent consideration of life and death together, as if joint concepts, causes a certain imaging of the "Grim Reaper" syndrome—of the individual being inexorably stalked by a relentless specter and inevitably being cut down too soon. Frustration and fear dog the footsteps, and try as one will, the shadow will not be eluded. In fact, it grows larger, until finally, of course, it engulfs the hapless individual. What is the sense of trying to escape the inevitable, or of trying to best an opponent whose track record is impeccable? Why bother? A sense of futility is incorporated into effort and there is a diminishing of purpose. Some of life's brightness is tarnished and, unchecked, continues to discolor experience, depressing the joy of life. Ample negative news and evidence of the grimmer aspects of life reinforce the effect and, curiously, at some critical juncture, may even be sought out. ("Misery loves company" is an old refrain.) Anything as large as warfare, of course, is beyond the comprehension to change, and death is hereby licensed and permitted wholesale rampage. One is helpless, if not hopeless, before the coming (inevitable) onslaught.

(Is warfare a testing ground for death? Is an old method of "meeting the Old Warrior" indulged in by the group? War was always a dangerous "game". Now, however, its repercussions guarantee death for the multitude. The odds have changed to a certainty; the "game", really, is no more.)

The concept of "death in life" is broadly maintained and, because it has found some acceptance and may have more than a little effect, should be reexamined. For some, perhaps, the preciousness of life is enhanced by continually calling to mind death's approach (with constant reminders that "we're getting older", "they're growing up", "it's too late", etc.). Viewing the end of life, there is sharp ongoing notice of each day lost. For many, a pervasive depression may lie at the roots of energy in anticipation of death, sapping the life force and leaving little to face the challenges, while for others there may be taken a desperado stance, a deliberate confrontation with death. Ever more dangerous and death-defying obstacles are undertaken, and when they are overcome, a sense of seeming immunity from death is built up. It is, of course, a courageous but pathetic example of bravado in the face of death certainty, bowing to a death-oriented mentality.

Actually, energy has shifted from a life-centered emphasis to a death-defying focus. Of course, death has won a slight edge. Its imminence is heightened, its effect enlarged, and it has become the acknowledged and immediate adversary—a haunting contender, a hated foe, a robber. It must be met, confronted, opposed, and headed off (although the ultimate contest is never in question).

A social debate on the subject of death, meanwhile, is a recent phenomenon. A conscious deliberation on this topic has been growing of late, becoming an active pursuit. Classes are given, information is intensely sought, experiences of the dying are researched. Healing, "out-of-body" occurrences, and life-restored happenings are avidly investigated and seriously considered. The subject hovers on the brink of the metaphysical, but strong efforts are made to bring the matter under conscious control. "Death and Dying" has become a legitimate course of inquiry and subject for study. As the phrase slips smoothly and alliteratively from the tongue and, with repetition, becomes a familiar sound, some fear may have been slightly mitigated.

It is a two-edged sword, however. Whereas some aspects of fear may have been somewhat allayed by consciously pursuing the subject of death, it may be at the too great expense of weakening the will to life. A certain pseudo- or super-rationality may be promoting curiosity that undermines one's instincts for life. A certain fanaticism may also be manifested. Rationale disclaims morbidity and seeks to proclaim acceptance of death in life. The statement is made repeatedly that "death is a part of life", and it has taken on an aura of fact. But is death a part of life?

The fact is that *death has no place at all in life*. A contradiction in terms, death is not an anomaly, deviation, or abnormality of life. It is no experience of life at all. Death's eventuality results in life's termination—or, more accurately, life's *finis* causes death. Death is the antithesis of life. It is non-life, the condition when life is ended. Acquaintance with the word, observation of departing life, experiencing grief, or memorializing do not make death a part of life. Acknowledgment of its factuality also does not make death any living experience. Rather, it is life's leaving or losing, the individual's grasp on life gone, one's final release of life, signifying termination, before death is pronounced. Death does not "approach". Life wanes. When life has departed and is no more, there is death.

There is a fine point here, but it is the difference between life and death and the focus thereon. The will to life is under constant attack by the overemphasis and inordinate, if not erroneous, concentration on death-and-dying and, possibly, is being undermined by it. Even as a stone is worn away by constant exposure and buffeting by the elements, the miasmic clutch and insistent emphasis on death may be a weakening agent. Absorbing all the innumerable messages of pain, suffering, and death and disease propounded by individuals and society in one mode or another may well become a surfeit of negativism for the human organism. Constant confrontation with this grim awareness is a crude sledgehammer attack on human sensibilities and may be classified as a form of cruel and unloving behavior or punishment.

Continually confronted with the "Grim Reaper", the self may enter into retreat, becoming alienated, splitting away. The inner self wherein lie the deepest instincts is largely safeguarded from harm and is generally held inviolate. It is not totally immune, however, and is, of course, susceptible to messages from oneself. Generally, the system is intent on protecting the entire organism, and harm is warded off as much as possible. Messages of death are generally discarded until, and/or unless, they build in mounting crescendo and become suffocatingly gross. At some saturation point, unless negated, they may be absorbed and ultimately self-delivered. At this stage, the "lesson" has become cumulatively lethal.

If one's instincts and one's cognitive knowledge enter into confrontation, consistency being desired, the weaker may change even to one's own detriment. If evidence is apparently irrefutable (majority held, constant repetition, unimpeachable source, etc.), inroads may be made to accept the unwelcome knowledge. In the case at hand, cognition will triumph over will. Rather than aligning for greater strength, a part of the self will be diminished.

It is suggested that, if permitted, death messages enter into one's psyche and are manifested both physically and psychologically via actual mannerisms. Physically, of course, all manner of illnesses and diseases may enter a body where defenses are being eroded. Behaviorally, alienating mannerisms may be affected, bizarre actions taken in defiance, and anger erupt inexplicably (not the least at children, who are still immune from the awful knowledge). Mentally, depressions in every state may be manifested, and despair at the "meaninglessness" of life will be rampant. There is conflict within—life instincts are being overcome by death messages. Incredibly, these messages are largely learned messages, culturally induced and mass approved, finally driven home by one's self. Undue exposure, false belief, and the generally negative milieu play no small part in the debacle. (Note: the fact of death is not here the issue. That individual life ends at some time is not the point. What *is* the point is that death is prematurely invited in and permitted hegemony over life.)

Natural apprehension and general curiosity seem to have combined into a morbid fascination with death. The pendulum has swung too far, and there is overmuch interest in and concern with this subject. It is as if a great majority is drawn to an abyss and is mesmerized into staring, then stepping, over the edge. Whereas a definite awareness records the fact of life's termination, this should not be twisted into an unholy fascination with it. The emphasis must remain on life.

One's life-preserving instincts, one's will to life, and pain- and death-avoiding impulses seem to be entirely correct responses and reactions for the human being and should be strongly heeded and firmly bolstered. The social compact should support the individual and the group in sustaining and enhancing life, rather than diluting or weakening it. The individual and collective emphasis, of course, should be on life and living. *Life and living.* Positive life-supporting energies should be wholesalely expended in accordance with biological, physiological, psychological, and environmental life needs rather than on the negative emphasis, where focus is currently mired. This death focus is not benign.

Furthermore, and contrary to fixed and imaginary concepts, death does not at all seem to be a rigid line of demarcation, set inexorably at some unalterable point. Indeed, the point of death appears to be rather flexible. It can be moved, staved off, postponed (and advanced). This seemingly heretical statement is soon enough proved. One has merely to read the statistics of countries in which the living standard is raised to note a corresponding decrease in death. One may simply note that improved medical treatment has saved lives and put off death. Lowered traffic speeds on highways have been observed to cut the death rate. Even the relatively recent emphasis on health, exercise, and improved nutrition has already caused a statistical response of fewer deaths. Death is not a fixed point, then. It is movable, susceptible to treatment and/or influence, capable of being pushed ahead (or back, as the viewpoint sees it).

There is an inverse relationship with life. As death declines, life is prolonged; or, rather, as life is lengthened, death is postponed. Death is actually dependent on life, for it is life that determines when the condition of death shall occur. (Although fascinating, the question of the point at which life can no longer be lengthened, or even if there is such a point, is immaterial for purposes here.) The fact is, of course, that it is *life* that is amenable to change. It is life that is shaped, stretched, or curtailed. It is life that moves, is meaningful, and, above all, is fascinatingly mysterious in all its labyrinthian and creative possibilities.

A positive attitude and strong will towards life plays no small part in retaining it, as can be attested to by many physicians. In *Man's Search for Meaning*, Viktor Frankl describes the vital importance of the will to life even under the most harrowing conditions. When all normal life-enhancing systems are gone, only the will to life may sustain it.[168] Currently, as it is embraced, even life's span seems to be gaining in longevity and stature. The "three-score-and-ten" measurement of human life span has been reached and is being advanced.

Willingness to drop the scales from one's eyes affords the illuminating perception that it is life that is and has been inexorable. Where life wills, death has had to sidestep, to wait, to make way. Can one still cling to the notion that death is a mystery? It appears, in fact, to be an end to mystery. The mystery is surely life. Where does it go? How does it operate? What will happen? Life is the mystery!

It is life that is the unknown. It is life that twists and turns, the spiral ever undulating, taking on different shapes and going off in different directions. It is the blade of grass that insistently pierces through the rock, the tree on the bluff clinging to earth, the salmon rushing upstream to spawn. It is the diamond-faceted reflection of human inclinations—the farmer who shepherds the lamb, the monk and nun in cloistered walls, the teaming masses rubbing shoulders in friendship or friction. It is the caterpillar that incredibly becomes the butterfly, the minnow and the whale, the eagle in the sky. It is the fertile earth that nourishes the whole, the globe that spins on its axis in response to a greater movement, an entire sphere warmed by a life-giving sun. All of it, all of it, is life and motion responding to the imperial command—live, survive, adapt, change, renew, create.

All forms of life on this planet are evidence of the innate dictate and tenacity of the will to live. This is not to say that life forms have not died out. But it is to state that, in one way or another, the chain of life in nature has continued and rewound itself. Order has overcome disorder. Evolution has been supreme over entropy. Directions have changed, lines have doubled back or fanned out, but ever the links have been formed and added on. These actions continue today. Silent. Unknown. Unperceived. But ever onward, forward, in tandem with time.

Infinitely mobile and creative, life is progressive, adaptive, and novel. As a bulldozer shovels the earth from its path, so life cuts a swath before it into which it surges and expands, continuing the action again and again, and yet again. When outward action is momentarily at a standstill, the motion is turned inward, and the sweeping action researches itself. What can change? Where is there an outlet? How to go on? The process is nurtured by the life force itself, and in this regard we are as mere instruments through which this life instinct directs and expresses itself.

Revealingly, it is observed that the old (pseudo) duo, life and death, is immeasurably altered and elongated when the equation becomes a term—*birth, life, and death.* At once, the perspective is changed. Death has been shunted to one side, and life is centered. It becomes clearer that birth and death are simply the entry and exit points of life, which is the main affair. Life is the tenured term, the tangible reality, the solid substance. It is the moving escalator, as it were, on which humanity stirs. Some getting on (at birth), and some getting off (at life's end), it is the bridge that connects the past and the future—a past stretching interminably into the hidden mists of time, and the future expanding infinitely and intriguingly into the reaches of the universe.

Humankind has played out this round of birth, life, and death since its evolution and, after ages of development, has at last begun to seriously look at itself, its history, and its home ground, the earth. Now it palpably finds that it holds the very nature of this panorama in its hands. Humanity's fate, the environment's, and perhaps the entire planet's stand in the balance. The cups of elixir and of hemlock are before us, and having tasted both the dregs and aphrodisiacs of life's vintage, we stand momentarily poised before the two.

Common sense, the intellect, and all of life's forces should be committed to matter-of-factly picking up and drinking the elixir of life. To survive, there can be no other choice, and any other thoughts must be summarily dismissed. Then what is the hesitation? What are we waiting for? Apparently, some are still waiting in tranced fascination before the hemlock. Instead of getting on with the business of life, some have become fixated with its bankruptcy. Some first want to bring death to terms, to "demystify" it, to disengage its tentacled grasp from minds and lives, to smash it, as it were. And some need another mystery that equals The Great Mystery, The Big Divide, The Last Encounter (or whatever other romantic notions have affixed themselves euphemistically to death). Yearning for the mystery that seems to surround death, some may need to have a substitute in hand on which to expend their passion.

The craving for excitement, adventure, and mystery that has been deposited illogically at death's door (while life has been kept waiting in the wings like an understudy) may now be credited to its rightful owner. The natural highs and lows of life have been ignored and effectively obscured by a smokescreen of negativity. However, the misdirected researchers who have found only the steely cold glint of the end of experience—a dead end—instead of the surprise and excitement in the unfolding play of life may have been unhappily assisted in this prospect by various cultural outlooks that have retained the death focus.

Weighted with innumerable problems and burdened by this negative focus, it has been almost forgotten that there is delight in simply being alive. The joy of living has been nearly eclipsed by a trumpet fanfare for death. But by shifting the untenable load, the view is enlarged and vistas brighten. Valued at last, the singular holding of life is prized for its own sake. Alive, pulsating, multifaceted, *life is its own reward.*

In the current frightful situation, will we heed the life force? It must be hoped so, fervently prayed for, and studiously worked at—for it will take the combined efforts of the many to extricate ourselves from the sorry predicament facing humankind that, were it not so tragically full of consummate danger, is utterly and completely ridiculous in that it is self-made. But at least therein lies the possible solution.

Clearly observed, death through mechanical means, as in warfare, is a killer of multitudes. Wars and weapons being manmade, resultant havoc is not an inevitable result of nature or cataclysmic upheaval; death via military devastation is a selected result, largely a matter of human choice or manipulation—and quite preventable.

(The concept of *preventive peace* is yet to be sincerely approached. Preventive peace is a step up the rung of human development in promoting life-affirming cooperation and human empathy, whereas warfare may be seen as representing a more primitive time in human development—brawn and might eclipsing the brain or operating it in errored service. Like preventive health, which is aimed at staving off illness and physical degeneration, preventive peace follows a similar concept by staving off conflicts and wars and by maintaining civil, if not optimum, relations between peoples and nations. This timely concept will be taken up more fully later.)

Resistance to wanton destruction and loss of life is consistent with the will and instinct to live and with the highest and noblest aims of humanity. However, the closer the mental orientation is to death, singly or grouped, the greater is the chance or pressure to activate warfare. There is correlation between attitude and action. The "glory of death", the "mystery of the Beyond", "joining one's ancestors in honor", seeking martyrdom, etc. are inextricably linked to viewpoints of death and may be facilitators of individual and group disaster. Certainly, normal concern for life is blocked or bypassed as the death vise grips the mentality. If the life concept is insufficiently developed and adhered to, inadequate controls safeguard the people. Too few institutionalized means for bolstering life-oriented relations are established, and deadly inroads against life are ever possible.

In past ages when wars were sudden acts of mayhem visited summarily upon a people and considered inevitable, sensibilities had to accommodate the terrible visitations and accompanying upheavals for sanity's sake. All manner of rationale was incorporated into attitude, not the least being to anticipate dreaded events and mentally prepare for them, accounting for the "inevitability" of war, man's "warlike nature", "wars bring people together". Now, however, such rationalizing and retention of fixed attitude is disastrous, leading humanity into a bog from which there may be no escape.

Whereas humans have devised diverse and wondrous ways for interacting and understanding—ways of science, economics, laws, medicine, politics, education, etc.—prime value reserves to itself the hard-won, time-filled, precious gift of life. Pretending that there are no harmful actions and blithely (or ruthlessly) blundering forth may no longer be excused. Since actions have consequences, spontaneity notwithstanding, they should be taken under serious advisement and their impact and consequences on humanity and environment seriously considered. The questions must be asked: Is it good for life? Is it good for humanity and for individual man and woman? Is it good for earth?

It must be expected that there is a vast reservoir of ability in human beings that, with prodding and use, will come to the surface. The inheritors of millions of years of development, individuals are each mobile storage houses of knowledge accumulated through the ages. Instincts, emotions, insights, and perhaps vastly more are stored meticulously within each living human being. This entity is a marvelous panorama of potential findings, a storehouse waiting only to be tapped. The phenomenon is boundless, having but one requirement—life itself.

Turning the focus from death to life is the necessary mental switch that must be made. This change in thought and attitude may be a complete turnabout for some or just a nudge and continuation of theme for others. It is consistent with the instinct for life and the will to live and aligns physical and psychological forces with biological imperatives. It is by no means novel, impossible, or without precedent. Certainly, the Hebrews made this quantum leap in mental attitude ages ago, and it has been their message to humanity consistently since: "Choose life!". (Their escape from Egypt millennia past was more than a physical emancipation. Their escape was also a blessed mental release from a culture fastened on worship of the dead. Now, centuries upon centuries later, Egypt itself has come out of Egypt and has come *to* Israel.) Choose life!

GOOD AND EVIL

It is apparent that there are certain conditions and vagaries the human being must contend with in focusing and concentrating on life and the business and meaning of living. There is particular concern with good and evil.

In the Mideast, some 2,500 or more centuries ago, that most remarkable document, the Hebrew Bible, was produced as a history and directive for human behavior and relationships. Since taking the concept of good and evil and putting it into the human mind by way of a beautiful allegorical theme—the serpent in the Garden of Eden—there has been a conscious grappling with this dilemma. Can this dichotomous phenomenon be considered and understood?

Since it is acknowledged that only God is perfect, yet that man and woman are "perfectible"—that is, capable of improvement—it is readily accepted that one is not expected to be as perfect as God. It seems to be required, however, to strive to be God-like. Without expectation of being all-good—that is, God—it is perfectly acceptable to strive in this direction for general improvement.

By definition, the concept of evil represents a condition worse than bad—the epitome of bad—that is, evil. Whereas humans are capable of debased behavior, they are not expected to be *all* bad—that is, evil. The ability to discern right from wrong being early inculcated, if not an inherent attribute, the expectation is that evil is to be avoided for its own sake. Often portrayed as an attracting force, it is also a strong repellent.

If the concepts of good and evil are seen as filling the world with dualism (similar to former notions of a static two-dimensional world and, perhaps in the manner of the Eastern representation symbolized by the *Yin* and the *Yang*—that is, two opposing forces extant in the world), there appear to be only two avenues or choices before humankind: good and/or evil. But all good is closed to humanity, there being no way to be God; and conversely, the alternative, all evil, is unacceptable in its entirety, being abhorrent in its own right. Where is the human being, then, since neither option is totally acceptable and viable for humankind? We are, it appears, in between—in the spectrum between the two extremes, in the range *between* good and evil.

The area *between* the two forces of good and evil is the place where humans optimally exist and operate. According to ancient eastern philosophy, this is the *Tao*, or way, between the polar conditions of good and evil, the process that mediates between these two antithetical forces (each of which is, in its own right, anathema to the human being). But whereas the *Tao* is fitted narrowly between the *Yin* and the *Yang* (the two constant forces filling the universe, in this view), with little room for human expression, there is, rather, a natural broad span between the forces that has been filled by humankind (or has spawned the human organism) and is itself a living force on earth. Humanity has apparently expanded into a dimension that is also part of nature (as the visible color spectrum is part of light between black and white), and that is uniquely suited for human habitation.

The human organism has discovered, created, or filled a different condition in the world. Having taken the measure of its home ground, tested its limits, and discovered a natural haven, humanity has validated itself, its existence, and its role. Without penetrating the territories of either pure good or all evil, it is suggested that there has been occupied or carved out a range or condition conducive to human viability. This range has fluctuating limits beyond which conditions deteriorate. Although the outer extremes are inimical to humanity and are best shunned, they have been invaded at times with correspondingly detrimental effects (e.g., wars, violence, Hitler, false gods, etc.).

The difference herein expressed is that humankind is not caught on the horns of a dilemma, as former thought conveyed. Humanity is not teetering precariously on a narrow ridge or fence, sandwiched helplessly or hopelessly between two unremitting forces, neither of which is suitable for the human being. Rather, there is a vast natural range between the two that is specifically suited to human living and action. It is here that humanity has its own niche in the world and plays out its role.

The idea that there is a specific dimension for human performance is to begin to let loose of the notion that humanity is held captive by two implacable forces, each of which is inimical to the human condition. After all, angelicism is no more (desirable) a human condition than is barbarism. Furthermore, it is to begin to acknowledge and respect that there are needs, choices, and effects in maintenance thereof.

If the polar opposites, good and evil, are seen as both attracting and repelling, there would seem to be a no-man's land surrounding each, a mutually exclusive barrier of sorts where humankind does not generally enter or care to go. Intent to be all-good (God) or all-bad (evil), therefore, is to abrogate the human condition and to negate one's own authenticity, and to be subject to all the consequences thereof. There are areas where humanity effectively ceases, it seems. Ample guideposts mark the way, if they are but heeded. The option of choice is fortunately available. The human dimension—the range for human occupation—is a non-rigid continuum. Within the framework of this expanse, viable options afford room for free exercise of expression. There is room for change; movement is possible and permissible. Precluding a solely deterministic viewpoint, the options of choice and decision making are operative. Matters are not fixed and preset. (There is a hint of borders being pushed back or carved out, in the manner of "green belts" overtaking deserts.)

In light of current dismaying conditions, and with understanding of the natural sphere for human navigation, there is an immense need to examine behavior and possible consequences thereof. The question of meaning and purpose again insistently arises and will be further considered shortly. There is urgency in more fully understanding the human condition in order to make correct choices and to implement meaningful decisions. As humanity and its home ground, earth, are better understood and accepted, the matter of good and evil may subside in prominence, since, in any event, the essence of each is seen as outside of the human realm.

The ability to navigate amidst conditions on earth, if not to create a positive milieu, may be the recognition *summa cum laude* that should be accorded the indomitable human being. It is scarcely comprehended, so elemental (and vital) is this ability. Perception of situation and being is barely begun.

TIME: PAST—PRESENT—FUTURE

The subject of time has surfaced several times on these pages, and not without reason. Human development has evolved over time, even as has the earth, although in comparison to earth-time—some 4.5 billions of years—the human is a relative newcomer. As noted earlier, humanity has been unfolding for millions of years, no less than two million years and perhaps for five to fifteen millions of years or more, which in human time is a very long period indeed. Actually, we are an old and experienced people on the face of a much older earth.

Time is shot through the human organism. To pretend that humanity is newly arrived and is a neophyte in development is to be selectively blind to fact and to sell the human being short. Treading through the long hallways of time, it cannot be otherwise than that the human being is a font of natural knowledge whose potential is scarcely known or tapped, and who is worthy of the respect that is usually accorded wisdom, age, and experience.

It is clear, of course, that time was ongoing at the dates when many began keeping track of it. At critical points in history, some earlier, some later, a totally new way or perceiving life and self on earth evidently manifested itself to humans of such fundamentally stunning impact as to conceive of the "beginning of time". Life took on a different connotation such as to begin numbering the days and seasons. From then on to this date, each day, week, month and season of the year has been tallied. Time became a fascinating and meaningful subject for daily and continuous reckoning.

In actuality, however, time—undifferentiated, invisible, and all-encompassing—has merely continued, extended from the mists of the past into the reaches of the future. The eternal cosmos stretches into infinite space in an expanding universe, and throughout it all is time. There was time before the onset of human observation and tracking, and should humanity suddenly depart, there will be time afterwards. Uninvolved and impervious, time is the great leveler, the natural chronicler of past, present, and future. What has changed is not time, of course, but the human awareness of it and of its meaning. But what was it that caused this fundamental shift in perception? What was it that made the need for numbering days, for counting weeks and years and for recording the passage of time, suddenly and necessarily vital?

Time was observed to be a shared event, touching all matter. Experienced by all, human and nonhuman alike, even earth itself responded to time. Repetition of observable celestial and terrestrial phenomena lent humanity a measure of understanding and confidence in the natural sequence of the physical world. One could plant, sow, and reap at certain times or prepare clothing and shelter for needed seasons. The day inexorably dawned after the night, and the spring after the winter. Each day arrived and demanded its due. With enlightened understanding, if not supreme confidence in the natural order and in the phenomenon of time, the human being shook off the clench of the past and took exquisite note of the present. Life in the present was more fully embraced, and the human life span took on new meaning.

Although vast amounts of time were invested in earth, and a sense of timelessness was felt and observed in the greater universe, note was taken of the short term of individual life. Barely born and matured, it seemed, early man and woman soon died, scarcely observing the actual term of life on earth. Later, much of the time was occupied with ancestor worship, appeasing the gods, preparing for death and its accompanying trip into the netherworld, etc., besides toiling for immediate necessities of life. Living in the present was largely obscured, if not bypassed. The present was scarcely lived at all. But with growing awareness of time, *now* was almost newly found. The sensation of life was expanded by adding the present and incorporating it into experience. With a great burst of energy, humanity became exquisitely conscious of itself and of time.

The human factor existed and mattered. Life mattered. The present, and life in this world, must be lived fully and responsibly. It was a time of consciousness and self-consciousness, of tremulous hope and plan, of responsible action, growth, and control. Its role perceived undeniably, including its limitations and its potential, human life became meaningful and its lifetime of great import and value. From a near nonentity in the natural scheme of things, from a speck in the cosmos of matter, the human being became a living force in the world. Surging into the natural sphere, into that special niche, humanity became viable.

As the value of human life became pronounced and as this notion was picked up in time, religions and philosophies arose in conjunction with different perspectives. Guidelines were extolled for greater humanness, for ethical living, for tolerance, understanding, and love. (Yet, after centuries of time, the lesson has not been globally learned. The value of life is not yet universally upheld. Clearly visible in the world at large, human forces that adhere to either life or death viewpoints, in greater or lesser degree, are in confrontation. The matter of life, as of time, has been imperfectly assimilated and grossly ignored, if not devalued.)

Life is intimately connected to time. It is a nonsequitur to state that without time, life is nonexistent. Time is expressed in all that lives. Only with time is life buoyed and viable, guaranteeing survival of the organism, as of the species. But they are not the same thing. Whereas life appears to be dependent on time, the reverse is not apparent. Time itself does not stop at life's end or begin at its onset. It flows on beyond the earth and is a constant in the universe.

Here on earth, however, in its enthusiasm for the present, for the here and now, and for the acquired (obsessive) need for speed, time has been caught up, cut out, and fractured into bits and pieces. In the race to outrun time, the mode seems to have almost disembodied time from its greater connection until, for all intents and purposes, there is almost no time left at all. Rupturing time in minutiae into fragments and particles until unity is destroyed and cohesion is lost may be as discontinuous as cutting the present off from both past and future. The effect is to dismantle the whole. The natural order is ignored or unseen in the haste to use time when, in fact, the frantic pace may be unnecessary and unnatural, since time is of a piece. And although it permits some handling, there may be a limit to time's manipulation.

Whereas the present is all there is—this moment, now—it is built on all the past and evolves unerringly into the future. It has not sprung into existence of itself, nor does it remain in isolation. The present is not a disembodied moment, a particle of time dropped by itself into the now. Coming from the past, this present (this now, this ultimate reality) passes into the future and itself becomes the past. It becomes the building block of every tomorrow, the basis for the future. Every act becomes a past, and every past upholds the present, which is the promise of tomorrow. In cyclical fashion, the process repeats itself endlessly in time. It is a rolling extension of yesterday that became today and, in its own revolution, extends unerringly into tomorrow. Time is an entirety, continuous, silently filling existence and space.

Time is visible in all that lives and is. Although it cannot itself be seen, it is experienced and absorbed into being and is expressed in living. Time is overtly expressed in the visible spectrum—in life and in matter—yet it is invisible and immaterial. To the material, however, it is of the essence.

Westerners live energetically in the present, with little apparent concern for the past and with small thought for the future (which is, presently, overcast). To discuss the past is largely to strike an unresponsive chord, and to actively debate the future is usually deemed futile. It is as if, seizing on the present with vim and vigor, it is so all-consuming as to eclipse what went before and what will follow. The culture is immersed in the present. Still, questions intrude: Does yesterday matter once it is past? How much of it is a factor in living today? And of what effect is today on the morrow? Can any part of the future be foreseen? Does the future affect today?

With little apparent enthusiasm for the subject, but sharply caught up in the real possibility of curtailment of the future, the mental apparatus is slowly turning to the seemingly excruciating subject of time—of past, present, and future. Dimly perceiving that there is linkage of necessity between the factors, there is grumbling acknowledgment of consequences of action, but still little enthusiasm for accepting responsibility. Like the ancients, for whom the act of birth seemed removed from the act of sex (there is a time factor here, too), there is just bare recognition of the fact that human ignorance and irresponsibility is to blame for the predicament facing humanity. It is of such gross nature as to be almost blinding.

The incredible lack of empathy for life and for the environment, not to mention fellow humankind, has resulted in a situation that is almost a-human and beyond human capacity to rectify. Somehow there has been disembodiment from the consequences of action and behavior. And anger has a great right to flash at the stupendous insensitivity. (But even anger is not so overwhelming as to lash at itself futilely. The organism wills to live and, willing, wills anger, fear, anxiety, depression, confusion, etc. to turn into energy sufficient to propel us past this dark place.)

The past is important to today, of course. We are its products, as is the terror today facing the human race due to past excesses. Humanity has been brought face to face with its own *finis*, not as God would will it but through its own carelessness. Yet at the same time, the human exuberance has resulted in perceiving an entirely new beginning. The future is vitally important, too. Whole vistas of unrestrained imagination have been unveiled. It is a pleasure to contemplate an expanded universe, to know there are endless worlds to see, to hope to expand human experience and human life. (And perhaps God forgives unwitting humanity and delights in it with us.)

Each of us is an organism in whom is embodied past, present, and future. The past is incorporated into experience and forms a firm foundation over which today is acted out. The fact that the past forms the foundation for the present should add respect and attention to this day's actions, since it, in turn, is of major consequence to the future. Readying to absorb new stimuli and to consider the changes engendered in future existence, an amount of selection, processing, and discarding of information is necessary. This is a seemingly difficult task. But in reality, it is exactly what the human being has been doing, consciously and unconsciously, for ages of time.

Memory is incorporated in the organism, refined to a high degree in humanity. It extends far into the past, linking time in constant evolution. Its primary function, undoubtedly, is to retain those factors that are essential to life, weeding out extraneous matter. In hierarchical fashion, memory has stored all that is necessary for the perpetuation of life. An ongoing function, memory is an aid to stability. There is no need for or fear of being overloaded—that is, being overburdened by the past—since another factor is operative on behalf of the future. The human perspective is already actively engaged in healthy anticipation of future time. The mind stretches to accommodate forthcoming events and readies the self for them.

The entire group is actually in constant anticipation of the future—the student planning for graduation, the employee contemplating vacation, the businessman signing a ten-year lease. Seeds are planted for later harvesting, bank deposits are made for children's college years, and people are urged to plan for their retirement. Predictions and forecasts of weather, economics, and production are made daily. The near or immediate past, yesterday, is clearly known, and the near or immediate future, tomorrow, is almost as well known, since it may well be a (near) duplication of today. Of course, the farther future, as the farther past, is less familiar, necessitating extended plans, imagination, memory, and records to be brought into play.

The year 2000 is frequently cited, and life in the twenty-first century is already worriedly or excitedly anticipated and planned for. The certainty is that it will come. And the apparent guarantee of ability to handle it is contained in the assurance of adequately handling the present, as was the case in the past. Why should it be different? It will not spring up unannounced. It will arrive in ample time, be heralded in advance, and be here when time is ready. It is exactly likely that when time is ready, so will be the human being to receive it.

The past and present already being viable parts of human experience, recognition of the phenomenon of future time incorporated in human mind and activity should not only build confidence in time but should also enlarge the sense of living it more fully. The past is relevant, the present is viable, and the future is anticipated. This trinity of time is linked together and is one piece. Honoring each dimension and incorporating it into memory, action, and imagination, the experience of time is reflected in cohesive continuity. Living in three dimensions of time, the human being is enriched and enlarged by the experience and is already anticipating experiences of another (fourth) dimension, space-time.

Timelessness and universalism are apparent in the large. The timeless qualities of the universe may have been early man's observations. Communing with nature and living close to the land may have instilled knowledge of the earth, and affinity with the spheres, within the human breast.

But in the min*ute*, in the near and in the particle, time is tim*ed*. Life is hurried. Leisure pace and thought are sacrificed, and contemplation is generally confined to singular or mundane matters. The specific is urgent, and the narrowed specialty is the mode. The serene devotee of universal time is not an integral part of Madison Avenue or Wall Street. And yet, capturing this moment *is* an essential part of living it. If this moment is lost—the now—there is mere substitution of past or future for it, and life is experienced on the fringes of existence, if not in the shadows. The fullness of time—past, present, and future—seeks incorporation and assimilation within experienced lifetime.

Retaining essences of the past and the future in present living, humanity can be expected to rise to the challenge and potential of eventually incorporating space-time into existence. Universal time is confronted upon penetrating the gravity barriers in the greater atmosphere beyond earth. Great reaches of space are observed, and great stretches of time are before the gaze. From this vantage point, time is seen as a seemingly single dimension, cradling all matter, humans included, in its intriguingly endless expanse, merging seamlessly with space. Time awaits and permits its adoption, as we know. (If there is ultimately some reservation as to its infinity, that is very long and very far away.) Time is the medium and the link that wends through all space and matter and is incorporated in all that is.

Meanwhile, humanity has discovered that there are limits to its own existence, even perhaps the earth's. Time, here, is running out, it seems. Having "played" with time, there is danger observed in continuing to devalue or ignore its integral part in existence. It has been diminished almost to the point of no return. Backtracking (on tiptoe, perhaps) is immediately necessary. For the human race, there is possible an end to existence, an end to time. Time is short. Time is of the essence. It cannot be overstated.

Yet, undaunted and simultaneously, the onward-pressing mind contemplates the nearer universe. The eye surveys the panorama and questions, "Is there a place for humankind in the greater extensions of space? Are there other intelligent beings somewhere? What are the risks in finding out?"

Humanity has been hard won over millennia of time and is carved, as it were, out of earth. It is scarcely yet aware of itself as the marvelous expression of creation it is. Still in its infancy with regard to self-knowledge, the human race is already straining to leave "home". There is a curiosity and, perhaps, yearning within as it gazes spaceward. First, however, a crash course is needed, in a manner of speaking, on knowledge and perception of self, on humanity in general, and on the (symbiotic) relationship to earth. And, of course, some pressing problems are in need of being straightened out.

Compellingly, what is the definition and conception of our own being? How do we wish to be perceived? How do we see ourselves? In short, what is a human being? Figure 3 reproduces the depiction of humankind, man and woman, in the time space capsule, a plaque carried on the Pioneer F (10) spacecraft when it was launched under the aegis of the National Aeronautics and Space Administration.[169] Should it be intercepted some far off time hence, the impression intended to be conveyed is that we are friendly beings. It would be quite ironic if these "friendly beings" should have meanwhile destroyed themselves. The time has come to take stock of ourselves.

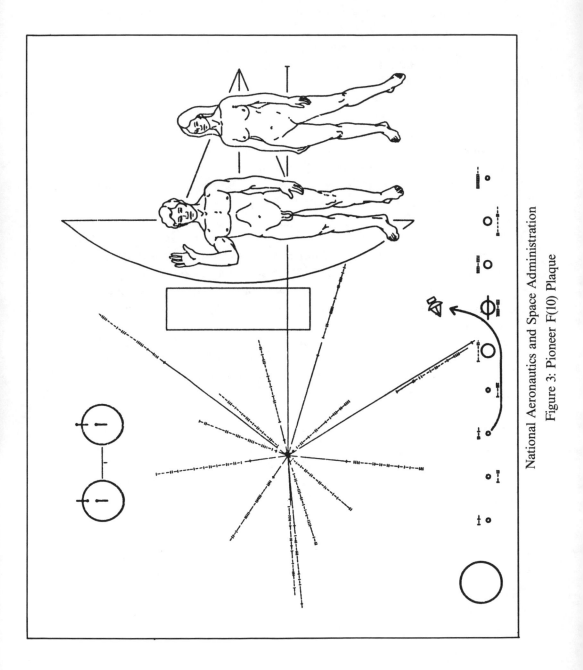

National Aeronautics and Space Administration

Figure 3: Pioneer F(10) Plaque

MEANING AND PURPOSE

It is time for self-knowledge. Whereas much has been learned about many things, there are blank spots in knowledge of our own humanity. What is the human race all about? Is there meaning and purpose in living? Who or what is the compleat or authentic human being? Is it a condition possible (for all) to attain? Alexander Pope's lines might well be recalled:

"Know then thyself, presume not God to scan;
The proper study of mankind is man."[170]

To seek meaning and purpose in living is to come to grips with one's self, with one's humanity, and with the human condition. It is to seek identification and authenticity and, that established, it is to give attention to the requirements for maintaining the whole.

To seek meaning and purpose in living is to begin to understand that there is a human condition and a role to fulfill within the framework. It is to realize that the human being craves substance in living, and that there is unease at unused options and opportunities. It is to know that there is a fullness in living that is possible (but experienced too rarely), and hence a quality of life that is essential to establish and sustain. However, desire or awareness is not enough to satisfy the need and condition. It must be matched and implemented by meaningful plans and action. To act as agents of humanity indicates knowledge of being human, and a friendship and love felt thereto. One must be friends with oneself and with humanity in general and have trust in the human potential.

The act of authenticity accepts one's own humanity and sets aside falsity, intentional or otherwise. In this regard, there is an immediate act of rectification that is necessarily urgent. What sense is there in seeking meaning and purpose in living if humans are willing to continue to submit to being solely identified as animals? While it is not in itself a bad word or demeaning to an animal to be so classified, it is a false and diminishing label as applied to human beings and acts as a reducing agent in its connotation.

To identify the entire human race as animals is an incomplete, if not erroneous, classification (although descendent lineage is not disputed). Animals and humans are divergent beings, and the lack of proper recognition of this plain fact is sheer neglect on the part of the academic and scientific community. Some greater facts of divergence were mentioned earlier, and of course, there are more—from biological and physiological characteristics to psychological and behavioral facts. To categorize the whole human race as animals is not only mislabeling an entire people, but is evidence of the poverty of understanding of humankind, one's own category. It is loud declaration of separation of self from humanity. It is an unconscionable admission.

Classification of organisms—taxonomy—was systematized by the noted Swedish naturalist, Carl von Linné (or Carl Linnaeus), some two hundred years ago. The Linnean system, still in use, groups organisms by considering similarities as well as ancestry. Figure 4 groups and itemizes the categories in descending order.

Kingdom	Group	Genus
Phylum	Order	Species
Class	Family	Variety[171]

Figure 4: Carl von Linné System of Classification of Organisms

Man has been identified as a member of the animal kingdom since, as a primate, he is not of the vegetable or mineral kingdom. Other classifications indicate, for example, that due to his nervous system, he is of the chordate phylum; breast-feeding infants indicate membership in the class of mammals; three families comprise the hominoid group, of which only one has survived, *Homo*; and *sapiens* is the only surviving species and variety (also called *sapiens*).[172] And there, for all the accomplishments, ideas, and events that have transpired involving humankind, the matter has rested. By scientific decree, the human race is still labeled "animal", differentiated only in kind.

Whereas science has been responsible for many inspiring break-throughs (and undoubtedly more will come), it is a relative neophyte in the study of man and woman as human. It is suggested that the classification and label are outdated in the face of current knowledge. Humankind has "graduated" from the animal kingdom. The need is to recognize human growth and development and to establish a new classification for human identity.

The following is suggested for adoption as a more worthy description of evolving humanity: Final identification of human beings with the animal kingdom is now reconsidered, and the sole labeling of humans as "animals" is overruled. Continuing with the system of naming the overall classification "kingdom", another descriptive adjunct more suited to the need is herewith submitted—the *Human Kingdom*. Collective humanity is demanding its recognition and due as human beings, members of the *Human Kingdom* on earth, its earned place in nature. No other label is valid; no other label is acceptable; no other label may be applied.

The self-concept and identification of humans as human beings of the *Human Kingdom* is necessarily important. In order to more easily see their behavior and projected needs and desires, humans must be able to see themselves in their own roles and in symbiosis with the rest of the environment. Yearning for meaning and purpose, the gateway to full humanhood must be purposefully stepped through.

The concept is not new at all, of course; the *Human Kingdom* is already existing and viable. Only the formal recognition and acknowledgment of the category and "ascension" is actually new. Only on paper is it new. (But that paper, that recognition, even that self-concept gives identification, evidence, and respect to the entire group and, in effect, raises the status of the whole.) Not merely an accessory to the act, humanity *is* the act, and there is room for the whole human race in this classification. Appendix F at the back of this book is designed as a tear-out for readers who wish to identify and join in this formal identification endeavor.

We have seen that time is essential to human beings, for it is the staff of life, the ingredient of individual and collective survival. The past having brought us here, the present wherein we are, and the future where we will be are all components of the whole, of time. It is the essence of life. Without life, of course, there is no humanly experienced time, and therefore no meaning or purpose to fulfill. Without life, human purpose and meaning are moot and irrelevant concepts. Essentially, then, the first priority is life. And within the living framework, *how* life is lived is a matter of vital importance.

Meaning and purpose are intricately entwined concepts for human beings, and of increasing concern. There is a hunger for meaningful living, for living a life well. But how is it to be done? How is life lived meaningfully? In fact, what does "meaning" mean?

The concept of *meaning* is a sophisticated notion and a directive in its own right. It asks: live for what, as what? Human beings are not simple amoebas. The development is eons old, and lessons and experiences of life have been amassed and assimilated over ages of time. One understands and feels that life has significance, human significance and import. There are human qualities and values demanding expression. *Meaning* is immediately linked to life and how it is lived.

Meaning in living, like a multifaceted diamond, has various aspects to its substance, some of which can only be suggested here. Certain reflections indicate, for instance, that authentic living is a vital requirement— that is, in order to find or fulfill meaning in living, it is necessary *to live authentically as human beings and according to human nature*. It is to nurture and develop feelings of humaneness, of enlarging that aspect of ourselves that is concerned with nobler living, human empathy and justice. It is to value creativity, love, and art equally with science, knowledge, and worldly affairs. And it is to place as high esteem on cooperation as on competition.

Humanity is remarkably able to live on several levels at the same time. There are commonalties with the universe, with earth, with other creatures, and with one's own kind. Within this enormous (limitless?) framework, there is the need to create or *make a life*, to have a *role*, and even to have a *goal*. Seemingly simple, even these few definitions or guidelines have eluded many who have narrowly interpreted human nature and the meaning of living humanly.

To live fully and completely as human beings with affinity and love for one's own kind—*to live authentically*—is to raise the caliber of life and living to a level commensurate with membership in the *Human Kingdom*. It is to accept the human level of being, to acknowledge the responsibility inherent in such acceptance, and to translate behavior accordingly. It is to utilize the human potential to its creative fullest, providing conditions that maximize and maintain this expression, and to derive satisfaction from outer and inner growth of the self and community.

To live authentically is to self-inquire if the individual life is worthy of the appellation "human". And since improving one's self is to improve the whole, the same query must be made of the group. Does the group do justice to the individual? Raising the caliber of the group is tantamount to improving one's own lot, since we are each born into community. Yearning to improve, the human must now earnestly decipher the nature of human nature and strive for conditions that enhance it. (Consensus and agreement will need to be reached on all that "human" actually means.) In the stretch for greater humanhood, demeaning restrictions are struggled against. Higher standards are sought as the individual reaches toward fuller humanity. To accept and settle for less is to denigrate the human potential and to leave unfulfilled the gnawing need for meaning in living.

To make a life is to engage life unashamedly in one's own behalf and, by so doing, to contribute to the improvement of the self and the whole.

(Hans Selye's "altruistic egotism" in *Stress without Distress*, 1974, may be recalled.)[173] It is an individual responsibility. It is to understand one's own special direction in actualizing a satisfactory style of living that will fulfill personal meaning and purpose (while hopefully maintaining or adding to societal and environmental good), and to have a measure of control over it. *To make a life* firmly establishes oneself with the human family, upholding time-won values and accomplishments, accepting responsibility for maintaining or improving the whole. This must be accomplished with the knowledge and understanding that the earth is the immediate source of sustenance and energy and with respect for the marvelous structure and chain of life within its perimeters. *To make a life* is not relegated to one sex alone but is the lifelong endeavor of both sexes, of all.

The above implies that there is a *role* to be played, and, of course, there is. The role that is to be fulfilled is the specific *human role*—the human man, the human woman—one that no other being on earth or in the known universe can play, create, or express. A human being is a specific kind of being, a viable member of one's own genus with affinity and love for one's own kind. Individually and collectively, it is to strive to fulfill one's own role, thereby adding to the balance and maintenance of the whole.

In general, for woman, it is to proudly develop the innate characteristics that contribute to her being, to throw off the yoke of habit and repression that has been hampering development and experience, and to accept responsibility for expressing her particular perception of the world. And, generally, for man, whose vast accomplishments have been dimmed by unbridled acceptance of the war system, and whose hegemony over woman has been so religiously guarded, it is to know that there is joy and adventure in life and living, and that the future holds amazing possibilites. Also, it is to welcome woman's release of human potential that each, together or individually, may live more meaningfully in balance with his or her own, and all, nature. To be authentic, each man, each woman, must fully develop this individual role, each being one of only two kinds of humans in all the world, yet *together* one within the *Human Kingdom*.

But, to what end is the *role* applied? Is it aimed at anything? Is there a goal? There is indeed. The *goal* is to develop all aspects of one's being in service of self, humanity, and nature. It is to live according to the highest potential, to be that human being destiny has decreed possible, and to live in the human range-continuum wherein is concern for ethics, values, justice, and peace. *The goal is to be the best human being it is possible for each to be at all stages of life*, to use in creative unison all attributes of human nature in service of life and nature, and to gladly and freely pass it on to all generations that follow.

Meaning and purpose are seen as near-inseparable concepts. If *meaning* is to live quite self-consciously as human beings, what is the *purpose* of life? Is it the same as *meaning*? If not, what is the difference?

There appears to be a sense of purposefulness about living, an intent. The organism wills to live; having gained life, its tenacity to live is not to be minimized. "The first priority is life." With knowledge of time embedded in its core (e.g., human and animal maturation and development, birds' flight patterns, fish spawning habits, etc.), life itself wills to live. Taken at its most basic level, an instinctive directive, the *purpose* of life is seen as fundamental and elemental at its core—it is to live. *The purpose of life is to live.* That which perpetuates life serves its purpose. Purpose dovetails with time in life's behalf, driving the organism to obtain and fulfill its basic needs (a pattern that may be a shared intention with other species). It is lifelong and maintains as life unfolds.

That which enhances life serves its purpose. The *quality* of life is inextricably bound up with life itself. Raising the standard of living, for example, is one way of enhancing life. "Standard of living" in our culture generally refers to the economic standard of the individual or nation. But material amenities are only one measuring stick in the overall quality-of-life category. Quality of life is of broader reference than the kind of car that is in the garage, or the washing machine or toaster.

Improving the quality of life by enhancing it is no fleeting notion, since it serves life's purpose in maintaining oneself and others in life and assists the need to live meaningfully. Raising the economic standard has helped, but as many have discovered, it is inadequate by itself in satisfying the need for meaningful living. Quality of life also refers to a style of life and meaningful way of living that satisfies an inner hunger, a cry for universal qualities and living beyond those of the marketplace, a cry, perhaps, for purposeful and meaningful occupation of time. (It may be that our perception of time must enlarge to accept the sense of timelessness that pervades the greater atmosphere and to permit its message to seep beneficially into our souls, calming our spirits and thus our actions.)

Time never ending and the evolutionary spiral always undulating, limitations can be overcome (with God's help) as each one strives to become the best human being he or she can. Whereas there is usually great emphasis on accepting one's limitations, on accepting less than the best, insufficient attention is paid to the fact that so very many with courage, creativity, trust, and faith transcend countless limitations in the stretch to reach higher goals.

To speak of meaning and purpose in life, therefore, is no little task. It is to understand that the human being is part of a great entity, descended through time and ascended into its own place in the nature of life on earth. It is to be a viable part of this forceful entity and to wish its survival, to accept its unfolding potential in full measure, and to be a willing participant in the evolving drama.

To speak of meaning and purpose in life is to accept responsibility for the human condition, to live according to its demands and promises, and to create the life that enhances self and community. To speak of meaning and purpose is to embrace life, nature, and time. It is to live fully in the present, remembering the past but readily leaving it, and to step forthrightly into the future.

Meaning and purpose have everything to do with human survival. They are life-oriented, accepting as well as directing the curious spiraling. It has to do with the courage of being and living humanly, and of creating, promoting, and maintaining optimum conditions for human growth and development. Finding meaning and purpose in life, and breathing meaning and purpose into it, is to find all.

PART III

BUILDING A CLIMATE

OF PEACE

CHAPTER TWELVE

PEACE BUILDING

Peace is a healing, building, and positive process in society, not only a refuge from the disintegration of war. It is a condition deeply needed in a world where many divisive forces are operative and where, in any event, closer contact between humans is occurring and more innovative and peaceful ways of interacting must be devised. Whereas the topic of nuclear war is being openly contemplated and discussed—a horrendous event that has moved into center stage of awareness—the need is great for peace to upstage and supplant this unhealthy potentiality.

The hands of the symbolic time clock of the *Bulletin of the Atomic Scientists* have been moved to indicate that the world is figuratively six minutes from midnight[174]—that is, almost on the threshold of war—and all efforts at containment and reversal of this trend are now imperative. The future is but fragilely holding.

Peace is more than the absence of war, of course. It is a system of relationships between consenting peoples and nations, a living contract buoyed by the support of its adherents. There is greater chance of success, naturally, if the process is widely recognized, respected, and supported. Escalating from private dream to public consciousness, the logical step now is to question how peace may be enlarged. How is peace to be widely implemented? Who and what are involved?

Creating the necessary cultural climate in which peaceful initiatives will become the expected solutions for manifold problems is essential for such directives to take firm hold and become effective instruments of policy and change. Building a social milieu wherein peace goals and objectives will continue and grow, replacing violence and warfare, is the initial step towards peaceful global transformation.

The fact that this country has established itself and its ideals on a moral basis—and projects this image in the world—augurs well for the success of this new direction. Americans have had the freedom and luxury of time, space, and experience to develop relevant notions of human rights and of individual and community relationships. Welding together a great nation of different people from disparate environmental locales, common idealism, determination, and fortitude have forged a firm standard for improved and nobler living. Such a people and such a land are the correct standard bearers and productive seed beds for creatively establishing and furthering peace objectives at home and abroad. (Yet such actions and behavior are in no way limited to the U.S.A.)

The muted state of peace information that has been available to citizens acknowledged (and deplored), however, indicates that there must be a concerted effort to bring cogent material to the public at large—a wholesale consciousness-raising of the community, as it were. Peace information, suggestions, and plans need to be widely circulated for the public to become knowledgeable and involved. Creative input of supporting citizens will further peace goals, and with the active involvement and support of the home base, peace stands a better chance of promotion elsewhere. But first we must be united and of firm resolve, willing to work for what is believed in, and willing to shape and create the future.

Acknowledging and upholding the general desirability of peace and the fact that it is within the realm of attainment, we have reached the time to *firmly state and widely broadcast* the message that peaceful means are to be established and adhered to as the basis for international relations and utilized for the resolution of conflicts. Verbalizing more than the wish for peace by giving it action and overt support, we must research multiple avenues for increasing peace plans and methods, and for bringing information to the foreground of public attention. A public matter, the people are invited to become energetically involved in shaping the world of their desires and needs. A feeling of singleness of purpose, of common striving and optimistic fulfillment, must prevail if the community's energies are to be successfully and creatively enlisted on behalf of peace.

Although offering a fresh approach to old problems, such a positive proclamation and plan may elicit negative as well as positive reactions. There must be the fortitude to brave skepticism, negativity, even hostility in publicly proclaiming the *need* for peace, the *desire* for peace, and the *intent* to build a viable network and support system for its wider institutional implementation. Since peace is in humanity's general interest—suggesting glimpses into the future, if not now representing the future itself—it may realistically be expected to receive eventual widespread support from the public at large. After all, peace is a deeply valued principle now seeking its assured place in human affairs.

Following the successful United States efforts for peace when then-President Jimmy Carter assisted Egypt and Israel in declaring a formal peace pact and, some fifty years earlier, when the United States, under then-President Woodrow Wilson, proclaimed the standard for international relationships that led to the eventual formation of the United Nations, America must again boldly stand up for peace as the fundamental and viable platform and system for relations between the countries on earth. The idea must be presented as a logical and timely plan for the entire family of nations. And, if done with dedicated determination, there is sufficient reason to believe that it will ignite of its own energy and flare through the world, lodging in minds as well as hearts and creating fertile ground for its wider advancement.

With the ability to transmit almost instantaneously the news of the day to many and distant parts of the globe, it would not take long before a wondering world listened to the news that America was truly taking peace to heart and researching its full possibilities. Nor, it is suggested, would it take long for the rest of humanity to realize that peace involves everyone everywhere, each individual being a viable part of the process, a valuable link, vital to the successful formulation and deployment of the whole endeavor. At this precarious time, in an embattled and tense global milieu, there is very little that would (or could) unite the earth's human population so much as the proclaimed intent and effort to hold up the standard of peace—not as an ideal only, but as a living system between the inhabitants on this planet.

At this point, a reminder may be necessary in order to proceed without a nagging concern. *Complete disarmament or elimination of all military preparedness is not advocated.* Although it is eminently clear that, in the face of modern nuclear technology and a shrinking world, continuing military solutions to international dissension may well lead to "the final solution", it is recognized that the military balance of forces is momentarily the accepted mode of national "security" and international "respect". Such a system cannot be dismantled overnight, nor should it be, given the hostile conditions. Obviously, lest others who are suspicious or contemptuous of the notion of a peace system operative in the world become foolishly emboldened, this country must not appear attractively weak to their military ambitions or overtures. Rather than declaring that a peace system should supplant the ancient (obsolete) war system *after* a war—that is, in the position of victor and vanquished (if "victory" is ever again possible)—this peace declaration must be made in relatively peaceful times.

An "instant" peace is unrealistic to expect, since peace is itself a process. It must be built step by step and expanded until it is ready to stand on its own and branch out, firmly rooted and sturdily constructed. (Also, it is reasoned, militarism will diminish as peace strengthens and spreads, the minimization of one depending on the growth of the other. Some time must necessarily be expected to transpire for equalization and exchange or transfer of ideas and behavior to occur.) The time for such building and growth has come.

POLITICIZING PEACE

The uppermost echelon of power authorized by the people is invested in the political system. Representing the people directly, mandated by them, parties, departments, and political representatives are empowered to stand in the people's stead. Assimilating various and multiple powers, these formal representations act in the people's behalf domestically and internationally. Publicly sanctioned, politics affords the right to act authoritatively, and due respect is given and received in the process.

The people's welfare is presumably secured by this social system and it has generally been assumed that all necessary bases are covered. However, it has become all too apparent that there is now a widening void where the people's actual physical welfare is concerned. They (we) are not at all secured from harm. A world war would decimate the population to the point where survival of the species is questionable. Humanity is at risk. There is possibility of extinction. Clearly, the need to avoid war and to prolong peace is in the general interest of the species' survival. But there is no formal peace program or department solely devoted to this need. Incredibly, peace has had more lip service than real service. This lack is no small oversight; it contributes to the unhealthy situation presently confronting humankind.

There are few who would deny that healthy change is necessary. The need to conserve, continue, and maintain peaceful relations in the world is not at all consistent with the actual condition. To bolster the foundation of peace and to further its application, certain measures must be instituted. A program of *preventive peace* is suggested.

Preventive peace is analogous to preventive health, as mentioned earlier. In medicine, which has been largely disease-oriented, a program of preventive health is being instituted. It is becoming clearer that prevention of disease is aided by a healthily functioning body. The individual is not a simple bystander to health but must accept responsibility for (maintaining) the condition of health. The same is true for the collective welfare of the people. The active involvement of the community is solicited; a comprehensive program to safeguard its members is needed.

The time to safeguard peace is in peacetime, as we can safeguard health when healthy. When a group is warring, as when life is ebbing, it is simply too late to begin a program for optimum well-being. By then the dangers are heightened, the prognosis is pessimistic, and the group, as the individual, is at risk. As preventive health is to the whole body, preventive peace is to the whole community, a condition to be kept fit and smoothly functioning. Its maintenance depends on some basic requirements within a certain framework.

Since governments act through the political machinery of hierarchical commands and departments, there is an immediate need to empower the peace process by supplying it with the needed setting recognized by people and establishments. An official *Department of Peace* is the first essential step in according peace the priority it deserves and demands.

But perhaps the suggestion for instituting a Department of Peace elicits a smile (for the naiveté of the idea) or causes surprise (for the novelty of the notion). Such reactions are understandable, but may be quite inappropriate. The idea for a Department of Peace may appear to be novel or naive, but it is neither new nor simple. Much as the author would like to take credit for such a sensible suggestion, it cannot be done (and, if publicity coverage was better and more evenhanded, the matter would be generally known).

The noteworthy proposition for a Department of Peace has been many times proffered in government circles, but, lacking vision or courage, members have not acted upon it (and news accounts have caused no ripples in public awareness, so preposterous has it evidently been deemed). Professor Frederick L. Schuman in *Why a Department of Peace*, 1969, has chronicled the many times it has been proposed that a Department of Peace be established under a Secretary of Peace in the government of the United States of America.[175]

Without repeating the historic attempts to institute a formal peace department in government circles, reaching back to the earliest days of the founding of this country, serious attempts at bringing the matter before the Senate have been made latterly in the 1930s, in the 1940s, and well into the 1960s.[176] Indeed, some *eighty-five bills* to create or establish a Department of Peace were introduced between 1955 and 1968, in the 84th to 90th Congresses, in the House or Senate of the U.S.A.[177] Appendix G reproduces House of Representatives Bill 6501, which was introduced in the 91st Congress in 1969 on behalf of creating a Department of Peace.

The wonder of it all is not that a Department of Peace has been championed by forward-minded representatives of the people, but that such news has escaped public attention for so long. It must be asked: What manner of sentiment is abroad in the land that would contribute to withholding such congressional attempts? And what manner of reporting finds such news "unnewsworthy"? (However, to be fair, the *sub rosa* general misunderstanding of peace plays no small part in this suppression.)

However much dismay may be felt at opportunities lost, there is no point in losing even more. The situation is critical, and the need is urgent. Now, almost at the point of no return, even the most obstreperous politician is aware of the negative possibilities inherent in war; lest we slide unbrakingly into a debacle, efforts at turning the situation around must begin in earnest. A Department of Peace is a most practical idea, a noble idea, exquisitely timely. The empowerment of elected or appointed officials in this government office must be mandated.

To have validity, authority, and power, as noted, official peace deliberations and actions must be properly established in the recognized pattern instituted by the people. They must be accompanied by all the accoutrements of respected offices and officeholders. This means that a Department of Peace must be properly headed by a Secretary of Peace, must support a functioning staff, and must be represented at all important levels and meetings. Its primary purpose would be to promote and extend peace, to research its potentials and risks, and, of course, to avoid war. That which is most needed in the world, peace, would be the focus, function, and goal of this most eminent government office.

Creating an executive department such as a Department of Peace is well within the jurisdiction of Congress; acts of Congress have established other departments, such as the Department of Energy, the Department of Health and Human Services, the Department of Education, etc. There is, of course, a War Department—or, as it is officially known, a Department of Defense.

One would like to think that the Department of Defense is sufficient to service the needs of the people in securing their safebeing. Time and tradition have combined to place the Defense Department in the political forefront, and it was seemingly understood that the people's well-being and security were safely harbored and their fears allayed by the notion of immunity from attack and adequate defense for safety. However, it is presently recognized that there is no immunity from attack, and the very means of defense are a threat to the people. Hair-trigger options are the province of belligerent men liable to misjudgments. The system of more and bigger weapons, of sophisticated hardware, of warfare, nuclear weapons, militaristic solutions to people problems, etc. all slant towards force, compounding the issues until they are almost unrecognizable and suffocatingly threatening.

A Department of Defense is stiffly focused on wars, on militarism, on *breaks* or threatened breaks in peace. It stands as a muscled arm of the people ready to repel or inflict physical harm. It is itself a violent (re)action. Just as the official tax collector of the Internal Revenue Service has little or nothing to do with employment or the conditions conducive to earning funds, a Defense or War Department has little to do with actual peace, with its needs and conditions, or with efforts to promote and enlarge the practice of it. That is the job of a specialized Department of Peace.

Ideally, all offices should be conducted so as to foster good public relations, but the practice does not necessarily succeed in doing so. Government offices are specialized to their own particular focus, and each has its own vested interest to follow—none of which is exclusively that most essential interest of all, peace. The job of specifically building and maintaining peace and friendly relations has been secondary or nonexistent.

A Department of Peace would be peace-empowered, people-oriented, and globally-minded. Necessarily, official representatives of this department would be(come) knowledgeable about the ways and customs of world peoples, be fluent in their languages, and understand their values and histories. At long last, demonstrating recognition of the viable existence of others, the United States could rid itself of the image of "The Ugly American", blustering into peoples' affairs without the least idea of the people. The matter of human rights would be enhanced and given greater credence with the establishment of a proper Peace Department. Such a department would concern itself with the warmth and sincerity of *human* relations rather than "foreign" relations.

It is important to pay strict attention to the needs of a Department of Peace, to respect the structural framework and organizational requirements, and to offer it not one iota less power, money, and time than competing departments. In fact, it would make more sense to invest a Department of Peace with as much (if not more) money, facilities, and personnel as the most respected and financially endowed office in the land, since it is peace that actually safeguards the people's welfare (and promises survival). Seeking to enhance cooperation and integration, efforts would be life- and peace-intensive, not death- and war-defensive.

Since future interactions will inevitably be occurring more frequently between the peoples and countries of earth, it is to be hoped and expected that such contacts will be conducted in an atmosphere conducive to maintaining optimum relations. Accordingly, a system of peace operative in the world must be finely tuned to the needs of people and the circumstances in which they find themselves.

Establishment of a climate receptive to the wider dissemination of a peace system involves knowledge and understanding of the condition. As noted, the cultural ground must be prepared and cultivated for the establishment and growth of peace practices. This involves a fair amount of education and communication. In addition to a Department of Peace, it is advocated that such information should naturally emanate from the extensive educational system so proudly developed in this country. One must again return to the subject of education, a deeply held value in the United States of America.

PEACE EDUCATION

The subject of peace should be frankly aired and openly discussed, as noted earlier. Since peace research and peace studies have opened the field of collective human behavior, it does not speak well for the academic pursuit of truth to withhold or discourage such vital study from students (and knowledge from the people). Peace is too much a matter of public concern to be withheld from public search and comment, and it should be as energetically engaged in in the classroom and the community as in the council.

The topic of peace and all its allied forms of organization must be freely discussed, researched, and analyzed and opened fully to the creativity of fertile minds. There is no good reason to keep this topical theme from all the avenues of knowledge and research; in relatively short order, discussions and findings should permeate the populace. There should be provided the opportunity to hear about peace, to read about it, and to consider its potential problems and prospects in full measure. Certainly, an informed people is better able to exercise its prerogatives and map its future plans.

The underlying basis of the educational perspective, as the community's, is called into question. With much of academia devoted to teaching and supporting the status quo—and much of that predicated on the history and system of war, an adversary system—the question of purposes and goals of education must be asked. What is the academic emphasis? Fundamental questions press for answers. What are the conditions of existence? What systems of global interactions are operative? What is stressed, competition or cooperation? What makes for human fulfillment? What enhances life? What diminishes it? Barely brushing at the perimeters of knowledge of basic human needs, these and other similarly focused questions should be in the forefront of the educational challenge. Discovering more about human beings and improving human conditions—and thus human life—is as necessary to living satisfactorily in the local community as to living neighborly in the world at large.

Education must investigate the nature of present institutionalized methods by which the communal "game" is played—that is, research the network of rules, sanctions, rewards, and punishments for living in a civilized world. A basically new education is needed if human life is to survive and thrive. Many educators and others have called for a broad review of social systems, especially the educational system[178] and, as noted, the political system—all of which determine much of the quality and style of life.

Academia must be as concerned with education for the future as with the past. Indeed, if there is to be a future in human terms as we know it, citizens must be educated to "wage peace" in a world striving to activate and sustain it. Whereas methodologies and approaches that are usually taught are not insignificant, their focus is largely irrelevant if still bound to a war system. The basic and fundamental aim of education is again called into question. What are students being educated for? What kind of world awaits their educated involvement? What will be their roles and contributions? Are current studies satisfying the need and the students?

There is a basic reorientation that must take place. Whereas the past is important in knowing and understanding what has happened, and although one's nation and environs are important for identity and citizenship, this does not constitute the total experience. The local history takes place within the larger context of the world, as does the past fit into the total time structure. Isolated, it does not tell the whole story; integrated, the parts fall into place. Incorporating global education in its teachings, peace education widens parochial history to world history, broadening the knowledge of existence and participation. That "no nation is an island unto itself" is factual as well as philosophical. Whereas the idea of one earth has raised the specter of world domination by power-hungry individuals or governments, the fact is that it *is* one earth. All areas and peoples are part of this panorama and are becoming more closely interrelated. It cannot be avoided. From this perspective, students must be educated to world awareness and involvement. At the least, the lessons will dovetail with experience and reality, and knowledge will become meaningful and relevant.

(Note: Inasmuch as peace is not yet an internationally accomplished fact, the need is for students to pioneer this approach as much as to prepare for it. In other words, not only is there a "west" in destination, but individuals must "*go*" west. There must be a willingness to engage in an area that is newly opening, to tread new ground, and to create new paths. Peace is not only a basic human need, it is a process, a direction, and a system.)

It is to be expected that (self-) interest and attention will engender enthusiasm and hope enough to lay to rest apathetic notions of the "impossibility" of peace. Instead, the subject and focus should enlarge interest, spark ideas and imagination, and become a natural and familiar theme. The matter of peace will be considered as how, when, and where—not if.

The process has begun. Touched on earlier, a whole new range of topics reflecting greater concern with the need for harmony in the world has quietly become part of the roster at some educational institutions. Although not yet upheld on all national curricula, new viewpoints are nevertheless being elicited at the college level as serious minded educators and students probe existing problems and potential resolutions. Whereas some schools have boldly incorporated the word "peace" into their class offerings, others skirt the word and use less provocative titling, such as world order classes, global studies, world community, international relations, etc. No matter what the title, however, determined seekers can find avenues of study and research that are progressively peace-oriented. It may be that students will still have to keep the overall theme fixed firmly in their own minds or be obstinate and persuasive in finding agreeable counselors as they map out the programs of their desires. But the route has been opened, as the following examples indicate.

At Dartmouth College, Hanover, New Hampshire, in the Department of Government, for instance, there has been a "Seminar on Problems of World Order". Interest has focused on contemporary international problems and the search for alternative models for the future. Peace, mediation, economic well-being, social justice, and ecological balance figured strongly in discussions.[179] At Princeton University, Princeton, New Jersey, in the Department of Politics, there has been an "Introduction to World Order", which was concerned with global transformation of politics.[180] And at Columbia University, New York, New York, there was interest in the "Less Developed Countries in World Politics".[181]

There has been a class on "Global Interdependence and Human Survival: an Introduction to World Order Studies" at the University of Iowa, Iowa City, Iowa.[182] An "Introduction to International Relations (World Politics on an Endangered Planet)" has been discussed at Purdue University, Lafayette, Indiana.[183] Meanwhile, Harvard University, Cambridge, Massachusetts, has offered a "United Nations Law Seminar: Problems of World Order Class", focusing on preferred nonviolent settlements of conflicts, peaceful change, economic order, etc.[184] Also at Harvard University, the Department of Social Sciences has discussed "Problems in Peace, Justice, and the Processes of Change".[185] Consideration was given to issues related to peace and war, oppression, justice, and environment.

While Colgate University, Hamilton, New York, has been concerned with the "Problems of World Community",[186] "Global Perspectives in Citizenship Education" was studied at Northern Illinois University at DeKalb, Illinois.[187] "World Food Politics" was on the curriculum at California Polytechnic State University, San Luis Obispo, California,[188] and "Human Rights and International Organizations" has been researched at the University of Denver, Denver, Colorado.[189] And, simply, "The Future of the World" has been pondered at the University of Texas, Austin, Texas.[190]

It is suggested that these and other such thought-provoking and future-minded studies be widely incorporated into the curricula and classrooms of the country. Taken to heart and mind, a surge of hope, optimism, and deeply relevant study and research would galvanize the entire system, if not the people. A great sweep would occur in education—a fundamentally new approach that would clear the cobwebs of antiquated material from spiderishly usurping the focus and creativity needed for living in the coming twenty-first century and beyond.

THE FOCUS WIDENS

There is change in global awareness occurring off-campus, too, as we have seen. Experiences of shortages, greater costs for energy, uneven distribution of resources, and concern for the environment are widely shared. Nuclear power is losing its enchantment for many, beginning to be seen as a sinkhole for funds, and nuclear armaments are widely decried. Debilitating economics have hit all segments of the population as world events have notably affected local conditions. Worldwide, dichotomously, both militarism and pacifism are growing.

Gains have been made toward the establishment of a National Peace Academy in the United States. A Commission on Proposals for the National Academy of Peace and Conflict Resolution was authorized in November 1978 by then-President Jimmy Carter, and funding for three appointments was provided in December 1979.[191] An interim report was presented to the President and the 96th Congress in September 1980, urging the creation of a Peace Academy, and in June 1984 the Senate approved such a proposal, attaching the United States Academy of Peace Act to S.2723 (the fiscal year Defense Authorization Bill).[192] Many national organizations have endorsed the concept of an Academy of Peace (which is currently being considered as the U.S. Institute for Peace), and it is not farfetched to predict that such an academy (or Institute) will be in operation before the end of this century, impacting for peace.

There is also diligent effort to establish a World Peace Tax Fund.[193] Public funding for the education, research, and promotion of peace in the world has been formally suggested, and Bill HR4897 for this eventuality was introduced into the 96th Congress in July 1979. Although limited to conscientious objectors to war, many are sympathetic to its premises.

A tax fund would appear to be an equitable way to support strong efforts at establishing and maintaining institutions, actions, and education for peace in the world. Since so much of our funds are spent on the military-industrial complex for our defense and security—which it can no longer provide—it is reasonable to conclude that means should be provided for that which will work toward fulfilling the actual need, peace. It makes more sense for our collective monies to be spent on that which will assist efforts to avoid war and continue peace than to be squandering precious funds and resources on how to blow up the world in a still more efficient manner.

As mentioned, during these past few years the subject of environmental issues has been looming ever larger on the horizons of awareness and permeating our consciousnesses. Pollution and atmospheric debris, defiled earth and seas, disappearing life forms and species, etc. have been causing consternation. Prophetic warnings are being issued against careless continuation of expedient and irresponsible behavior and desecration of the environment. Gradually seeping into collective mind, the message of the environmentalists has been absorbed sufficiently to admit the subject, if not yet fully the practice, of environmental attachment and responsibility. Practitioners and experts in the field have been earning a place of recognition and respect (although opinions and analyses of findings may be interpreted differently, or accepted with varying degrees of enthusiasm).

The environmental movement has driven home recognition and acknowledgment of our greater attachment to, dependence on, and responsibility for our planet, earth. In the ultimate sense, it is home to all that live as we know it. Husbanding of resources and respect for the environment are thrifty acts of self-preservation, since, combined, these are the sources of nourishment, energy, and life. Concern for wildlife, vegetation, and marine creatures, as well as for land use and the artificial and synthetic means used on it, is consistent with concern for the earth as a whole. Realizing that biology is a chain of interlocking life forms, understanding and appreciation are sought for the entire life phenomenon. Respect is engendered for the natural cycle of life, for generation and regeneration, even as astonishment at its unfolding is warranted. The whole life process is a marvel of development that can scarcely be contemplated or perceived without a sense of wonder.

Environmentalists are realists *par excellence*. Their message is a reminder that man and woman are part of the natural rhythm of earth and subject to all the fluctuations thereon. Whereas the whole field is relatively new, the message strikes an inherent chord. Care for "mother" earth is tantamount to care for self, since the well-being of the source is reflected in its progeny and products, humans included. Environmental consideration is naturally linked to the peace movement in its concern for life, symbiotic living, conservation, and evolutionary growth.

Off on another issue are the vociferous voices of present day anti-nuclear activists, as noted. Considered impudent by some, they are seen as life-and-survival protectors by others. Their dedication to preserving the living earth and its inhabitants from the creeping destruction of radiation—devastation that may linger for centuries and millennia—is to be seen in heroic measure. No less than in biblical times of David versus Goliath, the actions of these responsible humans are pitted against the might and machines of objective technology—technology that is admittedly fallible and unable to be utilized in guaranteed safety—and against those who would wield it at any price.

There have been many shocking incidents at nuclear reactors in the United States when mechanical equipment or individuals failed to perform as required.[194] Delays and shutdowns have often been necessary, and costs have escalated far beyond original expectations. It will be recalled that a near tragedy was painstakingly averted at Three Mile Island, Pennsylvania, in March 1979, and the world is aware of the catastrophe at Chernobyl, U.S.S.R., in April 1986.

The danger of contamination from nuclear radiation that persists for thousands of years is too high a price to pay for whatever benefits are promised. Irremediable catastrophe is simply not a bargaining chip to be condoned. The scientists must go back to the drawing boards or give it up. Technology, after all, is not sacrosanct. Trusteeship of the environment is considered a duty beyond price, power, or convenience. The call to life is carried beyond the moment's needs, and responsibility for consequences of action and usage is the cry of the anti-nuclearist. The earth may not be abused. What has taken eons of evolutionary development is to be marvelously respected and cared for. In this effort, the anti-nuclearists are distinctly conjoined with the environmentalists and the peace advocates in protection of life, land, and atmosphere. This translates into an environment and milieu safe for human (and other) habitation.

The residual arm of nuclear technology is devastatingly entwined in the production of nuclear armaments. The fact that there is already sufficient material to blow up the world many times over is itself shameful to admit. That supposedly sane people are suggesting continued and greater production of the same is to stoke the furnace of disaster to red-hot blast condition. Something is bound to give sooner or later. And that something is the completely foreseeable consequence of an accident, misjudgment, terrorist's threat, or irrational and irresponsible blind rage aimed at (self-) destruction.

Not only is the continued funneling of funds, resources, and brain power into more production of nuclear weapons mad and a symbol of decaying morality and inhumanity, it is visible sign of increasing impotence at understanding and resolving world problems. Fear, rather, is the hand at the controls as impatience is increased, obstreperous attitudes struck, and greater militancy projected. Willingness to resort to use of extreme measures of destruction that would disembowel whole human communities (in pretense of peace) is evidence of a great void in human empathy and imaginative leadership and ability—scarcely the mark of any great nation.

The fact is, peace cannot be forced. Permanent peace cannot be bought at the end of a cannon, bludgeon, or nuclear bomb. Peace requires the participation and support of willing partners in life, not the subdued remainders of decimated populations on contaminated lands. It must be enlisted and solidified between equals in residence on earth.

The subject of disarmament has been broached by concerned world citizens aware of the dangerous plight of themselves and the world in general. Enough literature has begun circulating and reaching the eyes of the populace to cause alarm at the stockpiles of weaponry (still proliferating) that can decimate the earth and its inhabitants. Sufficient unimpeachable knowledge is available to inform the citizenry of the brittle nature of human existence, and disarmament talks, arms control, and containment of the possible fury are evidence of informed attempts at attacking and diminishing the problem.

At the request of developing Third World nations, disarmament talks were formally initiated at the United Nations in 1978. Although the great issues were not resolved, precedent was set as the tentative nature of existence was brought before world member nations. A second United Nations Special Session on Disarmament was held in May-June, 1982, broadening information yet again; and a special United Nations meeting on arms and economics was held in August, 1987 (officially represented by 149 of the 159 member nations).

There is awareness that something must be done and a halt to madness made, but the subject is not simple. Different measures are aimed at defusing the overall danger. Urging reduction in weapons and other restrictive measures indicates the need for military restraint, the need to begin harnessing the military behemoth. Although this will undoubtedly continue to be deeply troublesome as the public becomes increasingly aware of deadly missiles poised and pointing in all directions, the problem is greater than only containment of weapons. Survival needs are now paramount. *The entire matter of war and peace is the issue.*

Many allied activities are impacting for a change in inter-nation behavior and for a turn to nonviolent modes of international conduct. It is logical to conclude that if peace is the intent and the goal, a great wash of peaceful plans and projects must be considered and carried out. Peace plans and projections are not made simply to assuage concerns about destruction, nor are they a "pollyanaish" approach to dim fears, however valuable that may be; they are deeply relevant approaches to world events and systems that touch lives all around the globe. Humanly oriented, the matter focuses on the cultures and patterns of living devised by various groupings of people, and it takes into consideration the insecurities and fears that have led to standing armies worldwide. It probes the reasons behind the institutions and established norms of human relationships (including religions and thought systems).

There are great differences in the way people think and interpret the world, but these differences must be appreciated, aligned, and bridged if there is to be greater peace in the world. Established patterns and life-styles have roots in longstanding images of the world, and there is a natural reluctance to change the focus. There is an innate wish to grow and develop, however, and with clear and evident reason, needed change is easier to adopt and adapt to. To begin with, there should be recognition of the desire for peace beating simultaneously in peoples' hearts all over the globe; translated into action, this alone can be sufficient to build the sturdiest of bridges to and between people everywhere.

It is apparent that many efforts need to be waged on behalf of peace—multiple ways that involve the human element and cooperative participation—ways, perhaps, that have yet to be devised. A revitalized perspective can galvanize the globe as a great "getting-to-know-you" attitude sweeps over the earth. Barriers between peoples can crumble as the world and its human inhabitants become more familiar (and less threatening) to one another. Seen at last as human beings no different than oneself, and separated only by thought systems in different stages of development and perspective (which, with continued international and cross-national interaction and communication, will become progressively more homogenized), *the process of peace begins at last on the most basic level, the human plane, the common ground of mutual humanity.*

CHAPTER THIRTEEN

THE HUMAN FOCUS

$\mathcal{T}$he frontier in need of present development is the human frontier, perhaps the most important frontier of all to approach. Since we have no other lens than the human one, it is this focus that must be brought to bear on all conditions involving humanity.

A human focus seems reasonable enough for human beings to decide for, but it has been a long time coming. There has been a seeming reluctance to turn the full gaze upon humankind—ourselves. For various and sundry reasons, it has seemed almost easier to champion the cause of nonhuman affairs or, at most, suffering human beings. Yet empathy must not rest solely or largely with the nonhuman element (animals, environment, machines), or only on the sinking individual. Worthy as these causes remain—and they are a measure of our humanity in raising the caliber of life for all—identification must include the total human family that has persisted in the face of untold obstacles and that continues its struggle to uphold human standards and persevere against heavy odds.

This is a period of transition. As humankind stands on the edge of annihilation from self-excesses or evolution into a seemingly limitless future, new pathways must be devised that will enlist widespread cooperation if the time to come is to be secured. There must be new understandings of our own kind. A self-searching gaze necessitates seeing the human being in the long view—as a being who has grown into humanity over an enormous period of time—who now seeks to build broader links in uniquely human design, in symbiosis with the living environment. It is time to shift the focus squarely upon ourselves, both glaring and loving, for greater enlightenment.

Presently, the "spotlight" has been showing the world vile and unlawful behavior in many places of the globe. It is almost as if all possible behavior is being displayed for human edification (much of which is reprehensible to civilized conduct). We are seeing the hatred of some who attack those who advocate or represent reasonable behavior. Their passion decries reason. Yet even here in this "reasonable" land, the confrontational method has brought ourselves and our adversary to an impasse that threatens the whole world.

It appears that passion without reason is volatile; conversely, reason without emotion is mechanical. Separately, these attributes are legitimate in, say, saving a child from an immediate life-threatening situation, or working on a mathematical problem. But as sole methods of interaction between human beings, each is plainly insufficient in generating meaningful and cooperative ties. Indeed, in their insistent, single-minded use there is a degree of self-centeredness and inhumanity displayed so gross as to virtually eliminate the other party. Where is the recognition and empathy between human beings?

Empathy between humans indicates an identification with others, an acknowledgment of the other's existence, an "I-Thou" relationship, as philosopher Martin Buber emphasized.[195] It is traveling on the same wavelength of life. Actually, every person in this world is sharing the living experience of being human beings on earth with every other person, and all, therefore, are traveling together on the same global human wavelength, whether or not there is consciousness or acknowledgment of the shared passage. (Of course, this shared experience becomes more intense and binding the closer the ties—same nation, community, household, etc.) Since we are journeying together, and since we now share a common fate, it behooves us to consider how to foster respectful, closer relationships, how to form bonds of identification and friendship, and how to relate as human beings. It might even be that by simply advising our adversaries that we are all in the same boat, so to speak, the belligerence might soften. If we are "kin", the feelings might thaw. In any event, it would be a human approach.

Humanity has been viable for ages of time. As noted, we are not neophytes in existence. There have been tremendous advances in learning and adapting, the latest being awareness of the finiteness of the global habitat and the fantastic possibilities of extending life into the greater universe. There is awareness that humans have the ability to observe, foresee, forestall, and even forecast some consequences of action and behavior, to improve the self and community, and to feel both shame and pride. There is the power to change course and to redirect the path. And there is both need and readiness to admit the idea of improved self, to grow stalwartly into the ennobled concept, and to uplift the global community. Notwithstanding the current dilemma, humans may rightly claim that they are a highly developed form of life on earth that has been laying the broad foundations of humanness over countless millennia. All the while, and perhaps more keenly acknowledged presently than before, there is awed awareness of the wide panoply of life in nature. But while the magnificent diversity of life is recognized, nothing detracts from the marvelous achievements and growth of humans over time and place. Indeed, it may well be that much besides humanity will flourish when humans accept responsibility for their rightful place in nature.

The history and generally forward development of human beings offers hope and enthusiasm for future possibilities. But the facts of history are only the perimeters of the human story. Closer attention is again directed to the personal, perhaps moral, inner development of the individual and the group. The capacity and advancement displayed in transcending, transforming, and *humanizing* the entire species is the real marvel of evolutionary development, as noted. It is the role that has been paralleling physical and emotional growth, if not propelling it.

Visually, homo sapiens sapiens, as a species, has a specifically human appearance. The job of *becoming* human, however, lies in the inner development as much as the outward—in the conception, perspective, and behavior of *being* human. This is translated into action *between* humans, thereby constituting the ground of human relationships. (Hitler's henchmen looked human, for instance, but their anti-human behavior belied the appearance.) Within the state or range of human behavior—the human continuum, earlier mentioned—there is ample room for role fulfillment, as against being only an undeveloped member of homo sapiens sapiens.

Cultural and psychological developments have accompanied the metamorphosis from species membership to authentic human being—the former being only the shell, the latter being the development of inherent human potential. Without manifestation or completion of the human content and appropriate behavior, the "shell" remains just a facade, and the human potential is unfulfilled and unrealized. Either development without the other is an incomplete process for humans. To be whole and united, the individual, as the populace, must be one in humanhood.

Humanness has been hard won over a great stretch of time. The prerogative of no one individual or nation, and the due of all, conditions for human development should be but are not everywhere beneficial or sufficiently ensured. Yet human fulfillment is a condition naturally sought by the evolving human being. Like reaching the surface from a great depth—as, indeed, from ages of time—achievement of authentic humanity is to fulfill the natural human potential, just as it is to physically develop and to psychologically mature. Now the human being and the human condition have come strongly to the fore and stand in a prominent position on the world scene. However, in critically examining the human entity faced with the dilemma of near-instant destruction, the patterns, behavior, and attitudes that have driven nations to present confrontations are carefully observed.

We can no longer be aloof from the responsibilities and consequences of individual and communal behavior. Modestly, the majority has generally refrained from judgmental determinations. Such unwillingness to pass judgment may be due to identification with all others—as in "there, but for the grace of God, go I". However, where humanity (or lack of it) is involved, such reticence may not be continued, since lack of involvement has amounted to tacit acceptance of the status quo. And look where it is!

Obviously, something is drastically wrong that has resulted in the fearsome possibility looming threateningly over the human race. Our understanding of one another, and of ourselves, is evidently incomplete or erroneous if it has resulted in this obscene condition. Perhaps our self-confidence has been so low or shallow as to have permitted the predicament to occur. Or we have basically misunderstood an elemental lesson of living on earth.

Culturally, it has largely been religion's role to attempt explanation of the unknown, to give expression to feelings and emotions of humanitarianism, and to guide behavior accordingly, although religion's own history has been less than exemplary in many instances. While one can only wonder at any religion's nondenunciation in ringing tones of inhuman acts everywhere on earth—its own compliance with the status quo indicating, at the least, a forbearance and tacit (albeit disapproving) acceptance, if not expectation, of immorality and inhumanity—the currently renewed emphasis on morality is public indication of a general dissatisfaction with the state of the world as it relates to human experience and existence. The turn to religion in recent times, or the *re*turn to religion, it is posited, is at least an attempt to seek improved modes of human behavior and interaction and to turn to a source or condition beyond the self for strength in achieving greater humanhood.

It is socially acceptable to seek religion's help in improving one's humanity. The practice of seeking divine guidance—however it has been done, in whatever form, or for whatever reasons or goals—indicates a belief in the ability to transcend limitations, as well as recognition or belief in powers greater than the individual's. That a community of members seeks divine inspiration potentially raises that community's transcendence. (Although, as at present, noting the debilitating climate of confrontation bristling in the world, to have waited until the world is on the brink of disaster, *in extremis,* before attempting change is, for one thing, extremely late, and, for another, neither heartening nor conducive to building confidence in the stated desire to achieve real change. Serious questions should be asked of oneself and of one's religion.)

The surcease that is gained in unashamedly seeking inspired intervention has given credence to the rationally unexplained phenomenon that has been variously called God, the Power, the Creator, the Source, etc. Religious practice has been retained over ages of time in virtually all societies in varying degrees of fervor and belief, notwithstanding some official antireligious stances extant in the world; at the least, this indicates an attempt to inculcate values and patterns of behavior that affirm humanhood while inspiring a humble spirit. Whereas overzealousness has at times caused highly irregular, irreligious, and a-human effects, at its best, religious belief is a source of comfort, direction, and strength.

For those who turn to divine intervention or for those who disavow metaphysical beliefs and insist on rational explanations, it can only be surmised that humans have an innate sense of the order of the natural world, a world of seemingly mixed blessings. In adapting to an environment of varied elemental factors in which the human must wend his or her way, different modes of discerning and coping have been devised. Unknowns have been creatively imagined via art, religion, philosophy, etc., while the scientific world has been busy scalpeling, labeling, and identifying specifics. Whatever explanations or terminologies are given to environmental phenomena, however, the conditions exist and have pre-existed. Acknowledgment and adaptation are still necessary, as, for instance, one does not jump off a tall building, no matter whether gravity has a name or not.

That humans have discerned and attempted to come to grips with all manner of phenomenal circumstances says volumes about our abilities, including innate knowledge and instinct, even if some questions are still unanswered. That the species has maintained in the face of all the conditions and vagaries stumbled upon (and largely met) is indication of the strength of the group. All the attributes have combined to form a marvelous species, a strongly willed collective—the human race.

Clearly, man and woman are not incidental to nature and the universe but are integral parts of the whole, acting on it and being acted upon. As a class, it is perceived in even more respectful manner. This strong entity is now face to face with itself and must understand the strength of the forces behind it. Humankind has been driven to overcome, to survive, and to carve out, as it were, a milieu in which life is worth the living.

A community of humans is not intent on diminishing or squashing humanity anywhere. To what end? It would be a negating act, an act of self-denial. Rather, recognizing humanness as a natural attribute and characteristic, an acceptance of other humans is involved. From the individual's specific awareness and behavior comes a wider embrace; there is identification with the whole human race. (To do otherwise—to subdue, enslave, diminish, or kill other humans—is an act of greatest self-debasement, an act of homicide, fratricide, and suicide, figuratively and literally.)

We have come round full circle.

Momentarily at a standstill, we stand both objectively and pugnaciously eyeing the other. There is no retreat.

Finally, of course, there is only acceptance and advancement.

There is acceptance of human beings everywhere, ourselves most of all. And in dawning enlightenment, it is apparent that we are better than we realized. We are *human* beings. There is realization that to be human is to be a special kind of being, and to act in a special kind of manner. As noted, there is a driving need for authentic and meaningful living, and awareness that humans have a role to play that "no other being may or can portray".

There are no peoples who are alone in human potential. It is peculiar to the species. Humanhood is not a prize for some. It is each person's birthright and, like all characteristics, must be individually nourished for optimum development. It must be consciously acknowledged and respected, individually and communally, as the time-honored heritage it is. More than enough time and experience has been absorbed in human development to differentiate between acceptable and non-acceptable behavior and ways of relating. Now it is time for selection and application of such knowledge in order that judgment and choice may be exercised in improving the human being and relationship.

Since (human) life is necessarily fundamental, it follows that all efforts at maintaining life and enhancing the quality of life should be pursued. Concern for the quality of life has new meaning if greater humanness, ethical behavior, and values are upheld as honored and expected manifestations of individual and group behavior. Whereas, for example, trade relations are important to economics, improved human relations are important to peace. (Eliminating warfare and violence from human annals is merely the next step up the ladder of human development.)

Human beings are enlarged by the depth, multiplicity, and time of their evolutionary development. The wealth and variety of the past may be translated into knowledge, and thus into readiness for action. A sense of united peoplehood may be embraced—not only for the communal sense of self, but for the elongated experience of humanity that each person may rightfully lay claim to. Whereas our nation is just over two hundred years old, human beings have been refining themselves for untold millennia, and this accumulation of time and experience should be consciously acknowledged and assimilated into awareness. Humanity has been viable for a very long time.

To be morally neutral or to be without concern or judgment of behavior is to be without benefit of one's natural ability to humanness, or discernment of same. It is to underutilize a natural attribute, or even to choose away from it—a disuniting act. The individual is not an innocent bystander in life. Personal involvement and individual responsibility are mandatory. To strengthen humanhood in society and to weave webs of peace, one's behavior, as the group's, must be considered vis-à-vis the "other", and the social norms established accordingly. Questions are raised: What is the personal obligation to self and the community? Is one's work uplifting or debasing to self and others? Is honor displayed in relationships—in business, neighborhood, family? Does the nation uphold its obligations to citizens and world communities? Does it behave equitably in its transactions? Who is concerned, and what evaluations take place?

There is responsibility to the self and community in strengthening humanity everywhere. We must be worthy of peace if its aims are to be projected globally. We must become quietly determined, but actively engaged, in assimilating the qualities of humanness that are prized among all peoples and in making them a lasting part of ourselves and communities. If, as self-identifying and self-accepting human beings, citizens of the world, we are willing to proceed *en masse* into humanhood, with all the growth and grandeur that is implied, it may just be that the process of human life on this planet will be uplifted and assured.

If behind all the noise and furor there was formerly the need to protect one's humanity by fighting and dying for it, that need must now be satisfied by striving and living for it. Whatever claims may have been previously made in warfare's behalf are now obsolete. Only by peaceful coexistence can life and its development proceed. Implementing ways and means to safeguard peace and civilization, and developing those aspects of ourselves that are generally recognized and valued as unalterably "human", using them in daily transactions everywhere, is the mandate for human survival and progress.

The ability to conceptualize—to recall as well as to forecast—is a richness of human capability. If by good fortune or even desperate thrust of instinct the collective should trust its humanity sufficiently to act in life's behalf by stoutly championing peace and resolutely denouncing war, the ills of the past will largely dissipate and fade away. A new era is before humankind if it rises to the challenge. Since fundamental ways of thinking, projecting, and living are involved, they are best served by all members of society, not just by designated officials, specialists, or "elitists". The people are the final arbiters of their own lives, and self-concern is healthy motivation. Together there is tremendous capability for restoring vitality, redirecting social mores, and improving the quality of life. There is a God-given chance to fulfill destiny.

Appreciation of earth and of the greater universe, of people and their continuing unfolding, all make for an enrichment of life in which the senses and the mind may enlarge and delight. Internally at peace, peace may be externally projected authentically and humanly in a seemingly miraculous new beginning. The path is before us, unbarred and untrammeled. We have merely to embark on it.

CHAPTER FOURTEEN

WHAT IS;
WHAT SHOULD BE;
AS IF

$\mathcal{T}$he dangerous juxtaposition at which the world's future is poised is more widely known daily. The possibility of irreparable harm is no longer an incredible notion or irrational fear as awareness of potential vast destruction settles into consciousness.

Huge amounts of money have been sunk into the weapons industry. In the face of indisputable evidence of potential cataclysm, of the experience of holocausts, and of countless advice and pleas to the contrary, the arms race continues—not only unabated, but stoked to flaming heat. The largest amount of money in military history is channeled into weapons accumulation that almost beggars description. If money and weapons can buy security, this country is seemingly prepared to expend its resources in doing so.

A then-record-breaking one hundred and ninety-eight billion, eight hundred million dollar ($198,800,000,000) military spending bill was authorized by the U.S. Congress for 1982 military appropriations, research, and development.[196] This mushroomed to approximately two hundred and sixty-eight billion dollars ($268,000,000,000) in 1985,[197] paving the way for the president's five-year defense program from 1984 through 1988 of one and one-half trillion dollars ($1,500,000,000,000),[198] a sum so vast that it is almost rendered meaningless in normal monetary considerations and transactions. (And there is already a dispute because a potential gap of *billions* of dollars exists between the Pentagon's estimate of national defense needs and the $1.5 trillion dollars earmarked for it.)[199]

Security is considered almost totally from the military standpoint, as most of its "eggs" are placed in one basket—the military container. We are loudly advised that huge defense needs are desperately warranted, and this viewpoint has harangued and badgered the people's representatives into meek compliance. Militancy is gaining its greatest power, not only from the huge arsenals that are being stocked but from the tunnel vision and mentality that is being channeled narrowly into militaristic perspectives.

As is increasingly apparent, however, security is rapidly diminishing, perhaps nonexistent, and the world is more dangerously tilting. Illogically, people are expected to studiously overlook the nature of weaponry that has become so lethal as to have the possibility of annihilating the proponents (themselves) as well as the opponents. Also, it is assiduously ignored that great sums were already placed by a trusting citizenry in the military's coffers, where, they assumed (and were scarcely advised to the contrary), matters were being properly handled as needed. Yet the relatively carte blanche military behavior and system has merely succeeded in bringing the state of the nation and world to the precarious position it is in. The destructive forces are already in place, continuing to proliferate, and the problems are no closer to resolution than ever.

We are asked to continue this path of proven folly even as we are led to believe that there is no other way than blind adherence to an outmoded, wasteful, and inhuman system. The inability of nihilating weapons to differentiate between friend and foe is terrifying, but most damning of all is the calculating mind that is willing to expend both. Our security has vanished—not only from outside enemies, but from our own forces. The military mind at highest levels is willing to consider the demise of large segments of its own population—indeed, it has been doing so for a long time. Confronted with failure, it blusteringly demands more of the same, compounding the failure. The effects of a nuclear holocaust are rationally considered, and some have cynically accepted that life could "probably" be rebuilt. A chilling example of inhuman consideration is before our eyes. (Rational mind without humanity is little different than a machine, each being devoid of feeling. We have the nazi machine as bitter example.)

Sole dependence on the military vehicle for life and security has passed its prime and usefulness. The military must be viewed and treated as the prepared might it is in service of the people, and *it* must be directed, not the other way around. The *people* are the authority and power and safeguard of continued survival. While the state or nation remains backed by its arsenal of war materiel and military forces that are of some deterrent value in the global impasse, human solutions to problems of seeming implacability must now and henceforth be sought. The need is urgent and clamoring for attention.

It is evident that technology has outstripped human political and social development. In order to apply it in a positive manner for humankind's benefit, the technological capacity must be contained and directed accordingly. Although mechanical performance may often be far greater than human ability (as in an automobile that is generally capable of traveling at 120 miles per hour but is restricted to 55 or 65 miles per hour, for safety's sake), the actual *permitted* performance must be solidly controlled by the human beings whom it is serving. Conversely, humanity must rise to greater capacity of human development. In order to remain masters of technological innovation (and masters of their own fate), people must demonstrate commensurate cultural growth and ability to control and tailor the mechanical might in service of life and needs. It will not do to let the machine overcome its makers.

It is clear that the past and present system of warmaking has placed an exhausted and near-emaciated people on the brink of human and environmental bankruptcy. Mayhem has correspondingly increased. Perhaps most critical of all, the dilemma is bereft of ideological content even as it is draining the lifeblood and resources of the people. There is little left of substantive or logical value in warfare other than the forces of habit, fear, and bragadoccio. It is a bluff that, if called, may find itself playing the impotent fool or mindless button-pusher, extinguishing vast panoplies of life (in which we, too, may be the pawns and victims). If the pattern is permitted to progress, one or the other superpower (a third one and a fourth one waiting in the wings) may temporarily gain control, reducing others to diminished status, while the style is continued in unremitting pattern until a crazed or inhuman state or individual unleashes a cataclysm. *There is no future in the whole degenerative situation.*

(The intent herein is not to engage or enlarge fear. There is fear enough in the present condition. Whereas fear can be a stimulant galvanizing one into action, it can also be an immobilizing agent freezing one into inaction. But the awareness and comparison of fearful consequences of tragic proportions confronting the world's peoples, while odious, might at least suggest that a method (war) incorporating extinction in its wake is hardly a mode to be utilized under any circumstances and is therefore no method or system at all to be rationally considered. The logic has simply gone out of it, as the heart did long ago.)

What is the answer? What is to be done?

Consider the obverse of war.

Peace is not new; it is not untried; it is not unheard of. Upheld and sponsored by societies, religions, and philosophies, peace is no newcomer to sensibilities and experiences. Ongoing, practiced, and familiar, peace and cooperation are the basis of civilization that has been building over time. At a critical point now, and gripping to maintain itself, civilization is seen as attempting to shed war as a group practice and supplant it with peace. At the center and heart of individual nations, civilization (peace) is reaching out in a unity of effort that must replace warfare.

Freeing the mind from its preoccupation with war and death, and placing it squarely on peace and life, the perspective certainly changes and is immensely unencumbered. One observes that peace has indeed become an established pattern and life-style that has enlarged beyond the self and the community and is engaged in by millions of people in many different ways. Actually, peace has almost surreptitiously invaded our homes and nation and become the established way of life. Yet in an almost schizo-phrenic manner it is ignored, denied, and deprecated, even as it is prayed for and yearned after. This denial must cease, and, with dawning reali-zation, peace must be perceived and acclaimed for its potent actualization.

The foremost need of peace is to believe it is possible. It needs to be taken seriously. Peace is a many-faceted process with multiple appendices. In its own right, peace is a basis and a system, having a psychology and morphology of its own, which should come as no surprise but, rather, as an awakening and illuminating discovery. Ranging widely from war deterrence to inter-nation and cross-nation cooperation, peace enhances the individual and the group, supporting and maximizing human develop-ment and conditions, ensuring the care and protection of the environment. Encompassing survival and evolution in its wake, peace is both the ship and the course whereby avenues into the future may be entered and directed. Peace has merely to be acknowledged, its banner upheld, and its patterns improved and extended. All manner of ideas and plans on behalf of peace and humanity are ready to be suggested and tried (limited only by the impoverishment of our minds, an aspect that is not readily accepted).

The matter of peace is pounding on the table of public sensitivities and, with little time left for conjecture, is demanding quick recognition.

There has been ample preparatory practice over time, however, and peace now seeks active public acceptance and support. What may seem unlikely to some, at first glance, may quickly find approval and fertile ground in others. Since the need is acute, there is enough reason to believe that the trend toward the study and research, support and practice of peace will accelerate. Cultural learning is relatively rapid and, once begun, spreads quickly and widely (especially in this, our communication and information age).

It is none too soon that the greater world problems are being considered. Futurists are insisting on longer projections as shortages appear likely or consequences of use become apparent. The poor and underprivileged are growing almost everywhere, especially in developing countries (Latin America, Africa, Asia, etc.),[200] which have more than three-fourths of the world's human population, and where a large percentage of the globe's vital natural resources are located. Problems of growing magnitude need serious attention and resolution.

Talk of scaling down expectations and life-styles may be of special application or greater interest to westerners, who have used a disproportionately large share of the world's resources—perhaps Americans most of all. But, talk of quality, health, and humanness may also be taken more to heart by westerners and may more than compensate for or equalize so-called deprivations. The opportunity to *be* more may be at hand.

The fact is that we are again at a point facing forward and backward at the same time. It is no special ability or trick to see the road traveled, since it is behind us, nor is it too difficult to see partially ahead and to have intimations of possible occurrences, since ample experience has shown the consequences of certain actions (for instance, warfare spells ruin, devastation, and death; peace stands for survival, cooperation, and life). It does not take any special skill to choose peace, merely the instincts of any living organism. But, as has been said, we are also a thinking and feeling people, and decisions must satisfy the mind as well as the heart.

What makes peace the answer to the modern dilemma, a critical point at which humankind is presently almost immobilized, and a veering away from a past mode of behavior that has been near-ingrained into consciousness? Peace has been an ongoing experiment in human relationships. It is a viable process and an ideal in its own right. It satisfies the need for ideology while providing practicality and incorporating methodology. Pragmatic and visionary, the setting and the goal, peace combines process, means, and content within its evolving condition. It is a potent idea, creative in its portent. Promising survival—that alone is sufficient to promote its condition—peace is a promise of change as well as stable balance and is exactly what is now needed. It offers a haven and a route and, if tightly grasped (like the brass ring) will sustain a people for a very long time to come.

Since the danger is consummate and the choice is so dramatic, simply recoiling from the abyss into which blind momentum is propelling humanity is insufficient. A complete turnaround is the active movement needed, a process of change set into motion that will forever dissuade warfare and enhance peace between the peoples on earth. Individually and collectively, energies, minds, and creative potentialities must be turned to the needs at hand in order to continue and hasten the progress and institution of peace as a viable condition for humankind.

A whole new world awaits our active involvement and participation. Although difficulties and impediments of formidable size lie immediately ahead, the direction is obvious. No more time need be wasted nor energies deflected from the course at hand. In agreement and in unison, instinct concurring with logic and affect, the directed strength of the populace is a tremendous asset in focusing attention and in funneling action where needed. Perhaps, at last, as conceived of thousands of years ago and preached for so long, humanity will unite as one in symbiotic coalition. An exciting era and voyage of discovery awaits the intrepid participants as the banner of peace is consciously picked up by a determined people anxious and eager to begin the shaping of a world.

WHAT SHOULD BE

How something "should be" is indicative of an ability to discern or conceive of a concept. It is a notion implying knowledge or foreknowledge in conception of plan and execution of follow-through. There is often a sense of fitness or rightness to a condition, even before it is actualized. A sense of how something should be (done) directs the process of completion and, if unsatisfactory, guides the correction.

This sense of *what should be* is an earned feeling. An extension of learning and experience coupled with expectation, an awareness or sense of form is exercised and brought to bear on a particular objective. From planning a hunt in ancient times to building a house, crossing the ocean or manning a space vehicle, projection is incorporated into plan, and a sense of "end" or goal directs the endeavor. *What should be* is a mental projection encompassing past experience, present knowledge, and future expectations. It is a goal-oriented direction, and its exercise is instrumental in molding coming events.

This process is an integral part of the creative effort. Artists, for example, have a strong sense of how something should be, "seeing" the completed work before it is done. On stage and in motion pictures, actors and actresses are relied upon to interpret correctly the intended concept or role. The better the artist, the truer the performance. The sense of how something should be guides director, actor, and ultimately patron and consumer alike. The public, too, has a strong sense of knowledge as to how something should be and, in accepting or rejecting the offering, exercises this awareness and judgment.

The matter of general expectation plays its part. From music making, say, to toaster production or bridge building, how something should be is embodied in the entire process. Conceived in the mind and committed to plan, the concept is carried from original idea to rendition or project completion. Skill, experience, and materials add to product sophistication and expectation. An aware consumer expects and demands professionalism (determined, of course, by the respective society and culture).

Whereas novel themes have interest, the greatest impact is supplied by forward-minded concepts and ideas. When assimilated, they become the standards against which others are compared and move cultural growth forward. The creative process does not conceive of static concept, of nonmovement or reached end. Why, therefore, should not creativity and peace become allies in continuation of the human story?

A civilized people, a cultured people, is aware of its own history and experience. The knowledge and experience of cooperation from centuries of civilization is rooted deeply within the populace, and the *expectation* of continued human linkage is part of the collective mind. We are scarcely without knowledge of civilized behavior. It is no novel situation, unknown or untested, and there can be few who do not innately feel that peace *should* exist between humans. Practiced locally and expected in daily life, should it not be the same elsewhere? And, if we would safeguard and keep it, should peace not be strengthened and extended globally?

The teachings of home, church, school, and state have been generally upheld. There are very few persons in our culture who can be said to have been early taught that, if angry, one steals, abducts, or kills others. It simply isn't done. How social behavior "should be" is taught, performed, and expected. Society reinforces the anticipated behavior and stands ready to punish offenders. While this explanation is necessarily simple and does not delve into the myriad complexities and problems of modern societies—many of which are due to insufficiencies and inhumanities of war-prone and death-oriented perspectives and conduct—there is nonetheless behind it all an awareness of how things should be. Humans have been around long enough to know, value, and respect civilized behavior.

Experience has proven that war breaks down the lessons and accomplishments of civilized society, diminishes humankind, and is unheeding of individual needs. Humanity is set aside, suffers, and is at risk; development is impeded, and evolution is hindered. Whereas any number of excuses may be cited, the fact is that the group or nation that foments mayhem and war in the face of present technology and circumstances is broadcasting its own developmental immaturity and limitations. It is no model for anyone anywhere, no matter what else is achieved; it cannot satisfy or fulfill human dreams. That satisfaction can only be achieved now by peaceful methods.

Humanity, life, and peace are inextricably linked. In the struggle for improvement the human reach has extended over time, from primordial origins to space voyager. Great obstacles have been overcome and many refinements incorporated. Now the collective hand is outstretched to life. Yet all it needs is the mental adoption. The mind must be life-oriented as well as the reach. And in adopting the life-orientation and permitting it to permeate the being, notions of negativity and death dissipate. Warfare, military confrontation, and technology turned against humanity are seen as the negative forms of behavior and thought they represent, belonging to past history. The false security of an obsolete methodology (warfare) is supplanted by a healthier mode (peace) in safeguarding the populace and ensuring survival of the species, and in raising the caliber and level of human interaction on the scale of life.

How should the state of global interaction be? *What should be* done? There should be instituted measures and societal support for peace, from a formal Department of Peace to international programs that serve to link people to people. As the military mentality (and enormous cost) is minimized, there should be an increase in social and human concerns. There should be confidence in humanity itself, a quiet pride in our own development, an intent to live meaningful lives. There should be the sense of unlimited opportunity, hope in the future, and amazement at the likelihood of coming adventures in space.

Peace is the human system that should be formally adopted in the family of nations. It should be announced and trumpeted all over the world. And information should be made available to all peoples in order that they become educated and familiarized with the notion and ready to participate in the creation of the world. All humans everywhere have the same tenancy on earth and an earned proprietary interest in it.

It is at this point—a beginning, so to speak—that humanity should start its collective self-appraisal. There are so many things that should be in our lives that they stand ready to spill out in random profusion, even as some remain mute in our hearts. *What should be is a fount of untold measure.* For example, there should be determination to grow in strength— mentally, physically, and humanly. Conditions of existence should be secured that foster the growth of individuals who are justly proud of their humanity. There should be instituted dialogue for greater understanding and comparison of diverse cultural philosophies and life-styles. There should be open discussion and comparison of the various expressions of family life—of raising healthy offspring, of better relations between men and women, and of the opportunities for personal growth and optimal well-being.

These are not peripheral issues or matters of small consequence. In the global meet, there may be concern about retaining life-styles, ethics, and values and of guarding and uplifting humanity. There is a great interest and curiosity in meeting one's counterpart wherever he or she lives in the world, and of learning new ways of "seeing" and "being". With respect for the many different cultures that have evolved, there is much to be learned, evaluated, added, or discarded. There is so much that needs to be done. Whereas much verbosity is paid in deference to the individual's rights, or to the fact that this is a "nation under God", all of it is quite meaningless unless the intent and meaning are absorbed and translated into action. If, in fact, the individual is of utmost importance and this is a nation under God, a lot of things should be different than they are.

Citizens of this land should be feeling of special worth, loved and protected, each and every one. They should not be part of a meaningless pool to be exterminated at the whim or result of power-crazed individuals whose fingers are poised tremblingly on facile technological buttons connected to holocaust bombs. Women, who comprise half the population, should not have to prove that they are "equal". Together, men and women should be raising sons and daughters all of equal worth before God, state, and humankind.

Then, where each individual is truly of worth, the marketplace should reflect the skills and production of a viable citizenry. The workplace should be humanized and wages fairly equalized. Service should be the hallmark of a sensitive sector. There should be greater distribution of goods and products, less unemployment, and more meaningful work. In such a milieu, product and production should reflect skill and care; individuals should feel that their work is an extension of themselves; and the national output should be the valued creation of a proud populace.

People should be making judgments as to what constitutes acceptable human behavior and what does not. They should be safeguarding their humanity, enriching and perpetuating it, all the while choosing to be the best human beings they can be. And they should be caring for the environment—the earth, their terrestrial abode. The populace should be healthier and live longer. There should be joy in learning, as in living, and awed recognition of the wonders of life. Thoughts and plans should be life-oriented, peace-projected and future-minded. There should be peace in the world.

"There should be peace in the world." Although many agree that peace "should" exist, indicating a feeling or awareness that peace has a place in human affairs, it is weakly espoused and inadequately expressed. Rather, peace should be stoutly defended and strongly championed. It should be solidly instituted and visibly enlarged as a viable system in human affairs.

Humanity should be casting a quizzical eye into the universal environs, for in all likelihood the coming century will bring excursions into space. Novel experiences lie shortly ahead, and there is not much preparatory time. Whatever it means and whatever it brings, the new age is almost upon us, and if we would be ready, we should be making preparations in earnest—educating ourselves, disciplining ourselves, instituting peace and cooperation among ourselves, etc.

Peace? Peace is merely that which should be—not an end in itself, but a beginning. Delayed overlong, peace should be recognized as the basis of human interaction. The foundation of human viability, it is acknowledgment that there is more to be gained from cooperation than from alienation and disintegration, that the human family is one entity, and that the earth is the natural habitat of all. It is recognition that diversity is natural and desirable, yet similarities bind us to each other.

There should be peace because civilized living demands it, humanity dictates it, survival commands it. Visualizing and anticipating its premises and conditions, we should be making peace a staunch global reality and making plans for the future. And knowing *what should be*, we ought to be getting on with it!

AS IF

The *as if* model is a technique for testing new modes of being and performing and plays an active role in preparing for future events. Actually, it is more than preparing for an event; the *as if* technique engages in mental presentation of the event itself in advance of its actual occurrence.

Not only imaging the occurrence, acting *as if* an event is taking place is to bring it into the present. It is to consider it from many sides and to prepare responses, needs, and actions in its behalf. The *as if* process, for instance, selects a desired result and considers it under present and future circumstances. The full weight of focused attention is brought to bear in hypothesizing, analyzing, and acting under the perceived conditions. It is making preparations for an incidence that is in the offing.

Acting *as if* an event is at hand is to consider its eventuality possible, its occurrence expected, its actuality imminent. It adds substance to conjecture and sets into motion a series of actions to pave the way, adding near-certainty to probability. In this way it seems the future is ascertained, familiarized, controlled and prepared for. Also, it is apparently made to happen. The future is expected *as if* it will occur as planned. That it does so when it does, of course, is a fortunate and remarkable coincidence (if not result).

Many activities use the *as if* principle, but because we have become accustomed to its usage, little is thought about it. As mentioned, actors and actresses act their parts *as if* they were the actual people being portrayed. The model is frequently used in visualizing a coming event—say, a scheduled tennis match or speaking performance. Plans for the future, perhaps five years hence, may activate the *as if* principle. Knowledge, practice, and mental preparations anticipate the event itself and may ensure a higher degree of performance and success.

A planning mode, the *as if* method is used in simulations of all kinds, providing an avenue for consideration and testing of problems and possible solutions. For instance, war games are an accepted and instituted methodology of military preparedness, and under relatively realistic conditions, all act *as if* the real thing is in progress. An apprenticeship method, *as if* experienced, is employed when neophytes attempt professional work. Children, of course, playact *as if* they were parents, teachers, cops, and robbers.

When the *as if* model is evoked, there is often preparation for the anticipated event by intense concentration on it—by thinking and planning ahead, by visualizing possible occurrences (including one's performance in it), and by acting out the perceived needs and part. In essence, one is prepared well in advance, and it is hoped that this readiness translates into an eased performance at the appropriate time; unfamiliarity at actual show time does not readily disrupt the practice—the less so, the more professional and accomplished the performer. Roles are taken on, positions prepared for, and plans readied *as if* one is an authority on any given number of subjects or activities in society. Acting *as if* one knows what one is about imparts confidence and, in time, a measure of expertise. The part is usually accepted, grown into, and modeled.

Confidence is expressed in the use of behavior that is natural and expected. Similarly, there is confidence in the ability to adapt, secure, and survive the needs and exigencies of the day. There is expectation in the natural order. One acts *as if* the morrow will arrive. Of course, one is expressing confidence and hope in life as it is known and experienced. There is a ready "willingness to suspend disbelief"—that is, fear is supplanted, and hope and belief implanted. Unambiguous daily actions indicate common acts of confidence in the extension of life and of time. People act *as if* life is forever.

Heretofore, insofar as humans have conceived and experienced it, life has been all-enveloping. It has stretched in all directions—before, behind, beside, ahead. Whereas individuals have died, the community and the species have been maintained and continued. Life has never been doubted. The seasons have come and gone. The recurrence of natural phenomena has been observed. Humanity has proliferated, along with all manner of terrestrial life. Now, however, a pall of doubt is pervasively being felt in the marrow of one's being about the ability of human (and other) life to survive. Observation discloses that the threat is from within; humanity is warring with itself and faces possible extinction from its own excesses.

No longer is the species assured on the path it is walking (stalking might be a better word). As much as the whales or snail-darters, humans are at risk. We are all endangered. Survival is no longer a given. Of course, time and the universe will continue, but human life may be curtailed and become absent from the universal scheme. Dichotomously, we are the threatened and the threatening species.

A profound change is noted that has been variously described as a juncture, a turning point, a crossroads, etc. The problem of war and militarism is manmade. As such, it is usually suggested, manmade problems may be solved by manmade solutions. That is true, but only up to a point—that point being where the problems, like a cancer, take on a life of

their own and threaten the host. It is posited that saving action to counter
the incredible threat to humankind and the environment must be quickly
taken before the point of no return is reached—while there is still choice.

In essence, the war system has proven itself to be a despoiler of life, a
misapplication of intellect, skill, and resources, and an immature use of
might. The flexing of more and bigger muscle is ludicrous in the face of
crying human needs. The unlimited consumption of resources in an era of
limited supplies on a finite earth, and the application of mind and labor in
the service of death and destruction, is evidence of a system, if not a
people, gone berserk, insanely seducing the rest of the populace into
blindly following its fatal dance of death. Continued conformity to inhospitable and inhuman intent is a travesty against humankind and earth itself.
Twisting mentality towards ultimate destruction, the habit of warfare is
gripping humanity in a cancerous clamp. Guaranteeing irreparable harm
to life and the environment, this monstrous habit is inexorably grinding
towards nihilation and extinction.

Clearly, that is not the way to go. War has become too costly to maintain on all fronts—human, material, and environmental—and it cannot be
further upheld in any conscience. The habit of millennia needs breaking,
and the chains of conformity must be stepped away from. Decisions for
change rise to the challenge and indicate needed reforms. One must look
to the end—not the "end" that doomsayers glumly decry (Armageddon or
any other feared and "predicted" end). The consequence of unbridled
hostility—a possible end, to be sure—is likewise totally rejected. One looks
to the desired end. *The desired end.*

The desired end, of course, is the end of the dangerous pattern the
world has fallen into, the closing down of an archaic system of warfare
and militarism that is no longer tenable in a modern world. The desired
end is the fulfillment of humanity's basic desire and need—the creation of
a "new" system that places peace, civilization, and life as the highest
priorities on all agendas. Peace, the pattern of life and civilization, is the
system to be upheld, while emphasis is shifted away from its nemesis, war,
with its retinue of death and destruction. Life is to be lived *as if* it is of
supreme value and worth, showcasing the growth and development of
human beings that are a credit to themselves and their race.

Acting *as if* life is the first good of humanity and environment, and *as
if* the individual is the fullest expression of it, questions soon arise: How
may survival be ensured, peace secured, and life lived to its utmost
potential? How may creativity be released and joyfully enlisted? Will the

realization seep in that individuals seek authentic human living in a meaningful manner as naturally as flowers seek the sun? Since old myths and notions of peace as passive can be laid to rest, what new and ongoing actions in the coming years will ensure an energetic, progressive, yet tranquil mode of life? How will peace be safeguarded in an actively inter-acting world? What will provide for equitable opportunities for men and women? What life-styles will evolve to assure peace, justice, and *la joie de vivre?* What are the enduring principles? What is the common ground?

No act of great courage or immense moral conviction is involved. No vastly different behavior is suggested. The ways, means, facts, problems, and solutions for peace in the world exist right now. Countless individuals have been pointing the way, and common sense is clamoring for its say. It was understood long ago that the end (TELOS) toward which one strives exists now.[201] The goal—peace—needs merely to be planned and prepared for in a manner similar to other human practices. (As the philosophers have noted, "being" and "becoming" are two sides of the same coin, existing simultaneously.)

One method of implementation is eminently simple. It is to act *as if* peace exists. Acting *as if* peace is a global *fait accompli* is to observe the requirements, frailties, and risks according to the facts. And by acting *as if* peace is a living reality (as indeed it partially is) one concentrates on the needs, zeroes in on the problems, and focuses on solutions. Note is taken of the imperfections that abound in societal, national, and international relations. The gaps, limitations, and strengths are acknowledged, and plans are made to improve and promote the whole. A prodigious amount of work and complexity of ground must be covered. All possible methods must be implemented, from politicization of the peace process in govern-ment circles to communication and participation of the citizenry and the wider community. Acting *as if* peace is a desirable system for human interaction, the people are actively involved in its strengthening, in paving the way for its successful deployment, and in preparing for life in a peaceful world.

Living "as if people mattered" and *as if* peace is a viable reality is to introduce a new attitude and level of existence. There are so many things to be considered. How will we behave to one another? What will be different? What will be the same? Will all occupations and services now in operation still be useful? (Of course, it is expected that the weapons makers will necessarily convert facilities to peacetime uses, releasing valuable mate-rial, labor, and funds for vital social needs. In fact, *industry, labor, and management should be considering the problems and solutions of peace in full measure.*)

Globally, who is concerned and responsible for the good of the earth? Where and to whom may greater suggestions and grievances be taken? Who will make (worldwide) decisions, and how will they be implemented? How will the perspectives and opinions of women be added? In this latter regard, it is suggested that women now act *as if* they are equal—as they are—and demand their equal due. Women must begin to understand and forthrightly act out their roles in society, utilizing their particular perspectives and making them known. The world, after all, is peopled by two sexes.

All are involved in shaping a future, and it will not do to remain on the outside of peace as passive or neutral observers. That which is most fervently desired and most religiously petitioned is at hand. It lies within our grasp. The product of centuries, the consequence of civilization, the legacy and inheritance of humanity is positioned squarely before us and awaits the firm grip of the individual and the dedicated grasp of the multitude. Like a flaming torch, it must be raised aloft to permit bright illumination and a clear, unencumbered view. One does not wait for or expect peace to descend in a miraculous drop, like the pot of gold at the end of the rainbow. One realizes that the path itself, the process, *is* the pot of gold and can "give end-pleasure". "The road to peace *is* peace."

There is ample evidence of peace working in local enclaves, in cities, states, and nations. Now it must be approached *as if* peace is the mode of interaction between all nations—in essence, *as if* peace is/will be the accepted form of human interaction on earth. All manner of worldwide communications need to be implemented to reach the global community to enlist support, friendship, and creative involvement. (Having respect for the sensitivities and fears of others, the purpose is to reach them, not to upstage, startle, or cause suspicion of motives.) It is one earth. We are one species, one people.

Peace in the world is not an unattainable ideal or ephemeral wish. It is desirable; it is possible; it is beneficial. Peace is the realization of the hopes, plans, and pragmatic efforts of countless people over time. A viable system, the extension of peace permits the flourishing of human potential, the thriving of the environment, and the continued exploration of the surrounding universe. It is the recognition of the value of life, the dignity of the individual, and the process of human relationships. It goes hand in hand with survival, is intimately attached to time and space, and is the ground of future growth and evolution. The culmination of an age-old search and, simultaneously, a guiding beacon, peace is the premise and condition for a new beginning.

It is to be hoped and strived for that the world will be the congenial habitat of ennobled men and women, proud of their uniquely human roles, and joined in the common endeavor of raising the caliber of life on earth as the search is continued for authenticity and adventure in the unfolding panorama and mystery of life. Poised at an apex in human history and development, there is no other movement but energetically and peacefully forward into life and community. In the language of space, "all systems are go!"

APPENDIX A

PEACE ORIENTED ORGANIZATIONS

Alternatives, Inc.
1924 East Third
Bloomington, Indiana 47401

American Council for the United
Nations University
1211 Kenbar Court
McLean, Virginia 22101

American Friends Service
Committee
160 North 15th Street
Philadelphia, PA 19102

American Jewish Committee
165 East 56th Street
New York, New York 10022

American Peace Society
4000 Albermarle Street, N.W.
Washington, D.C. 20016

Another Mother for Peace
407 North Maple Drive
Beverly Hills, California 90210

The Arms Control Association
11 Dupont Circle, N.W.
Washington, D.C. 20036

Better World Society
1140 Connecticut Ave., N.W.
Washington, D.C. 20036

Carnegie Endowment for
International Peace
11 Dupont Circle
Washington, D.C. 20036

Center for Concern
3700 13th Street, N.E.
Washington, D.C. 20017

Center for Defense Information
1500 Massachusetts Avenue, N.W.
Washington, D.C. 20005

Center for Global Perspectives
218 East 18th Street
New York, New York 10003

Center for the Study of Democratic
Institutions
P.O. Box 4068
Santa Barbara, California 93103

Center for U.N. Reform Education
600 Valley Road
Wayne, New Jersey 07470

Center for War/Peace Studies
218 East 18th Street
New York, New York 10003

Clergy and Laity Concerned
Human Rights Coordinating Center
1114 G Street, S.E.
Washington, D.C. 20003

Commission to Study the
Organization of Peace
866 UN Plaza
New York, New York 10017

Conference on Peace Research in
History
Department of History
University of Toledo
Toledo, Ohio 43606

Consortium on Peace Research,
Education and Development
(COPRED)
University of Illinois at
Urbana-Champaign
911 West High Street, Room 100
Urbana, Illinois 61801

Council for a Livable World
100 Maryland Avenue, N.E.
Washington, D.C. 20002

Council for a Livable World
Education Fund
11 Beacon Street
Boston, Massachusetts 02108

Council on Religion and
International Affairs
170 East 64th Street
New York, New York 10021

The Cousteau Society
930 West 21st Street
Norfolk, Virginia 23517

Farmers and World Affairs
101 North 7th Street
Camden, New Jersey 08102

Federation of American Scientists
307 Massachusetts Avenue, N.E.
Washington, D.C. 20002

Fellowship of Reconciliation
Box 271
Nyack, New York 10960

Friends of the Earth
124 Spear Street
San Francisco, California 94105

Fund for Peace
345 East 46th Street
New York, New York 10017

Global Education Association
552 Park Avenue
East Orange, New Jersey 07017

Greenpeace
1611 Connecticut Avenue, N.W.
P.O. Box 3720
Washington, D.C. 20007

International Council of Women
777 UN Plaza
New York, New York 10017

International League for Human
Rights
777 UN Plaza
New York, New York 10017

International Peace Academy, Inc.
777 United Nations Plaza
New York, New York 10017

Institute for World Order
777 UN Plaza
New York, New York 10017

Jane Addams Peace Association
777 UN Plaza
New York, New York 10017

Members of Congress for Peace
Through Law
201 Massachusetts Avenue, N.E.
Washington, D.C. 20002

Mobilization for Survival
3610 Locust Walk
Philadelphia, Pennsylvania 19104

National Audubon Society
950 Third Avenue
New York, New York 10022

National Council for a World Peace
Tax Fund
2111 Florida Avenue, N.W.
Washington, D.C. 20008

Physicians for Social Responsibility
1601 Connecticut Avenue, N.W.,
#800
Washington, D.C. 20009

Planetary Citizens
777 UN Plaza
New York, New York 10017

The Planetary Society
P.O. Box 40185
Santa Barbara, California 93140

Promoting Enduring Peace
P.O. Box 5013
Woodmont, Connecticut 06460

SANE: A Citizen's Organization for
a Sane World
318 Massachusetts Avenue, N.E.
Washington, D.C. 20002

Sister Cities International
1625 1 Street, N.W., Suite 42426
Washington, D.C. 20006

Union of Concerned Scientists
1384 Massachusetts Avenue
Cambridge, Massachusetts 02238

War Resisters' League
339 Lafayette Street
New York, New York 10012

Women's International League for
Peace and Freedom
1213 Race Street
Philadelphia, Pennsylvania 19107

Women Strike for Peace
637 West 127 Street
New York, New York 10027

World Federalist Association
418 7th Street, S.E.
Washington, D.C. 20003

World Future Society
4916 St. Elmo Avenue
Washington, D.C. 20014

World Peace Through Law Center
839 17th Street, N.W.
Washington, D.C. 20006

World Peacemakers
2852 Ontario Road, N.W.
Washington, D.C. 20009

World Policy Institute
777 United Nations Plaza
New York, New York 10017

Worldwatch Institute
1776 Massachusetts Ave., N.W.
Washington, D.C. 20036

World Without War Council
175 Fifth Avenue
New York, New York 10010

FAMILIAR PEACE WORDS AND PHRASES

peaceful
peacemaker
peace of mind
peace day
peace conference
peace table
peace pipe
peace treaty
peacemaking
peace and quiet
rest in peace
home of peace
peace and security
peace and love
peace and order
peace and world order
peace candidate
peace officer
peace prize
peacekeeping
keeping the peace
war and peace
peace and war
peace research
peace now
go in peace
peace building
peace activities
peace prayers

pray for peace
prayer for peace
peace talks
peace words
shalom
peacetime
peace community
at peace
peace-abiding
peaceable
appease
peaceless
peacelessness
peace pledge
peace with honor
peace party
peace candidate
peace and freedom
peace offering
peacelike
peace studies
peace corps
disturbing the peace
peace for all mankind
peace on earth
climate of peace
waging peace
peace action
peace and conflict

peace seeker
seeker of peace
peace activist
peace education
peace network
global peace
international peace
preventive peace
peace institute
peace academy
peace center
positive peace
negative peace
peace process
peace initiative
peacenik
peace and disarmament
peace advocate
peace concept
peace bridge
peace walk
peace march
peace run
hold one's peace
bike for peace
peace be with you
ways of peace
peaceful coexistence
world peace, etc.

PEACE EDUCATION AND RESEARCH CENTERS OUTSIDE OF THE UNITED STATES

AUSTRALIA

Monash University
Politics 378
Melbourne, Australia 3168

Peace Research Centre
Research School, Pacific Studies
Australian National University
GPO Box 4
Canberra, ACT 2601, Australia

University of Queensland
External Studies, XV201, XV202
St. Lucia, Queensland
Australia 4067

BELGIUM

Centre of War Sociology Institut de
Sociologie de l'Universite Libre de
Brouxelles
44 trenne Jeane
Brussels 1050, Belgium

University of Leuven
Center for Peace Research
Luc Reychler
Van Evenstraat 2B
Leuven B-3000, Belgium

University of Peace
Boulevard du Nord, 4
5000 Namur, Belgium

CANADA

Canadian Institute for International
Peace and Security
P.O. Box 3425, Station D
Ottawa, Ontario K1P 6L4, Canada

Canadian Peace Research Institute
119 Thomas Street
Oaksville, Ontario, Canada L6J 3A7

Peace Research Institute
25 Dundana Avenue
Dundas, Ontario, Canada L9H 4E5

Waterloo, University of
Institute of Peace Studies
Conrad Grebel College
Waterloo, Ontario
Canada N2L 3G6

DENMARK

Center of Peace and Conflict
Research
Vandkunsten 5
1467 Copenhagen K, Denmark

Hesbjerg Peace Research College
5491 Blommenslyst
Hesbjerg 50, Denmark

Institute of Political Studies
University of Copenhagen
Rosenborggade 15, 2nd F
DK-1130, Copenhagen, Denmark

ENGLAND

J. D. Bernal Peace Library
70 Great Russell Street
London WCI B 3BN, England

Centre for the Analysis of Conflict
University College London
4-8 Endsleigh Gardens
London, W.C., 1 H OEG, England

International Confederation for
Disarmament and Peace
6, Endsleigh Street
London, W.C. 1, England

Pugwash Conferences on Science
and World Affairs
9 Great Russell Mansions
60 Great Russell Street
London WC1B 3BE, England

Richardson Institute for Conflict and
Peace Research
Politics Department
University of Lancaster
Lancaster LA1 4YF, England

University of Bradford
School of Peace Studies
Bradford, West Yorkshire BC7-1DP,
England

FINLAND

Institute of Political Science
University of Tampere
P.O. Box 607
33101 Tampere 10, Finland

Tampere Peace Research Institute
Hameenkatu 13B A
P.O. Box 447
SF-33101 Tampere 10, Finland

World Peace Council
Lonnratinkatu 25 A 6 krs
00180 Helsinki 18, Finland

FRANCE

The Atlantic Institute for
International Affairs
24 Quai du 4-Septembe
Boulogne-sur-Sienne, France

and
120 Rue de Longchamp
Paris 75116, France

Centre Interdisciplinaire de
Recherches sur la Paix et
D'Etudes Strategiques
54, Boulevard Raspail
75006 Paris, France

Institut Francais de Polemologie
7, Rue Gutenberg
75 Paris XV, France

INDIA

Gandhi Peace Foundation
Indian Councl on Peace Research
221-223 Deen Dayal
Ypadhyaya Marg, New Delhi 11002,
India

Peace Research Centre
Gujarat Vidyapith
Ashram Road
Ahmadabad 380014, India

Program on Peace and Global
Transformation, UNU
Exchange Building, 1st Floor
13 Alipur Road
Delhi 110 054, India

ISRAEL

Israeli Institute of International
Affairs
Tel Aviv POB 17027, Israel

The Harry S Truman Research
Centre for the Advancement of
Peace
The Hebrew University of Jerusalem
Mount Scopus Campus
Jerusalem, Israel

University of Haifa
Peace Studies Program
Haifa, Israel

ITALY

Forum on the Problems of Peace
and War
Villa Arrivabene
Piazza Alberti 1, 50136 Firenze, Italy

Instituto Italiano di Polemologia e di
Recherchi sui Conflitti
Via Arco 1, Milano, Italy

JAPAN

Institute for Peace Science
Hiroshima University
Higashi - Sendamarchi
Hiroshima, Japan

International Peace Research
Institute
MEIGAKU (PRIME)

Meiji-Gakvin University
Kamikurata 1518
Totsuka-ku, Yokohama, Japan

Japan Peace Research Group
Institute of Social Science
University of Tokyo
Hongo 7-3-1, Bunkyo-ku, Tokyo 113,
Japan

Nagasaki Institute for Peace Culture
Nagasaki Institute of Applied
Science
536 Aba-machi
Nagasaki-shi 851-01, Japan

Peace Studies Association
Waseda University
4-5-4, Asagaya-Kita
Suguinami-hu, Tokyo 166, Japan

The Society of Prayer for World
Peace
5-26-27 Nakakokubun
Ichikawa, Chiba 272, Japan

Soka University
Peace Research Institute
1-236, Tangi-cho
Hachioji-shi
Tokyo 192, Japan

The U.N. University
Toho Seimei Building
15-1 Shibuya 2-chrome
Shibuya-ku, Tokyo 150, Japan

LATIN AMERICA

Consejo LatinoAmericano de
Investigacion Para La Paz
Apartado Postal 20-105
Mexico D.F., Mexico

International Peace Research
Association
IUPRJ
Rua Paulino Fernandes 32
CEP 22270 Rio de Janeiro RJ, Brazil

(formerly at Mershon Center,
199 West 10th Avenue
The Ohio State University
Columbus, Ohio 43201)

Instituto de Estudios Internacionales
University of Chile
Avda. Condell 249, Santiago
Casilla 14187, Sucarsal 21, Chile

Departamento de Ciencias Humanas
Universidad National Agraria, La
Molina
Apartado 456
Lima, Peru

U.N. University for Peace
P.O. Box 199
Escazu, Costa Rica

(On September 27, 1978,
then-President of Costa Rica,
Rodrigo Carazo, proposed the
establishment of a University for
Peace in Costa Rica within the
context of the United Nations
University. A report was submitted
to the Secretary-General, approved
by the General Assembly, and signed
by 22 member-nations as of
December 9, 1981. Now, although
still a fledgling, the U.N. University
for Peace is in operation in Costa
Rica.)

NETHERLANDS

Nederlands Instituut voor
Vredersvrangstukken
Alexanderstraat 7
Postbus 740, The Hague,
Netherlands

Peace Research Center
Institute of Political Science
University of Nijmegen
Verlengde Groenstraat 43
Nijmegen, Netherlands

Polemological Institute
University of Groningen
Heresingel 13
9711 ER Groningen, Netherlands

NIGERIA

Department of Teacher Education
University of Ibadan
Ibadan, Nigeria

Peace Research Institute of Nigeria
Department of Political Science
University of Nigeria
Nsukka, Nigeria

NORWAY

International Peace Research
Institute, Oslo
Radhusgata 4
Oslo 1, Norway

Peace Education Commission
International Peace Research
Association
Institute of Social Science
University of Tromso
2000 Tromso, Norway

PHILIPPINES

Mindanao State University
Southern Philippines
Center for Peace Studies
Marawi City, Philippines

SWEDEN

Department of Peace and Conflict
Research
Uppsala University
P.O. Box 278, S-75105
Uppsala 1, Sweden

Department of Peace and Conflict
Research
University of Goteborg
Viktoriagotan 30
S-41125 Goteborg, Sweden

Department of Peace and Conflict
Research
Lund University
Dag Hammerskjolds Vag 2
S-223 64 Lund, Sweden

Nobel Stiftelsen (Foundation)
Sturegatan 14
P.O. Box 5232, S-10245
Stockholm, Sweden

Stockholm International Peace
Research Institute
Sveavagen 166
113 46 Stockholm, Sweden

and
Pipers Vag 28
S-171 73 Solna, Sweden

SWITZERLAND

Geneva International Peace Research
Institute
41, Rue de Zurich
CH-1201 Geneve, Switzerland

International Peace Bureau
41 Rue de Zurich
1201 Geneva, Switzerland

Women's International League for
Peace and Freedom
1, Rue de Varembe, C.P. 28
1121 Geneva 20, Switzerland

APPENDIX D

ACADEMIC CENTERS FOR PEACE STUDIES AND PEACE RESEARCH IN THE UNITED STATES OF AMERICA

*Institutions so marked indicate that Peace Studies may be individually arranged, that the program is in formation, or that the emphasis is global and international without the title of Peace Studies being used. (There may be some institutions who have withdrawn their programs since first listed. Also, there are many institutions, including religiously oriented ones, that have developed or are developing Peace Studies and World Order programs not listed here. The field is burgeoning.)

*American University
School of International Service
4400 Massachusetts Ave., N.W.
Washington, D.C. 20016

Akron, University of
Center for Peace Studies
302 E. Buchtel
Akron, Ohio 44325

Alaska, University of
Peace Arts Committee
College, Alaska 99701

Amherst College
Peace and World Security Studies
Amherst, Massachusetts 01002

Antioch College
Antioch International Peace Studies
Yellow Springs, Ohio 45387

*Augsberg College
Department of Theology
Minneapolis, Minnesota 55405

Beloit College
Peace Studies Program
Beloit, Wisconsin 53511

Bethel College
Peace Studies Department
North Newton, Kansas 67117

Berkeley, University of California at
Peace and Conflict Studies
Room 120, Building T-8
Berkeley, California 94720

Boston College
Program for the Study of Peace and War
Chestnut Hill, Massachusetts 02167

Brandeis University
Peace Studies Program
Waltham, Massachusetts 02154

California Institute of Integral
Studies
Peace/War and Global Studies
765 Ashbury Street
San Francisco, California 94117

*California State University, Los
Angeles
Center of the Study of
Armament/Disarmament
5151 State University Drive
Los Angeles, California 90032

California State University,
Sacramento
Peace Studies Center
Sacramento, California 95819

California State University, San
Francisco
Peace Studies Program
San Francisco, California 94132

Chapman College
Peace Studies Program
Orange, California 92666

Claremont Graduate School
International Relations and Peace
Studies
Scripps College
Claremont, California 91711

Colgate University
Peace Studies Program
Hamilton, New York 13346

Colorado, University of, at Boulder
Conflict and Peace Studies
Department of Philosophy
Campus Box 331
Boulder, Colorado 80309

and
Concentration in Social Conflict
Department of Sociology
Campus Box 327
Boulder, Colorado 80309

*Columbia University
International War and Peace Studies
New York, New York 10027

Cornell University
Peace Studies Program
180 Uris Hall
Ithaca, New York 14853

*Dubuque, University of,
Peace Studies Concentration
Department of Political Science
2050 University Avenue
Dubuque, Iowa 52001

*Duke University
Conflict Resolution Program
Department of Political Science
Durham, North Carolina 27706

*D'Youville College
Peace Studies Program
520 Parker Avenue
Buffalo, New York 14201

Earlham College
Interdisciplinary 40
Richmond, Indiana 47374

and,
Earlham School of Religion
Peace and Global Studies
(Undergraduate)
Peace and Justice Studies (Graduate)
Richmond, Indiana 47374

Edgewood College
Independent Studies in Peace and
Conflict Resolution
Madison, Wisconsin 53711

Florida State University
Program in Peace Studies
234 Williams Building,
Tallahassee, Florida 32306

Georgetown University
Center for Peace Studies
410 Maguire
Washington, D.C. 20057

*Glassboro State College
Law/Justice Studies
Glassboro, New Jersey 08028

Goshen College
Peace Studies
Goshen, Indiana 46526

*Graceland College
Department of Philosophy
Lamoni, Iowa 50140

Gustavus Adolphus College
Peace Education Program
St. Peter, Minnesota 56082

Hamline University
Department of History
St. Paul, Minnesota 55104

Hampshire College
Five College Program in Peace and
World Security Studies
Amherst, Massachusetts 01002

Harvard University
Psychology and Social Relations
2600
Cambridge, Massachusetts 02138

Haverford College
Center for Nonviolent Conflict
Resolution
Haverford, Pennsylvania 19041

Hawaii, University of
World Order Program
Department of Political Science
Honolulu, Hawaii 96822

and
Hawaii, University of
Conflict Resolution,
Peacemaking and Mediation
2424 Maile Way, Porteus 620
Honolulu, Hawaii 96822

Illinois, University of, at
Urbana-Champaign
Institute of Communications
Research
222B Armory Building
505 E. Armory Avenue
Champaign, Illinois 61820

*Indiana University of Pennsylvania
Department of Political Science
Indiana, Pennsylvania 15705

International Peace Academy, Inc.
777 United Nations Plaza
New York, New York 10017

Irvine, University of California
Concentration in Global Peace and
Conflict Studies
Social Science Tower 531
Irvine, California 92719

Iowa, University of
Center for World Order Studies
College of Law
Iowa City, Iowa 52240

Juniata College
Peace and Conflict Studies
Huntingdon, Pennsylvania 16652

Kent State University
Center for Peaceful Change
Kent, Ohio 44242

La Verne College
Peace Studies Program
La Verne, California 91750

Manchester College
Peace Studies Institute
North Manchester, Indiana 46962

Manhattan College
Peace Studies
Manhattan College Parkway
Riverdale, New York 10471

*Mankato State College
Department of History
Mankato, Minnesota 56001

Maryland, University of
World Order Studies
College Park, Maryland 20742

*Massachusetts Institute of Technology
Center for International Studies
Cambridge, Massachusetts 02138

Massachusetts, University of
Peace and World Security Studies
Hampshire College
Amherst, Massachusetts 01002

Michigan, University of
Department of Political Science
Ann Arbor, Michigan 481069

Minnesota, University of
World Order Program
Center of International Studies
Minneapolis, Minnesota 55455

Missouri, University of
Peace Studies Program
101 Professional Building
Columbia, Missouri 65211

Missouri, University of
Community Conflict Resolution,
M.A. Program
St. Louis, Missouri 63121

Monmouth College
Center for Peace Studies
West Long Branch, New Jersey 07764

New York, State University of,
at Albany
Peace Studies Program
Albany, New York 12222

New York University
Peace Studies Program
6 Washington Place, Room 466
New York, New York 10003

North Dakota, University of
Center for Peace Studies
Box 8158 University Station
Grand Forks, North Dakota 58202

Notre Dame University
Institute for International Peace
Studies
Box 639
Notre Dame, Indiana 46566

Ohio State University
Mershon Center for Education
199 West 10th Avenue
Columbus, Ohio 43201

Oregon State University
Peace Studies Program
College of Liberal Arts
Corvallis, Oregon 97331

Pennsylvania, University of
Conflict Analysis and Peace Science
Department of Regional Science
3718 Locust Walk
Philadelphia, Pennsylvania 19104

Pittsburgh, University of
Peace Studies Program
College of Arts and Sciences
5000 North Willamette Boulevard
Portland, Oregon 97203

*Princeton University
Center of International Studies
Corwin Hall
Princeton, New Jersey 08544

*Purdue University
Department of Political Science
Lafayette, Indiana 47907

Reconstructionist Rabbinical College
Shalom Center
Church Road and Greenwood Ave.
Wyncote, Pennsylvania 19095

Santa Barbara, University of
California
Interdisciplinary Program in Global
Peace Studies
3834 Ellison Hall
Santa Barbara, California 93106

Santa Cruz, University of California
Peace and Strategic Studies
Colwell College
Santa Cruz, California 95064

St. Joseph's College
Program for the Study of Peace and
Human Development
City Lane at 54th Street
Philadelphia, Pennsylvania 19131

*St. Louis University
Department of Political Science
221 North Grand Boulevard
St. Louis, Missouri 63103

The School for International
Training
World Issues Program
49 Kipling Road
Brattleboro, Vermont 05301

Smith College
Program in Peace and World
Security Studies
Northampton, Massachusetts 01063

Southern Illinois University
Peace Studies Program
Peck Building, Room 3212
Edwardsville, Illinois 62026

Stanford University
Research Center
Hoover Institute on War, Revolution
and Peace
Stanford, California 94305

*State University of New York at
Albany
Department of Political Science
New York, New York 12222

State University of New York at Old
Westbury
Politics, Economics and Society
Program
Box 210
Old Westbury, Long Island
New York 11568

Stephens College
Program in Nonviolence and
International Affairs
Department of History
Columbia, Missouri 65201

Swarthmore College Peace
Collection
McCabe Library
Swarthmore, Pennsylvania 19081

Syracuse University
Program in Nonviolent Conflict and
Change
305 Sims V
Syracuse, New York 13244

Tufts University
Peace and Justice Studies Program
11 Miner Hall
Medford, Massachusetts 02155

*Union College
Department of Political Science
Schenectady, New York 12306

*Utah State University
Policy Research Program
Logan, Utah 84322

Warren Wilson College
Peace Education Program
701 Warren Wilson Road
Box 5063
Swannanoa, North Carolina 28778

Wayne State University
Center for Peace and Conflict Studies
5229 Cass Avenue
Detroit, Michigan 48202

Whitman College
Peace and World Order Studies Program
Walla Walla, Washington 99362

Wilmington College
Peace Resource Center
Box 1183
Wilmington, Ohio 45177

William Patterson College of New Jersey
Peace Studies Program
300 Pompton Road
Wayne, New Jersey 07470

Wisconsin, University of
Center for Conflict Resolution
420 North Lake Street
Madison, Wisconsin 53706

Wisconsin, University of, at Stevens Point
Peace Studies Program
Stevens Point, Wisconsin 54481

Wittenberg University
Global Studies Minor
P. O. Box 720
Springfield, Ohio 45501

*Yale University
Political Science Department
Box 3532 Yale Station
New Haven, Connecticut 06520

APPENDIX E

GLOSSARY OF TERMS
FOR WAGING PEACE*

ACTION LINE. Newspaper or television forum for resolving consumer complaints.

ADJUDICATION. Resolution of disputes through a court.

ARBITRATION. Process of having a third person settle a dispute, may or may not be binding.

BILATERAL NEGOTIATIONS. Direct or face-to-face negotiation between two parties to a dispute.

CONCILIATION. The process of having a third person reconcile two parties to a dispute.

CONFLICT. A dispute, disagreement, or clash of interest; may range from nonviolent to violent.

ESCALATION. An increase in intensity or magnitude (of a conflict).

GO-BETWEEN. A third party who assists by delivering communications between parties in a conflict.

LITIGATION. The process of using the courts to resolve a conflict.

MEDIATION. The process of using a third party to assist in bringing about a compromise to resolve a dispute.

MULTILATERAL NEGOTIATIONS. Face-to-face negotiations among the several parties in a conflict.

NEGOTIATION. Mutual discussion and arrangement of a resolution to a conflict.

OMBUDSMAN. An independent person appointed to hear and investigate complaints.

PLURALISTIC SOCIETY. A society with a multiplicity of ideologies, values, and life-styles.

POLARIZATION. The breaking up of a relationship or society into two or more hostile camps.

SOVEREIGNTY. The independent and supreme power or authority of nations.

THIRD PARTY INTERVENTION. The process of having a third party assist in resolving a conflict; roles may range from go-between, mediator and arbitrator to judge.

UNILATERAL ACTION. Independent action or decision by one party in a conflict; may range from avoidance or submission to individual violence or war.

*Source for "Glossary of Terms for Waging Peace":

Global Paper, Waging Peace, 1979, guide, in connection with television program over the PBS System, April 29, 30 and May 1; Public Relations/Advertising Department, WQED/Channel 13, 4802 Fifth Ave., Pittsburgh, PA 15213; p. 8.

Please note: A comprehensive survey of the state of conflict resolution has been issued by *Peace and Change*, Volume VIII, Number 2/3, ISSN 0149-0508, Summer 1982, Special Issue—Conflict Resolution, Special Editor—Maire A. Dugan, published at Kent State University, Kent, Ohio 44242.

APPENDIX F

TEAR-OUT PAGE

Please fill out legibly and mail to the publisher of this book for forwarding to educational and scientific institutions or departments and others deemed appropriate.

STATEMENT OF HUMAN DECLARATION

Name _____ M ___ F ___

Address _____

City _____ State _____ Zip _____

Country _____

STATEMENT:

As an integral part of humanity, I belong to the HUMAN KINGDOM on earth with all the rights and privileges thereof and responsibilities thereto. I do hereby refuse to be finally labeled as an animal, and demand to be classified in accordance with this Statement of Human Declaration.

_____
Signature

Age (circle one): 19 and under; 20-39; 40-59; 60-79; 80 and over.

(Optional: If classification certificate is desired, include $4.00 check or money order with this statement payable to the publisher of this book. Please allow approximately eight weeks for processing and mailing.)

91st CONGRESS
1st Session

H. R. 6501

IN THE HOUSE OF REPRESENTATIVES

FEBRUARY 6, 1969

Mr. HALPERN (for himself, Mr. ADDABBO, Mr. BRASCO, Mr. BOLAND, Mr. BUT-
TON, Mr. BURTON of California, Mr. CONYERS, Mr. DULSKI, Mr. EDWARDS
of California, Mr. EILBERG, Mr. FULTON of Pennsylvania, Mr. GRAY, Mr.
HAWKINS, Mrs. HECKLER of Massachusetts, Mr. HELSTOSKI, Mr. MOORHEAD,
Mr. NIX, Mr. PELLY, Mr. PODELL, Mr. REES, Mr. REUSS, Mr. ROSENTHAL,
Mr. ROYBAL, and Mr. RYAN) introduced the following bill; which was
referred to the Committee on Government Operations

A BILL

To promote the peaceful resolution of international conflict, and
for other purposes.

1   *Be it enacted by the Senate and House of Representa-*

2   *tives of the United States of America in Congress assembled,*

3   That this Act may be cited as the "Peace Act".

4   DECLARATION OF PURPOSE

5   SEC. 2. The Congress declares that the United States has

6   an urgent and continuing responsibility to seek international

7   peace and has undertaken obligations to seek international

8   peace under the Kellogg-Briand Pact of 1929, the Nurem-

9   berg Charter of 1945, and article I, paragraph 1, and article

VI--O

J. 98-001-G——1

2

1   II, paragraphs 3 and 4, of the United Nations Charter. It

2   is the purpose of this Act to meet these responsibilities and

3   obligations and to provide the means to seek and achieve the

4   peaceful resolution of international conflict.

5   TITLE I—DEPARTMENT OF PEACE

6   ESTABLISHMENT OF DEPARTMENT

7   SEC. 101. There is hereby established at the seat of gov-

8   ernment, as an executive department of the United States

9   Government, the Department of Peace (hereafter referred

10   to in this Act as the "Department").

11   FUNCTIONS OF THE DEPARTMENT

12   SEC. 102. (a) The Department shall be responsible for

13   carrying out the purposes of this Act. In achieving such pur-

14   poses, the Department shall—

15   (1) develop and recommend to the President ap-

16   propriate plans, policies, and programs designed to foster

17   peace;

18   (2) exercise leadership in coordinating all activi-

19   ties of the United States Government affecting the pres-

20   ervation or promotion of peace;

21   (3) cooperate with the governments of other na-

22   tions in research and planning for the peaceful resolution

23   of international conflict, and encourage similar action by

24   private institutions;

25   (4) encourage and assist the interchange of ideas

3

1   and persons between private institutions and groups in

2   the United States and those in other countries; and

3   (5) encourage the work of private institutions and

4   groups aimed at the resolution of international conflict.

5   (b) In carrying out its functions under section 102 (a)

6   (1), the Department shall include such recommendations

7   as it deems appropriate for the pacific settlement of current

8   international controversies in which the United States Gov-

9   ernment has or claims an interest. Such recommendations

10   may include specific proposals for the arbitration or adjudica-

11   tion of legal or justiciable disputes, the diplomatic settlement,

12   through compromise, of poltical disputes, and such other

13   procedures, with or without past precedents in international

14   practice, as the Department determines most likely to achieve

15   a nonviolent resolution of a controversy.

16   PERSONNEL OF THE DEPARTMENT

17   SEC. 103. (a) There shall be at the head of the Depart-

18   ment a Secretary of Peace (hereafter referred to in this Act

19   as the "Secretary"), who shall be appointed by the Presi-

20   dent, by and with the advice and consent of the Senate.

21   (b) There shall be in the Department an Under Secre-

22   tary of Peace, who shall be appointed by the President, by

23   and with the advice and consent of the Senate. The Under

24   Secretary of Peace (or, during the absence or disability of

25   the Under Secretary, or in the event of a vacancy in the

4

1 office of Under Secretary of Peace, an Assistant Secretary

2 of Peace or the General Counsel, determined according to

3 such order as the Secretary shall prescribe) shall act for,

4 and exercise the powers of, the Secretary during the absence

5 or disability of the Secretary or in the event of a vacancy in

6 the office of Secretary. The Under Secretary of Peace shall

7 perform such functions as the Secretary shall prescribe from

8 time to time.

9 (c) There shall be in the Department four Assistant

10 Secretaries of Peace and a General Counsel, each of whom

11 shall be appointed by the President, by and with the advice

12 and consent of the Senate, and who shall perform such

13 functions as the Secretary shall prescribe from time to time.

14 (d) The Secretary is authorized to appoint and fix the

15 compensation of such officers and employees, and prescribe

16 their functions and duties, as may be necessary to carry out

17 the purposes and functions of this Act.

18 (e) The Secretary may obtain the services of experts

19 and consultants in accordance with the provisions of section

20 3109 of title 5, United States Code.

21 TRANSFER OF FUNCTIONS TO DEPARTMENT

22 SEC. 104. (a) There are hereby transferred to the Sec-

23 retary all functions which were carried out immediately

24 before the effective date of this title—

25 (1) by one of the following agencies or offices:

5

1   (A) the Agency for International Develop-
2   ment;

3   (B) the Arms Control and Disarmament
4   Agency; or

5   (C) the Peace Corps;

6   (2) by a component of one of such agencies or
7   offices; or

8   (3) by the Secretary of State insofar as such
9   function relates to a function transferred under this
10   subsection from an agency, office, or component referred
11   to in paragraph (1) or (2).

12   (b) There are hereby transferred to the Secretary all
13   functions which were carried out immediately before the
14   effective date of this title—

15   (1) by the International Agricultural Develop-
16   ment Service, Department of Agriculture; or

17   (2) by the Secretary of Agriculture, insofar as the
18   function relates to functions transferred under this sub-
19   section from such Service.

20   (c) Section 2 of the United Nations Participation Act
21   of 1945 (22 U.S.C. 287) is amended by inserting at the
22   end thereof the following new subsection:

23   "(h) The Secretary of Peace shall advise the President
24   with respect to the appointment of any person to represent

6

1 the United States in the United Nations, or in any of its

2 organs, commissions, specialized agencies, or other bodies."

3   (d) The functions, powers, and duties of the Secretary

4 of State, and the other offices and officers of the Depart-

5 ment of State, relating to specialized agencies as defined in

6 article 57 of the United Nations Charter, are transferred to

7 the Secretary of Peace.

8   (e) Within one hundred and eighty days after the

9 effective date of this title, the President may transfer to the

10 Secretary any function of any other agency or office, or

11 part of any agency or office, in the executive branch of the

12 United States Government if the President determines that

13 such function relates primarily to functions transferred to

14 the Secretary by the preceding subsections of this section.

15   TRANSFER OF AGENCIES AND OFFICES

16   SEC. 105. (a) All personnel, assets, liabilities, con-

17 tracts, property, and records as are determined by the Di-

18 rector of the Bureau of the Budget to be employed, held,

19 or used primarily in connection with any function transferred

20 under the provisions of section 104, are transferred to the

21 Secretary. Except as provided in subsection (b), personnel

22 engaged in functions transferred under this title shall be

23 transferred in accordance with applicable laws and regula-

24 tions relating to transfer of functions.

25   (b) The transfer of personnel pursuant to subsection

7

1   (a) shall be without reduction in classification or compen-

2   sation for one year after such transfer.

3   (c) In any case where all of the functions of any

4   agency or office are transferred pursuant to this title, such

5   agency or office shall lapse.

6   ADMINISTRATIVE PROVISIONS

7   SEC. 106. (a) The Secretary may, in addition to the

8   authority to delegate and redelegate contained in any other

9   Act in the exercise of the functions transferred to the Secre-

10   tary by this title, delegate any of his functions to such offi-

11   cers and employees of the Department as he may designate,

12   may authorize such successive redelegations of such functions

13   as he may deem desirable, and may make such rules and

14   regulations as may be necessary to carry out his functions.

15   (b) The Secretary is authorized to establish a working

16   capital fund, to be available without fiscal year limitation, for

17   expenses necessary for the maintenance and operation of such

18   common administrative services as he shall find to be desir-

19   able in the interest of economy and efficiency in the Depart-

20   ment, including such services as a central supply service for

21   stationery and other supplies and equipment for which ade-

22   quate stocks may be maintained to meet in whole or in part

23   the requirements of the Department and its agencies; central

24   messenger, mail, telephone, and other communications serv-

25   ices; office space, central services for document reproduction,

8

1   and for graphics and visual aids; and a central library service.

2   The capital of the fund shall consist of any appropriations

3   made for the purpose of providing capital (which appropria-

4   tions are hereby authorized) and the fair and reasonable

5   value of such stocks of supplies, equipment, and other assets

6   and inventories on order as the Secretary may transfer to

7   the fund, less the related liabilities and unpaid obligations.

8   Such fund shall be reimbursed in advance from available

9   funds of agencies and offices in the Department, or from

10   other sources, for supplies and services at rates which will

11   approximate the expense of operation, including the accrual

12   of annual leave and the depreciation of equipment. The fund

13   shall also be credited with receipts from sale or exchange of

14   property and receipts in payment for loss or damage to prop-

15   erty owned by the fund. There shall be covered into the

16   United States Treasury as miscellaneous receipts any surplus

17   found in the fund (all assets, liabilities, and prior losses con-

18   sidered) above the amounts transferred or appropriated to

19   establish and maintain such fund.

20   (c) The Secretary may approve a seal of office for the

21   Department, and judicial notice shall be taken of such seal.

22   (d) In addition to the authority which is transferred

23   to and vested in the Secretary by section 104, as necessary,

24   and when not otherwise available, the Secretary is author-

25   ized to provide for, construct, or maintain the following

9

1 for employees and their dependents stationed at remote

2 localities:

3   (1) emergency medical services and supplies;

4   (2) food and other subsistence supplies;

5   (3) messing facilities;

6   (4) motion picture equipment and film for recrea-

7   tion and training; and

8   (5) living and working quarters and facilities.

9 The furnishing of medical treatment under clause (1) and

10 the furnishing of services and supplies under clauses (2)

11 and (3) of this subsection shall be at prices reflecting rea-

12 sonable value as determined by the Secretary and the pro-

13 ceeds therefrom shall be credited to the appropriation from

14 which the expenditure was made.

15   (e) (1) The Secretary is authorized to accept, hold,

16 administer, and utilize gifts and bequests of property, both

17 real and personal, for the purpose of aiding or facilitating

18 the work of the Department. Gifts and bequests of money

19 and the proceeds from sales of other property received as

20 gifts or bequests shall be deposited in the Treasury of the

21 United States in a separate fund and shall be disbursed upon

22 order of the Secretary.

23   (2) Upon the request of the Secretary, the Secretary

24 of the Treasury may invest and reinvest in securities of

25 the United States or in securities guaranteed as to prin-

10

1   cipal and interest by the United States any moneys con-

2   tained in the fund provided for in paragraph (1). Income

3   accruing from such securities, and from any other property

4   held by the Secretary pursuant to paragraph (1), shall

5   be deposited to the credit of the fund, and shall be disbursed

6   upon order of the Secretary.

7   (f) The Secretary is authorized to appoint, without

8   regard to the provisions of title 5, United States Code,

9   governing appointments in the competitive service, such

10   advisory committees as may be appropriate for the purpose

11   of consultation with and advice to the Department in the

12   performance of its functions. Members of such committees,

13   other than those regularly employed by the United States

14   Government, while attending meetings of such committees

15   or otherwise serving at the request of the Secretary, may be

16   paid compensation at rates not exceeding those authorized

17   for individuals under section 103 (e), and while so serving

18   away from their homes or regular places of business, may

19   be allowed travel expenses, including per diem in lieu of

20   subsistence, as authorized by section 5703 of title 5, United

21   States Code, for persons in the Government service employed

22   intermittently.

23   (g) (1) The Secretary is authorized to enter into

24   contracts with educational institutions, public or private

25   agencies or organizations, or individuals for the conduct of

11

1   research into any aspect of the problems related to the

2   programs of the Department which are authorized by statute.

3   (2) The Secretary may from time to time disseminate

4   in the form of reports or publications to public or private

5   agencies or organizations, or individuals such information

6   as he deems pertinent on the research carried out pursuant

7   to this subsection.

8   (3) Nothing contained in this subsection is intended

9   to amend, modify, or repeal any provisions of law adminis-

10 tered by the Department which authorize the making of

11 contracts for research.

12   TECHNICAL AMENDMENTS

13 Sec. 107. (a) Section 19 (d) (1) of title 3, United

14 States Code, is hereby amended by inserting before the

15 period at the end thereof a comma and the following:

16 "Secretary of Peace".

17 (b) Section 101 of title 5, United States Code, is

18 amended by inserting at the end thereof the following:

19 "The Department of Peace."

20 (c) Subchapter II of chapter 53 of title 5, United

21 States Code (relating to executive schedule pay rates), is

22 amended as follows:

23 (1) Section 5312 is amended by adding at the end

24 thereof the following:

25 "(13) Secretary of Peace."

12

1   (2) Section 5314 is amended by adding at the end

2   thereof the following:

3   "(54) Under Secretary of Peace."

4   (3) Section 5315 is amended by adding at the end

5   thereof the following:

6   "(92) General Counsel, Department of Peace.

7   "(93) Assistant Secretaries of Peace (4)."

8   (4) Section 5317 is amended by striking out "34"

9   and inserting in lieu thereof "36".

10   ANNUAL REPORT

11   SEC. 108. The Secretary shall, as soon as practicable

12   after the end of each fiscal year, make a report in writing

13   to the President for submission to the Congress on the

14   activities of the Department during the preceding fiscal

15   year.

16   SAVINGS PROVISIONS

17   SEC. 109. (a) All orders, determinations, rules, regu-

18   lations, permits, contracts, certificates, licenses, and

19   privileges—

20   (1) which have been issued, made, granted, or

21   allowed to become effective in the exercise of functions

22   which are transferred under this title, by (A) any

23   agency or office, or part thereof, any functions of which

24   are transferred by this title, or (B) any court of com-

25   petent jurisdiction, and

13

1   (2) which are in effect at the time this title takes

2   effect, shall continue in effect according to their terms

3   until modified, terminated, superseded, set aside, or

4   repealed by the Secretary, by any court of competent

5   jurisdiction, or by operation of law.

6   (b) The provisions of this title shall not affect any pro-

7   ceedings pending at the time this section takes effect before

8   any agency or office, or part thereof, functions of which are

9   transferred by this title; but such proceedings, to the extent

10   that they relate to functions so transferred, shall be continued

11   before the Department. Such proceedings, to the extent they

12   do not relate to functions so transferred, shall be continued

13   before the agency or office, or part thereof, before which

14   they were pending at the time of such transfer. In either case

15   orders shall be issued in such proceedings, appeals shall be

16   taken therefrom, and payments shall be made pursuant to

17   such orders, as if this title had not been enacted; and orders

18   issued in any such proceedings shall continue in effect until

19   modified, terminated, superseded, or repealed by the Secre-

20   tary, by a court of competent jurisdiction, or by operation of

21   law.

22   (c) (1) Except as provided in paragraph (2) —

23   (A) the provisions of this title shall not affect suits

24   commenced prior to the date this section takes effect, and

25   (B) in all such suits proceedings shall be had,

14

1   appeals taken, and judgments rendered, in the same

2   manner and effect as if this title had not been enacted.

3   No suit, action, or other proceeding commenced by or against

4   any officer in his official capacity as an officer of any agency

5   or office, or part thereof, functions of which are transferred

6   by this title, shall abate by reason of the enactment of

7   this title. No cause of action by or against any agency or

8   office, or part thereof, functions of which are transferred by

9   this title, or by or against any officer thereof in his official

10   capacity, shall abate by reason of the enactment of this title.

11   Causes of actions, suits, or other proceedings may be asserted

12   by or against the United States or such official of the De-

13   partment as may be appropriate and, in any litigation

14   pending when this section takes effect, the court may at any

15   time, on its own motion or that of any party, enter an

16   order which will give effect to the provisions of this sub-

17   section.

18   (2) If, before the date on which this title takes effect,

19   any agency or office, or officer thereof in his official capacity,

20   is a party to a suit, and under this title—

21   (A) such agency or office, or any part thereof, is

22   transferred to the Secretary, or

23   (B) any function of such agency, office, or part

24   thereof, or officer is transferred to the Secretary,

25   then such suit shall be continued by the Secretary (except

15

1 in the case of a suit not involving functions transferred to

2 the Secretary, in which case the suit shall be continued by

3 the agency, office, or part thereof, or officer which was a

4 party to the suit prior to the effective date of this title).

5 (d) With respect to any function transferred by this

6 title and exercised after the effective date of this title, refer-

7 ence in any other Federal law to any agency, office, or part

8 thereof, or officer so transferred or functions of which are

9 so transferred shall be deemed to mean the department or

10 officer in which such function is vested pursuant to this

11 title.

12 (e) Orders and actions of the Secretary in the exercise

13 of functions transferred under this title shall be subject to

14 judicial review to the same extent and in the same manner as

15 if such orders and actions had been by the agency or office,

16 or part thereof, exercising such functions, immediately pre-

17 ceding their transfer. Any statutory requirements relating to

18 notice, hearings, action upon the record, or administrative

19 review that apply to any function transferred by this title

20 shall apply to the exercise of such function by the Secretary.

21 (f) In the exercise of the functions transferred under

22 this title, the Secretary shall have the same authority as

23 that vested in the agency or office, or part thereof, exercising

24 such functions immediately preceding their transfer, and his

25 actions in exercising such functions shall have the same force

16

1   and effect as when exercised by such agency or office, or

2   part thereof.

3   CODIFICATION

4   Sec. 110. The Secretary is directed to submit to the

5   Congress within two years from the effective date of this title,

6   a proposed codification of all laws which contain functions

7   transferred to the Secretary by this title.

8   EFFECTIVE DATE; INITIAL APPOINTMENT OF OFFICERS

9   Sec. 111. (a) This title, other than this section, shall

10   take effect ninety days after the enactment of this Act, or on

11   such prior date after enactment of this Act as the President

12   shall prescribe and publish in the Federal Register.

13   (b) Notwithstanding subsection (a), any of the officers

14   provided for in subsections (a), (b), and (c) of section 103

15   may be appointed in the manner provided for in this title, at

16   any time after the date of enactment of this Act. Such officers

17   shall be compensated from the date they first take office, at

18   the rates provided for in this title. Such compensation and

19   related expenses of their offices shall be paid from funds

20   available for the functions to be transferred to the Depart-

21   ment pursuant to this title.

22   TITLE II—INTERNATIONAL PEACE INSTITUTE

23   ESTABLISHMENT OF INSTITUTE

24   Sec. 201. There is hereby established within the De-

25   partment the International Peace Institute (hereafter re-

26   ferred to in this Act as the "Institute"). The Institute shall

17

1 furnish training and instruction to prepare citizens of the

2 United States for service in positions or programs relating

3 to the field of promoting international understanding and

4 peace.

5   OFFICERS, STAFF, AND INSTRUCTORS

6   SEC. 202. (a) The Secretary may appoint or assign, on

7 a full- or part-time basis, such officers, staff, and instructors

8 as the needs of the Institute require.

9   (b) The Secretary may assign or detail, on a full- or

10 part-time basis and with the consent of the head of the

11 United States Government department or agency concerned,

12 any officer or employee of the executive branch of the United

13 States Government to serve on the faculty or staff of the

14 Institute. During the period of his assignment or detail, such

15 officer or employee shall be considered as remaining in the

16 position from which assigned or detailed.

17   SUPERVISION OF INSTITUTE

18   SEC. 203. The supervision and charge of the Institute

19 shall be under such officer or officers as the Secretary may

20 appoint for or assign to that duty, and under such regula-

21 tions as the Secretary may prescribe.

22   BOARD OF TRUSTEES

23   SEC. 204. (a) There is hereby established within the

24 Institute a board of trustees (hereafter referred to in this

25 Act as the "Board") which shall advise the Secretary on the

26 operation of the Institute. The Board shall be composed of—

18

1   (1) the Secretary (ex officio) ;

2   (2) two officers of the Department designated by

3   the Secretary;

4   (3) two Members of the Senate, of different polit-

5   ical parties, appointed by the President of the Senate;

6   (4) two Members of the House of Representatives,

7   of different political parties, appointed by the Speaker

8   of the House of Representatives;

9   (5) the Chairman of the Atomic Energy Commis-

10   sion, or his designee;

11   (6) the Chairman of the Federal Council on the

12   Arts and the Humanities, or his designee;

13   (7) one member from the National Academy of

14   Sciences, to be appointed by the President after con-

15   sultation with the President of the Academy;

16   (8) two educators of prominence appointed by the

17   President;

18   (9) two prominent persons associated with the

19   advancement of world peace, appointed by the Secre-

20   tary; and

21   (10) the United States Ambassador to the United

22   Nations.

23   (b) Members of the Board shall be appointed for two-

24   year terms and shall be eligible for reappointment.

25   (c) The Board shall visit the Institute annually. With

19

1 the approval of the Secretary, the Board or its members

2 may make other visits to the Institute in connection with

3 the duties of the Board.

4   (d) The Board shall inquire into the morale and dis-

5 cipline, the curriculum, instruction, physical equipment, fiscal

6 affairs, academic methods, and other matters relating to the

7 Institute that the Board decides to consider.

8   (e) Within sixty days after its annual visit, the Board

9 shall submit a written report to the President of its action,

10 and of its views and recommendations pertaining to the

11 Institute. Any report of a visit, other than the annual visit,

12 shall, if approved by a majority of the members of the Board,

13 be submitted to the President within sixty days after the

14 approval.

15   (f) Each member of the Board may be allowed travel

16 expenses, including per diem in lieu of subsistence, in accord-

17 ance with the provisions of section 5703 of title 5, United

18 States Code, for persons in the Government service em-

19 ployed intermittently.

20   ADMISSION OF STUDENTS

21   SEC. 205. (a) The authorized number of students at the

22 Institute shall be one hundred and fifty.

23   (b) The Institute shall operate as a coeducational in-

24 stitution and students shall be selected for admission to the

25 Institute on the basis of merit, as determined by a com-

20

1   petitive examination to be given annually in each State,

2   the District of Columbia, and the Commonwealth of Puerto

3   Rico, at such time, in such manner, and covering such sub-

4   ject matter as the Secretary may prescribe.

5   (c) No individual shall be eligible for admission to the

6   Institute unless he is a citizen of the United States who has

7   been awarded a bachelor's degree upon graduation from a

8   college or university located in the United States or a degree

9   which the Secretary determines is generally recognized as

10 the equivalent of a bachelor's degree upon graduation from

11 a college or university located in a foreign country.

12 STIPENDS AND TRAVEL AND TRANSPORTATION ALLOWANCES

13   SEC. 206. Each student of the Institute shall be en-

14 titled to receive—

15   (1) a stipend in an amount determined by the

16   Secretary to be within the range of stipends or fellow-

17   ships payable under other Government programs pro-

18   viding for the education or training of graduate students;

19   and

20   (2) reasonable travel and transportation allowances,

21   including transportation for his immediate family, house-

22   hold goods, and personal effects, under regulations pre-

23   scribed by the Secretary, but such allowances shall not

24   exceed the allowances payable under section 5723 of

25   title 5, United States Code.

21

1   COURSE OF INSTRUCTION AND TRAINING

2   SEC. 207. (a) The course of instruction and training for

3   students at the Institute shall be prescribed by the Secretary,

4   shall be for a period of one year, and shall, insofar as con-

5   sistent with the purposes of this title, be acceptable for credit

6   toward a graduate degree at accredited colleges and uni-

7   versities. In prescribing such course of instruction and train-

8   ing, the Secretary shall provide that special emphasis be

9   placed on such studies as will best prepare students for leader-

10   ship in the nonviolent resolution of international conflicts and

11   in the promotion of international understanding and peace.

12   Upon satisfactory completion of the prescribed course of in-

13   struction and training, students shall be awarded a Federal

14   certificate of participation.

15   (b) The course of instruction and training at the In-

16   stitute shall, during each year of its operation, be organized

17   as prescribed by the Secretary, except that one month of each

18   such year shall be devoted to annual leave for all students.

19   AGREEMENTS BY STUDENTS

20   SEC. 208. Each student selected for admission to the In-

21   stitute shall sign an agreement that, unless sooner separated,

22   he will—

23   (1) complete the course of instruction at the Insti-

24   tute; and

25   (2) accept, if offered, an appointment as an officer

22

1   or employee of the United States or, in the discretion of

2   the Secretary, employment with an international orga-

3   nization or private agency or foundation determined by

4   the Secretary to be engaged in activities relating to the

5   promoting or achieving of international understanding

6   and peace, in any position for which such student is

7   qualified by reason of his special training at the Institute,

8   for at least the one-year period immediately following

9   the awarding of his certificate from the Institute or the

10   completion by him of any period of full-time graduate

11   study approved by the Secretary.

12   AUTHORIZATIONS; ACQUISITION OF PROPERTY

13   SEC. 209. (a) There are authorized to be appropriated

14   such sums as may be necessary to carry out the provisions

15   of this title.

16   (b) The Institute shall have power to acquire and

17   hold real and personal property and may receive and accept

18   gifts, donations, and trusts.

19   TITLE III—JOINT COMMITTEE ON PEACE AND

20   INTERNATIONAL COOPERATION

21   ESTABLISHMENT OF JOINT COMMITTEE

22   SEC. 301. There is hereby established a joint congres-

23   sional committee to be known as the Joint Committee on

24   Peace and International Cooperation (hereinafter referred to

25   as the "joint committee"). The joint committee shall be com-

26   posed of seven Members of the Senate, to be appointed by

1   the President of the Senate, and seven Members of the

2   House of Representatives, to be appointed by the Speaker of

3   the House of Representatives. The party representation on

4   the joint committee shall as nearly as may be feasible reflect

5   the relative membership of the majority and minority parties

6   in the Senate and the House of Representatives, respectively.

7   FUNCTIONS

8   SEC. 302. It shall be the function of the joint committee—

9   (1) to make a continuing study of matters relating

10   to the Department of Peace;

11   (2) to study means of coordinating programs in

12   order to further the purpose of this Act; and

13   (3) as a guide to the several committees of the

14   Congress dealing with legislation relating to the Depart-

15   ment of Peace, to file a report not later than May 1 of

16   each year (beginning with the calendar year 1971)

17   with the Senate and the House of Representatives con-

18   taining its findings and recommendations with respect

19   to the Department of Peace, and from time to time to

20   make such other reports and recommendations to the

21   Senate and House of Representatives as it deems

22   advisable.

23   VACANCIES; SELECTION OF CHAIRMAN

24   SEC. 303. Vacancies in the membership of the joint

25   committee shall not affect the power of the remaining mem-

24

1   bers to execute the functions of the joint committee, and shall

2   be filled in the same manner as the original selection. The

3   joint committee shall select a chairman and a vice chairman

4   from among its members.

5   HEARINGS; STAFF; ASSISTANCE

6   SEC. 304. (a) In carrying out its duties under this title,

7   the joint committee, or any duly authorized subcommittee

8   thereof, is authorized to hold such hearings; to sit and act at

9   such times and places; to appoint and fix the compensation of

10   such experts, consultants, technicians, and staff personnel; to

11   procure such printing and binding; and to make such expendi-

12   tures as it deems advisable.

13   (b) With the prior consent of the department or agency

14   concerned, the joint committee is authorized to utilize the

15   services, information, and facilities of the departments and

16   establishments of the United States Government and private

17   research agencies.

18   AUTHORIZATION; EXPENSES

19   SEC. 305. (a) The expenses of the joint committee,

20   which shall not exceed $200,000 for each fiscal year, shall

21   be paid from the contingent fund of the Senate from funds

22   appropriated for the joint committee, upon vouchers signed

23   by the chairman of the joint committee or by any member

24   of the joint committee duly authorized by the chairman.

25   (b) Members of the joint committee, and its employees

25

1   and consultants, while traveling on official business for the

2   joint committee within or outside the United States, may

3   receive either the per diem allowance authorized to be paid

4   to Members of the Congress or its employees, or their actual

5   and necessary expenses provided an itemized statement of

6   such expenses is attached to the voucher.

REFERENCES

1 Margaret Mead, "Warfare is Only An Invention—Not a Biological Necessity.", *Peace and War*, Eds., Charles R. Beitz and Theodore Herman (San Francisco: W. H. Freeman and Company, 1973), p. 118.

2 Albert Einstein in *Einstein on Peace*, Edited by Otto Nathan and Heinz Norden, (New York: Schocken Books, 1960), p. 124.

3 Grenville Clark and Louis B. Sohn, *Introduction to World Peace Through World Law*. "Toward Consensus: and the World Order Models Project of the Institute for World Order", by Saul H. Mendlovitz and Thomas G. Weiss, (Chicago: World Without War Publications, 1973). pp. 74-97, p. 94. Secondary Source.

4 John G. Stoessinger, *Why Nations Go To War*, (New York: St. Martin's Press, 1974).

5 *Encyclopedia of the Social Sciences*, Volume II, David L. Sills, Editor, (USA: The Macmillan Company and The Free Press, 1968), s.v. "Peace," by Johan Galtung, pp. 487-496, and,

Los Angeles Times, September 20, 1982, Part 1, pp. 1, 3, 12, 13, 14.

6 *International Encyclopedia of the Social Sciences*, 1968 Edition, The Repertory on Disarmament and Peace Research Institutions cited s.v. "Peace" by Johan Galtung, pp. 487-496, p. 495.

7 Theodore Lentz, *Towards a Science of Peace*, 2nd Ed. (New York: Bookman Associates, Inc., 1954/61).

8 Quincy Wright, *A Study of War*, 2nd Ed., (Chicago: University of Chicago Press, 1942/65).

9 Lewis F. Richardson, *Arms and Insecurity: A Mathematical Study of The Causes and Origins of War*, Edited by Nicholas Rashensky and Ernesto Trucco (Pittsburgh: the Boxwood Press; Chicago: Quadrangle, 1960a).

10 Lewis F. Richardson, *Statistics of Deadly Quarrels,* Edited by Quincy Wright and C.C. Lienau. (Pittsburgh: The Boxwood Press, 1960b).

11 Clinton Fink, "Editorial Notes", *Journal of Conflict Resolution* 16 (December 1972), pp. 463-467, p. 464.

12 *Harvard Magazine*, (Cambridge: Harvard Magazine, Inc., November-December 1980), "Danger: Nuclear War," by Jonathan A. Leonard, pp. 21-25.

13 F. Hilary Conroy, "The Conference on Peace Research in History: A Memoir," *Journal of Peace Research* 4 (1968), pp. 365-374, p. 366.

14 Asbjorn Eide, "The Draft Statutes of IPRA,: *International Peace Research Newsletter*, Volume XVIII, No. 2 (The Netherlands: August 1980), pp. 5-11.

15 Philip P. Everts, "Developments and Trends in Peace and Conflict Research, 1965-1971: A Survey of Institutions," *Journal of Conflict Resolution*, Volume XVI, Number 4, (Beverly Hills: Sage Publications, December 1972), pp. 477-510.

16 Elise Boulding and J. Robert Passmore, *Bibliography on World Conflict and Peace*, (Boulder, Colorado: Institute of Behavioral Science, University of Colorado, 1974); and,
Hannah Newcombe, ed., *Voice of Women's Peace Library* , Bibliography, International Women's Year, 1975, Development Education Centre, 200 Bedford Road, Toronto, Ontario, Canada; and,
Burns H. Weston, Sherle R. Schwenninger, Diane E. Shamis, editors., *Peace and World Order Studies*, A Curriculum Guide, (New York: Transnational Academic Program, Institute for World Order, 1140 Avenue of the Americas, New York, N.Y. 10036 March 1978); and,
Barbara J. Wien, ed. *Peace and World Order Studies, Fourth Edition, A Curriculum Guide,* (New York: World Policy Institute, 1984).

17 Quincy Wright, *A Study of War*, 2nd Ed., (Chicago: University of Chicago Press, 1942), pp. 1092-3.

18 Ibid., 1942/65, p. xiv.

19 Ibid., p. 864.

20 Sylvia Hornstein, *The Psychology of Peace and War*, (Rohnert Park, CA: Sonoma State College, 1977), p. 31.

21 Allen Newcombe, "Initiatives and Responses," *Peace Research Reviews* 3 (June 1969). p. 19.

22 Francis A. Beer, "World Order and World Futures," *Journal of Conflict Resolution*, Vol. 23, No. 1, (Beverly Hills: Sage Publications, March 1979).

23 Ibid., p. 177.

24 Saul H. Mendlovitz and Thomas G. Weiss, "Toward Consensus: The World Order Models Project of the Institute for World Order," *Introduction to World Peace Through World Law*, Grenville Clark and Louis B. Sohn, (Chicago: World Without War Publications, 1973), pp. 74-97, p. 80.

25 William O. Douglas, "The Rule of Law in World Affairs," *Center Report*, (Santa Barbara: Center For the Study of Democratic Institutions, February 1976), pp. 14-17, p. 17.

26 Ibid., p. 15.

27 Thomas Jefferson, Thomas Jefferson Memorial, Washington, D. C.

28 Grenville Clark and Louis B. Sohn, *World Peace Through World Law*, 3rd Ed., (Cambridge, Mass.: Harvard University Press, copyright 1958, 1960, 1966 by the President and Fellows of Harvard College.)

29 Benjamin B. Ferencz, *A Common Sense Guide to World Peace*, (London: Oceana Publications, Inc., 1985).

30 Albert Einstein in *Einstein on Peace*, edited by Otto Nathan and Heinz Norden, (New York: Schocken Books, 1960), p. 82.

31 Ibid., p. 168.

32 Ibid., p. 169.

33 Mahatma Gandhi, in *All Men Are Brothers*, ed., Krishna Kripalni, (Paris: UNESCO, and New York: The Columbia University Press, 1958/Chicago: World Without War Publications, 1972), p. 109.

34 Ibid., pp. 74, 78, 79, 165, and,
Gene Sharp, "The Meanings of Non-Violence: A Typology," *Journal of Conflict Resolution*, 3, 1959, pp. 40-66, p. 58.

35 Mahatma Gandhi, in *All Men Are Brothers*, ed., Krishna Kripalni, (Paris: UNESCO, and New York: The Columbia University Press, 1958/Chicago: World Without War Publications, 1972) pp. 78, 79, 127.

36 Ibid., p. 111.

37 Ibid., p. 166.

38 Martin Luther King, Jr., *Strength to Love*, (New York: Harper and Row, Publishers 1963), p. 140.

39 Ibid., p. 140.

40 John A. Garraty, *Woodrow Wilson*, (New York: Harper & Row, Publishers, 1956), p. 151.

41 William E. Leuchtenberg, *The Perils of Prosperity* 1914-1932, (Chicago: University of Chicago Press, 1958), p. 48.

42 *Charter of the United Nations*, (New York: United Nations, 1945), p. 1.

43 Ibid., p. 3.

44 *The Random House Dictionary of the English Language*, The Unabridged Edition, Jess Stein, Editor-in-Chief, (New York: Random House, Inc., 1966/1981), "Major Dates in World History", p. 1930.

45 Frederick J. Libby, *To End War*, (Nyack, New York: Fellowship Publications, 1969) pp. 61, 65.

46 Ibid., pp. 52-59.

47 Charter, Women's International League for Peace and Freedom, 1213 Race St., Philadelphia, PA 19107. Publisher: *Peace and Freedom.*

48 *The Foundation Directory*, 5th Ed., s.v., "Carnegie Endowment for International Peace," (New York: United Nations Plaza and 46th St., N.Y. 10017; also, 11 Dupont Circle, Washington, D.C. 20036; also, 58 Rue de Moilledeau, 1211 Geneva, 16 Switzerland. (Donor—Andrew Carnegie), p. 219, and,
The Foundation Directory, 8th Edition, Marianna O. Lewis, Executive Editor, Alexis Teitz Gersumsky, Senior Editor, (New York: The Foundation Center, 1981) s.v. "Carnegie Endowment for International Peace," paragraph #479, p. 73.

49 *Awards, Honors and Prizes* 2, 2nd Edition, Managing Editor, Paul Wasserman (Detroit: Yale Research Co., 1972), s.v. "International and Foreign," p. 329.

50 Clinton Fink, "Editorial Notes," *Journal of Conflict Resolution* 16, (December 1972), pp. 463-647, p. 463.

51 *Great Books of the Western World* #43, Editor-in-Chief, Robert Maynard Hutchins, (Chicago: William Benton, Publisher, Encyclopedia Brittanica, Inc., 1952), "American State Papers," 'The Declaration of Independence,' (Thomas Jefferson), p. 1.

52 *The World Book Encyclopedia*, C, Volume 3, (Chicago: Field Enterprises, Inc., 1957), "Calendar," pp. 1116-1120, p. 1117.

53 *Time*, by Samuel A. Goudsmidt, Robert Claiborne and the Editors of Life (New York: Time Incorporated, 1966), pp. 60, 62, 74.

54 Ibid., p. 73, and,
World Book Encyclopedia, C. Volume 3 (Chicago: Field Enterprises, Inc., 1957), "Christian Era", p. 1423.

55 Ibid., (*Time*), pp. 72-73, and,
    Ibid., (*World Book Encyclopedia*), p. 1423.

56 *Time*, by Samuel A. Goudsmidt, Robert Claiborne, and the Editors of Life
    (New York: Time, Incorporated, 1966), p. 9.

57 Ibid., p. 50.

58 Ibid., pp. 55-57.

59 Max I. Dimont, *Jews, God and History*, (New York: Simon and Schuster,
    1972), p. 33 and,
    The World Book Encyclopedia, Volume 3, C, (Chicago: Field Enterprises,
    Inc., 1957), "Calendar," pp, 1116-1120, p. 1117.

60 *Time*, by Samuel A. Goudsmidt, Robert Claiborne, and the Editors of Life
    (New York: Time, Incorporated, 1966), pp. 69, 72.

61 *Encyclopedia Judaica*, Volume 5, C-Dh, (Jerusalem, Israel: Keter Publishing
    House, Ltd., 1971), "Calendar,", p. 43.

62 Ibid., "Historical," p. 48.

63 *Time*, by Samuel A. Goudsmidt, Robert Claiborne, and the Editors of Life
    (New York: Time, Incorporated, 1966), p. 58.

64 Ibid., pp. 62, 66.

65 Ibid., p. 70.

66 Ibid., p. 101.

67 Ibid., p. 101.

68 *Encyclopedia Judaica*, Volume 4, b, (Jerusalem, Israel: Keter Publishing
    House, Ltd., 1971), "Bible", pp. 814-967, pp. 822, 831, and,
    Barry W. Holtz, Editor, *Back to the Sources*, (New York: Summit Books,
    1984), p. 31, and,
    J. Bronowski, *The Ascent of Man*, (Boston: Little, Brown and Company,
    1973), p. 70, and,
    Max I. Dimont, *Jews, God and History*, (New Jersey: New American
    Library, 1962), p. 40.

69 *The Holy Scriptures*, according to the Masoretic Text, (Philadelphia, PA:
    The Jewish Publication Society of America, 1917/1960), "Isaiah," Chapter 2,
    Verse 4, p. 481, and,
    Encyclopedia Judaica, Volume 9, IS-JER (Jerusalem, Israel: Keter
    Publishing House,Ltd., 1970), "Isaiah," pp. 43-71, pp. 46, 51.

70 Kenneth E. Boulding, *The Meaning of the 20th Century: The Great
    Transition*, (New York: Harper and Row, Pub., 1964), p. 1.

71 J. Bronowski, *The Ascent of Man*, (Boston: Little, Brown and Company,
    1973), pp. 59-60.

72 Ibid., p. 95.

73 Ibid., p. 69.

74 E. Adamson Hoebel, *Anthropology: The Study of Man*, 4th Ed. (New York: McGraw-Hill Co., 1958/1972), p. 422.

75 J. Bronowski, *The Ascent of Man*, (Boston: Little, Brown and Company, 1973), pp. 89, 102, and,
Kenneth E. Boulding, *The Meaning of the 20th Century: The Great Transition*, (New York: Harper and Row, Publishers, 1964), p. 3.

76 J. Bronowski, *The Ascent of Man*, (Boston: Little, Brown and Company, 1973), p. 69, and,
E. Adamson Hoebel, *Anthropology: The Study of Man*, 4th Ed. (New York: McGraw-Hill Co., 1958/1972), pp. 9-10.

77 J. Bronowski, *The Ascent of Man*, (Boston: Little, Brown and Company, 1973), p. 88.

78 Ralph L. Beals and Harry Hoijer, *An Introduction to Anthropology*, 4th Ed. (New York: Macmillan Company, 1971), p. 27.

79 Ibid., pp. 29-31.

80 Ibid., p. 29.

81 *Valley News*, January 19, 1979, Section 1, p. 3, quote by Dr. Tim White, Anthropologist, U. C. Berkeley.

82 Ralph L. Beals and Harry Hoijer, *An Introduction to Anthropology*, 4th Ed. (New York: Macmillan Company, 1971), p. 29.

83 *Human Nature*, (P.O. Box 9100, Greenwich, Conn. 06835, November 1978), S. L. Washburn, "What We Can't Learn About People From Apes," pp. 70-75, p. 73.

84 Ralph L. Beals and Harry Hoijer, *An Introduction to Anthropology*, 4th Ed. (New York: Macmillan Company, 1971), p. 3.

85 Ibid., p. 23.

86 *Human Nature*, (P.O. Box 9100, Greenwich, Conn. 06835, November 1978), Luigi Giacommeti, "Thumbs Up," pp 40-47, p. 40.

87 E. Adamson Hoebel, *Anthropology: The Study of Man*, 4th Ed. (New York: McGraw-Hill Co., 1958/1972), p. 307.

88 *Human Nature*, (P.O. 9100, Greenwich, Conn. 06835, November 1978), S. L. Washburn, "What We Can't Learn About People From Apes," pp. 70-75, p. 70.

89 Ralph L. Beals and Harry Hoijer, *An Introduction to Anthropology*, 4th Ed. (New York: Macmillan Company, 1971), p. 3.

90 J. Bronowski, *The Ascent of Man*, (Boston: Little, Brown and Company, 1973), p. 59.

91 Ibid., p. 45.

92 Ibid., p. 50.

93 E. Adamson Hoebel, *Anthropology: The Study of Man*, 4th Ed. (New York: McGraw-Hill Co., 1958/1972), p. 157.

94 J. Bronowski, *The Ascent of Man*, (Boston: Little Brown and Company, 1973), p. 46.

95 *Human Nature*, (P.O. Box 9100, Greenwich, Con. 06835, November 1978), S. L. Washburn, "What We Can't Learn About People From Apes"), p. 75.

96 J. Bronowski, *The Ascent of Man*, (Boston: Little, Brown and Company, 1973), p. 59.

97 *Daily News*. July 25, 1986, "Fossils Date Earliest Life Beyond 3.5 Billion Years Ago," News, p. 11.

98 *Los Angeles Times*, April 2, 1980, "Team From UCLA Discovers Rock That is Oldest Evidence of Life," by George Alexander, p. 21.

99 Ralph L. Beals and Harry Hoijer, *An Introduction to Anthropology*, 4th Ed. (New York: Macmillan Company, 1971), p. 24.
Figure 1—Ibid., p. 24.
Figure 2—Ibid., pp. 19-60.

100 Quincy Wright, *A Study of War*, 2nd Ed. (Chicago: University of Chicago Press, 1942/65), p. 1514.

101 Karl W. Deutsch, "Preface," *A Study of War*, by Quincy Wright, p. xi.

102 Will and Ariel Durant, *The Lessons of History* (New York: Simon and Schuster, 1968), p. 81.

103 Quincy Wright, *A Study of War*, 2nd Ed. (Chicago: University of Chicago Press, 1942/65), p. 163.

104 Ibid., p. 163.

105 Kenneth E. Boulding, *The Meaning of the 20th Century: The Great Transition*, (New York: Harper and Row, Pub., 1964), p. 4.

106 John G. Stoessinger, *Why Nations Go To War* (New York: St. Martin's Press, 1974), p. 2.

107 Ibid., p. 224.

108 E. Adamson Hoebel, *Anthropology: The Study of Man*, 4th Ed. (New York: McGraw-Hill Co., 1958/1972), p. 242.

109 *Valley News*, "Son of Leakey: Boning Up on Prehistory," by Brian Alexander, September 28, 1978, Section 3, p. 1.

110 Karl W. Deutsch, "Preface," *A Study of War*, by Quincy Wright, 2nd Ed. (Chicago: University of Chicago Press, 1942/65, p. xi.

111 Kenneth E. Boulding, *The Meaning of the 20th Century: The Great Transition*, (New York: Harper and Row, Pub., 1964), p. 76.

112 William Eckhardt, "The Factor of Militarism," *Journal of Peace Research* 2 (1969), pp. 123-132, p. 123.

113 Quincy Wright, *A Study of War*, 2nd Ed. (Chicago: University of Chicago Press, 1942/65), pp. 291-2.

114 Ruth Leger Sivard, *World Military and Social Expenditures 1978*, (Leesburg, Virginia: WMSE Publications, 1978), p. 8.

115 *Daily News*, U.S./World, November 24, 1986, p. 9.

116 Lester R. Brown, *State of the World 1984*, (New York: W. W. Norton & Company 1984), p. 205. Secondary source, from: World Military Expenditures 1973-83, "SOURCE: Stockholm International Peace Research Institute, *World Armaments and Disarmaments, SIPRI Yearbook 1983*, (New York: Taylor & Francis, Inc., 1983)."

117 John Kenneth Galbraith, "Foreword", *World Military and Social Expenditures* 1978, by Ruth Leger Sivard (Leesburg, Virginia: WMSE Publications, 1978), p. 3.

118 Ruth Leger Sivard, *World Military and Social Expenditures 1978*, (Leesburg, Virginia: WMSE Publications, 1978), p. 8.

119 Quincy Wright, *A Study of War*, 2nd Ed. (Chicago: University of Chicago Press, 1942/65), p. 248.

120 Anthony C. Beilenson, 23rd Congressional District, California, 96th Congress, *Newsletter,* December 1979.

121 Will and Ariel Durant, *The Lessons of History* (New York: Simon and Schuster, 1978), p. 81.

122 Kenneth E. Boulding, "Future Direction in Conflict and Peace Studies," in *The Journal of Conflict Resolution*, Volume XXII, Number 2, (Beverly Hills, California: Sage Publications, June 1978), pp. 342-354, p. 343.

123 International Peace Academy, *Coping with Conflict*, Volume 5, (New York: International Peace Academy, Inc., 1981/82), pp. 1-8.

124 Dr. E. Suzanne Richert, *Waging Peace*, (Pittsburgh: WQED, April/May 1979).

125 Norman V. Walbek, "Global Public Political Culture," *Peace Research Reviews*, Volume 5, Number 2, (Oakville, Ontario, Canada: Canadian Peace Research Institute, November, 1973), pp. 1-128, p. 1.

126 *New Options*, Mark Satin, Editor, "Reforming the U.N.: Alternative to Any More Irangates", December 29, 1986, Issue No. 34, (Washington, D. C.: New Options, Inc., 1986).

127 Mahatma Gandhi, *All Men Are Brothers*, compiled and edited by Krishna Kripalani (Paris: United Nations Educational Scientific and Cultural Organization, 1958; New York: The Columbia Press, 1958/1972), p. 75.

128 Kenneth E. Boulding, *Stable Peace*, (Austin, Texas: University of Texas Press, 1978), p. 7.

129 Ibid., p. 25.

130 *Time* Magazine, February 12, 1979, p. 20.

131 *Daily News,* August 27, 1984, U. S. World, p. 2.

132 *Los Angeles Times*, June 19, 1981, Part 1, p. 22.

133 Albert Camus, *Neither Victims Nor Executioners*, (Chicago: World Without War Publications, 1972), pp. 48-49.

134 Kenneth E. Boulding, *The Meaning of the 20th Century: The Great Transition*, (New York: Harper and Row Publishers, 1964), p. 90.

135 Charles Osgood, "Suggestions for Winning the Real War With Communism," *The Journal of Conflict Resolution*, 3, (1959), pp. 295-325, p. 295.

136 Warner Levi, "On The Causes of War and the Conditions of Peace," *The Journal of Conflict Resolution*, 4 (1960), pp. 527-542, p. 533.

137 Albert Einstein in *Einstein on Peace*, Edited by Otto Nathan and Heinz Norden, (New York: Schocken Books, 1960/1972), p. 632.

138 Ibid., p. 633.

139 Mahendra Kumar, *Current Peace Research and India*, (Rajghat, Varanaski, India: Gandhian Institute of Studies, 1968), p. 62.

140 Will and Ariel Durant, *The Lessons of History*, (New York: Simon and Schuster, 1968), p. 86.

141 Ibid., p. 83.

142 Knud Larsen, "Aggression and Social Cost," *Peace Research Reviews* 5, Number 1, (Oakville, Ontario, Canada: Canadian Peace Research Institute, 1973), p. 37.

143 Morton Deutsch, in *The War-Peace Establishment* by Arthur Herzog, (New York: Harper and Row, Publishers, 1963), p. 187.

144 Stephen Nelson, "Nature/Nurture Revisited," *The Journal of Conflict Resolution* 18, (June 1974), pp. 285-335.

145 Ibid., p. 304.

146 Ibid., p. 293.

147 Ibid., p. 295.

148 Ibid., p. 314.

149 Jean Piaget, *Main Trends in Psychology*, (New York: Harper and Row, Publishers, 1970), p. 20.

150 Knud Larsen, "Aggression and Social Cost," *Peace Research Reviews*, Volume 5, Number 1, (Oakville, Ontario, Canada: Canadian Peace Research Institute, 1973), pp. 7-8.

151 *Human Nature*, (P.O. Box 9100, Greenwich, Conn. 06835, November 1978), S. L. Washburn, "What We Can't Learn About People From Apes," pp. 70-75, p. 70.

152 Jonas Salk, *The Survival of the Wisest*, (New York: Harper and Row, Publishers, 1973), p. 15.

153 Arthur R. Cohen, *Attitude Change and Social Influence*, (New York: Basic Books, 1964), p. 56.

154 *The Consolidated-Webster Encyclopedic Dictionary*, Editor-in-Chief, Franklin J. Meine, Ph.B, MA, (Chicago: 1954/61), p. 65.

155 Kenneth E. Boulding, *The Meaning of the 20th Century: The Great Transition,* (New York: Harper and Row, Pub., 1964), p. 156.

156 Ibid., p. 157.

157 Leon Festinger, *A Theory of Cognitive Dissonance*, (Stanford, CA: Stanford University Press, 1957), pp. 3, 5, 9, 11.

158 Ibid., p. 18.

159 Ibid., p. 20.

160 Ibid., p. 21.

161 Arthur R. Cohen, *Attitude Change and Social Influence*, (New York: Basic Books, 1964), p.x.

162 Abraham H. Maslow, *Toward a Psychology of Being*, 2nd Edition, (New York, D. Van Norstrand Company, 1968), p. 4.

163 A. H. Maslow, *Motivation and Personality*, (New York: Harper & Row, Publishers, 1959), p. 79.

164 Ibid., pp. 80-196.

165 Abraham H. Maslow, *The Farther Reaches of Human Nature*, (New York: Penguin Books, 1978/The Viking Press, 1971), p. 42.

166 Lester R. Brown, *World Without Borders*, (New York: Vintage Books, a division of Random House, 1972), p. 9.

167 E. Adamson Hoebel, *Anthropology: The Study of Man*, 4th Ed., (New York: McGraw-Hill Co., 1958/1972), p. 35.

168 Viktor E. Frankl, *Man's Search for Meaning*, (New York: Washington Square Press, 1963).

169 National Aeronautics and Space Administration, Photograph, Pioneer F Plaque (310 mission). Courtesy of NASA.

170 Alexander Pope, (1688-1744), "An Essay on Man," Epistle 2.

171 E. Adamson Hoebel, *Anthropology: The Study of Man* , 4th Edition, (New York: McGraw-Hill Book Company, 1958/1972), p. 85, and, *Audubon*, Volume 86, Number 5, (New York: The National Audubon Society, September 1984), "The Obscure Fame of Carl Linnaeus" by Bil Gilbert, pp. 102-114.

172 E. Adamson Hoebel, *Anthropology: The Study of Man*, 4th Edition, (New York: McGraw-Hill Book, Company, 1958/1972), pp. 85-86.

173 Hans Selye, *Stress without Distress,* (Philadelphia, PA: J.B. Lippincott Company, 1974).

174 *Daily News,* December 18, 1987, Nation/World, "'Doomsday Clock' is turned back" by Elizabeth Shogren, p. 7.

175 Frederick L. Schuman, *Why A Department of Peace?,* (Beverly Hills, CA: Another Mother for Peace, 1969), p. 9.

176 Ibid., pp. 13, 10.

177 Ibid., p. 14.

178 Professor William H. Boyer, "Planning Education and Systems Change," reprinted from *Educational Forum*, Volume XXXIX, No. 4, (West Lafayette, Indiana: Kappa Delta Pi, May 1975).

179 *Peace and World Order Studies*, A Curriculum Guide, Editors Burns H. Weston, Sherle R. Schwinninger, Diane E. Shamis, (New York: Trans-national Academics Program, Institute for World Order, 1978), p. 96.

180 Ibid., p. 77.

181 Ibid., p. 230.

182 Ibid., p. 114.

183 Ibid., p. 47.

184 Ibid., p. 99.

185 Ibid., p. 85.

186 Ibid., p. 93

187 *Peace and World Order Studies*, Fourth Edition, A Curriculum Guide, Barbara J. Wien, Editor, (New York: World Policy Institute, 1984), p. 185.

188 Ibid., p. 226.

189 Ibid., p. 371.

190 *Peace and World Order Studies*, A Curriculum Guide, Editors Burns H. Weston, Sherle R. Schwinninger, Diane E. Shamis, (New York: Transnational Academic Program, Institute for World Order, 1978), p. 315.

191 *Campaign Update*, Vol. IV, Issue 1, (Washington, D. C.: National Peace Academy Campaign, Winter 1981).

192 *Peace Chronicle*, (Urbana, IL: Consortium on Peace, Research, Education and Development, August 1984), p. 1.

193 The National Council for a World Peace Tax Fund, 2111 Florida Ave., N.W., Washington, D. C. 20008.

194 *Los Angeles Times*, "The Nation", (Los Angeles: Los Angeles Times, July 27, 1981), p. 2.

195 Martin Buber, *I and Thou*, (New York: Charles S. Scribner's and Sons, 1970), Walter Kaufmann translation.

196 *Los Angeles Times*, December 15, 1981, Part 1, p 2.

197 *Daily News,* November 24, 1986, U. S./World, News p. 9

198 *Los Angeles Times,* December 16, 1981, Part 1, pp. 1, 14.

199 *Los Angeles Times,* January 9, 1982, pp. 1, 16.

200 Ruth Leger Sivard, *World Military and Social Expenditures 1981*, (Leesburg, Virginia: World Priorities, 1981), p. 20.

201 Abraham H. Maslow, *The Farther Reaches of Human Nature*, (New York: Penguin Books, 1978/The Viking Press, 1971), p. 108.

ORDER FORM

NuAge Books
Post Office Box 7535
Van Nuys, CA 91409

Please send the following book by Sylvia Hornstein:

_____ copies of *Rx: PEACE, The Promise and The Future,* $ _____
hard cover, @ $18.95 each,

CALIFORNIANS: Please add 6½% Sales Tax $ _____

SHIPPING: $1.95 for the first book, and 50¢ $ _____
for each additional book,
per package.

TOTAL $ _____

Please mail to:

Name _____

Address _____ Apt. #_____

City _____ State _____ Zip_____

Phone (___) _____
     day

and,

Name _____

Address _____ Apt. #_____

City _____ State _____ Zip_____

Phone (___) _____
     day

Check or money order is to be made out to: *NuAge Books.*

Please allow approximately six to eight weeks for delivery.

Fifteen per cent (15%) discount rates available for quantity group study or gift purchases of ten or more. Please contact NuAge Books, Post Office Box 7535, Van Nuys, CA 91409.